ACCIDENTAL SOLDIER

ACCIDENTAL
SOLDIER

A Memoir of Service and Sacrifice
in the
Israel Defense Forces

DORIT SASSON

SHE WRITES PRESS

Published 2016
Printed in the United States of America

ISBN: 978-1-63152-035-8
Library of Congress Control Number: 2015950699

Book design by Stacey Aaronson
Map creation by Mike Morgenfeld

For information, address:
She Writes Press
1563 Solano Ave #546
Berkeley, CA 94707

She Writes Press is a division of SparkPoint Studio, LLC.

For Haim
my one and only lamplighter
And for our children,
Ivry and Ayala, my precious gems

AUTHOR'S NOTE

No memory is ever alone; it's at the end of a trail of memories,
a dozen trails that each have their own associations.

—Louis L'Amour

To write this book, I delved into memory of this event and time of my life and supplemented the process with research, personal journals, and notes. At times, I changed names to preserve anonymity. There are no made-up events or characters in this story. Many people and events that had no impact on the truth of the story have been omitted.

CONTENTS

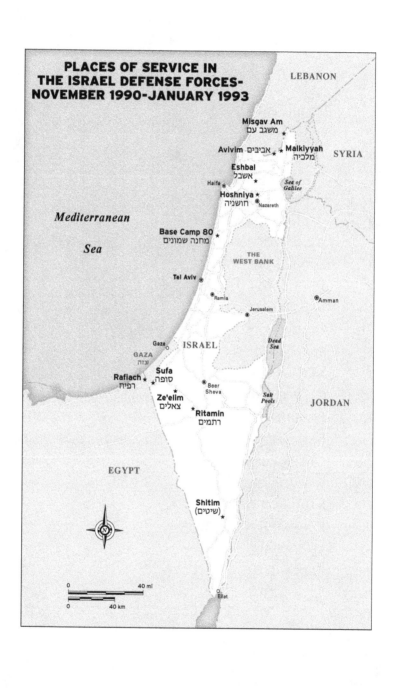

PLACES OF SERVICE IN THE ISRAEL DEFENSE FORCES-NOVEMBER 1990-JANUARY 1993

LEBANON

SYRIA

Misgav Am
משגב עם

Avivim אביבים ★ Malkiyyah
מלכיה

Eshbal
אשבל

Haifa

Sea of Galilee

Hoshniya חושניה
Nazareth

Mediterranean

Sea

Base Camp 80
מחנה שמונים

THE WEST BANK

Tel Aviv

Ramla

Amman

Jerusalem

Gaza

ISRAEL

Dead Sea

GAZA
עזה

Sufa
סופה

Rafiach
רפיח

Beer Sheva

Salt Pools

JORDAN

Ze'elim
צאלים

Ritamin
רתמים

EGYPT

Shitim
(שיטים)

0	40 mi
0	40 km

Eilat

1

LIVING THE QUESTIONS

I AM WAITING AT THE KOACH JUNCTION TO HITCHHIKE back to the kibbutz, mesmerized by the peach-colored Mount Hermon in the far distance, when an Israel Defense Force soldier—clad in white, which means he's part of the Air Force—slams the door of the vehicle he's just gotten out of. I've watched these soldiers hitchhike for the past three weeks, ever since I got here. This particular one makes his way past the yellow line of the *trampiada*—a curved cement stop made especially for soldiers—and approaches me. To my right, another mountain looms before me, its features in better focus: I can make out the red kalaniyot flowers native only to Israel, interspersed with other wildflowers, dotting its surface.

The countryside here is pristine. There are still quite a few hours left in the day, but already a cool breeze runs through my T-shirt. It gets cold in this part of the woods, which tells me that by the time I reach the kibbutz, I'll probably need a sweatshirt.

"Do you know when the bus is coming?" the soldier asks in Hebrew.

"I think the buses are all finished for the day," I say politely, also in Hebrew.

"I guess that means we have no choice but to hitchhike, right?" he says. He seems a bit jittery, but there's a huge grin plastered on his face.

I'm startled by such a question. Soldiers get rides from civilians all the time here, because the Israel Defense Forces are the lifeline of the nation. They serve to protect the country. So his chances of getting a *tramp*, or hitchhike, are high. But I'm just a kibbutz volunteer—this is my third trip to Israel and my first hitchhiking experience. I'm not so sure anyone will pick me up.

It's five in the afternoon and the buses to this area of the Galilee are all finished for the day, but if I can't find someone to give me a ride, I can always call my aunt and uncle; they live at Kibbutz Malkiyah, tucked back in the Galilean Mountains.

Perhaps this soldier senses the "Israeli" part of me because of my Mediterranean features—the hazel eyes and dark brown hair I inherited from my Israeli father. Plus, I'm not sitting with the rest of the volunteers, who are all Swedish and Danish and are camped right on the main road, yapping in their native tongues. At this point, I slip in and out of Hebrew and English just like I would with a pair of well-worn sweats. I'm tickled by this moment, and can't help but wonder why the heck would an IDF soldier ask me about the bus schedule, since they aren't really dependent on them. No IDF soldier has ever even approached me before.

I have zero experience hitchhiking in the States, and even though it's my first time, I feel comfortable doing it here. Perhaps it's because, like most Americans my age, I've been influenced by Hollywood movies and my image of soldiers is glamorized. Maybe it's because there's a certain camaraderie of trust and solidarity here in Israel—the understanding I have here that I'm being protected all the time. Whatever the reason, I don't hesitate to stand out in the middle of the road and stick out my index finger with my elbow comfortably resting on my side, just as I've observed others doing in the few short weeks since I arrived here.

Just then, a car approaches, and the driver signals that they're about to stop.

Hey, I did it, I think. *My first hitchhike!*

But instead of stopping alongside me, it stops farther up the road. The soldier turns around, sees it has stopped, and runs toward it. He talks to the driver through the passenger-side window while carefully holding his M16. Within a few minutes he's back and the civilian vehicle is off.

He runs back still holding his M16.

"It's not going where you need to go?" I ask.

"No, they're going to a different place."

"Oh." I notice he doesn't use the words "camp" or "army base," making this IDF world still a bit mysterious and a bit secretive.

I'm eager to use my university Hebrew. If Mom were here, she'd grab my shoulders and whisper fiercely, "Watch out, they've got guns. Don't get too close." But their guns don't shake me up; here, I can take a step closer, eavesdrop a bit.

The soldier steps out onto the road again with his index finger out, moving his boot in heel-toe-heel-toe fashion. Bustling bright. Olive skin. Dark hair. Curly. Just like my Israeli father.

It's the summer of 1989. I'm eighteen years old. Just a few months ago, my father, Israeli-born and raised, offered me money to travel around the world. It was my last chance to explore my options: Would I postpone another year at SUNY Albany, or travel? As a freshman, I was unhappy and aimless.

3

Dad complicated my life by holding up a picture of a twenty-two-year-old named Tania Aebi who'd made headlines in *The New York Times* by traveling around the world in a small boat. The newspaper clipping showed her entering New York harbor with a big wave and wide smile. I wanted to be *that* free. No obligations to school. I read the last words of the article over and over again: *She intends to write a memoir of her travels one day.*

"You see, Dorit? This is what it means to travel the world," Dad said, grinning and pointing to the boat with an *I-told-you-so* sort of look.

The idea of traveling around the world worried me, though: would I have enough money, even with Dad's help? What if I didn't want to go back to school after that? How would I manage so long on my own? Where would I possibly go, and who would I go with? Nobody I knew was traveling around the world. Still, the idea of stepping outside my comfort zone was appealing. So I decided to start small, and to focus on the one country I knew something about: Israel.

I seized the idea of volunteering on my aunt's kibbutz way before I really knew what a kibbutz was. Volunteering, I reasoned, would be an inexpensive way to visit the country. She and I corresponded in the fall of 1988 via airmail. I yelped when I received a red and blue envelope with Hebrew writing on it and with the word ISRAEL spelled out in English on the front.

"No problem," she'd written in response to my initial letter. "I spoke to the person in charge of volunteers. We have a place on Kibbutz Malkiyah for you."

What a perfect deal. I could still travel in Israel, I'd be with Dad's family, and since I'd be working and Dad was paying for the flight, I wouldn't need to shell out much money. I had finally found a way to break free from the two opposing forces of my life: my dad and my mom.

Mom was a child prodigy and a Julliard graduate, and today she is a classical pianist scared of anything that's unfamiliar, including Israel. She and her family escaped the Nazis in the mid-1930s, when she was an infant, leaving her home country of Spain for Panama. Eventually they left for the US, where she settled in New York. She concertizes around the world, and Israel is the one country that triggers fear and insecurity in her; unfortunately, I've inherited quite a bit of her fear.

She's always told me I have to "be somebody," and that starts with getting a college education. But starting when I was eleven, she left me in charge of taking care of my brother so she could practice with legendary masters on the Upper West Side. And she always came back late—too late. She's a New Yorker through and through, and so despite the prevalent crime and unsafe streets of the '70s and '80s, she always took either the bus or subway home.

After one late night practicing for an upcoming performance with Leonard Bernstein at Carnegie Hall, Mom told me I should consider becoming a teacher. "It's the one thing you can fall back on," she said. Aside from teaching Holocaust survivors a music survey course I designed at a vacation center somewhere in Pennsylvania a year or two ago, I have very little teaching experience, but the idea of pursuing a stable profession is appealing. She and my dad are both artists, so I know what it's like on the other side. She doesn't want to see me struggle, and I don't want that either. Plus, it's hard to follow your passion when all the freshmen in your graduating class are declaring pre-med and law majors. But I want to do the "right" thing, and I still don't know what that "right" thing is. It's frustrating.

Then there's Dad, a Fulbright graduate and visual artist who sees the world through oils and canvas. Between my two parents, he's the more logical and subtle one. So I'm following his philosophy of exploring my options without ruling college out—except that I'm staying with my Israeli family rather than actually traveling around the world, which makes me feel like I'm taking a shortcut.

"Dorit," he said to me in earnest, "I'll *give* you the money. Just take it and go!"

"I don't want to!" I'm defiant—a practice I've learned well from years of maneuvering between Dad and Mom, especially since Dad testified in court that Mom wasn't fit to be a primary caregiver and then moved out. I was twelve at the time.

"You'll regret it," he says. "Believe me."

"Nope, I don't think so," I say smugly. Years later, I will regret that I didn't take him up on his offer. How much does Mom's fear and anxiety control me? Dad is fully aware of her controlling tendencies, but he has no idea how much they influence my decisions.

By the time this volunteer stint rolled around, I had finally managed to tap into that "higher-up" that I today call my "Jedi" voice and had conquered my fears. *If Tania can do it, so can I*, I reassured myself. *It's Israel—a country I've visited before, the homeland of my family. I'll be staying with my aunt and uncle. I'm somewhat familiar with kibbutz life.*

Dad didn't say much when I said, "I'm going to volunteer on Malkiyah." This time there was no defiance in my voice and Dad wasn't trying to fight my decision. But we both knew that going to Israel was a deviation from the grander scheme of things. Perhaps I'd placated him in some way with the fact that I was going to volunteer in *his* homeland, but I'm sure at least a part of him was disappointed by my choice.

By the time my round-trip ticket was bought and my bags were packed, I was less jittery. The dots of earlier memories were starting to connect. I began vaguely to recall my aunt and uncle's kibbutz from two previous family visits—the first at age five and the second at twelve. I remembered that it took at least twenty minutes to get to, driving along a very circuitous, narrow road. In the car, sandwiched between two grownups, the twelve-year-old in me paid special attention to the darkness on both sides of the car.

"Where are we?" I asked.

"On the way to Malkiyah," someone said.

A barbed wire fence came into view under dim lights. "And what's that over there?" I asked, pointing.

"Lebanon," my aunt said. I almost could taste the *Leben*, a thin, unsweetened yogurt that Mom often bought and thickened with jam so it would appeal to my American taste buds. *Leben, Lebanon*—similar sounds. I remembered how I turned up my nose when I discovered the Leben wasn't sugary and processed like the other yogurts at the grocery store. This time, though, I was ready to taste other experiences.

∞

I LOOK AT MY WATCH. IT'S JUST THIS SOLDIER AND ME hitchhiking farther up the road for almost an hour. The Swedish and Danish volunteers just a few meters away don't really seem to care how they'll end up getting back to the kibbutz, and they're still jabbering away.

Just when I'm about to pull out a token to make a call to my aunt, an army Jeep turns onto the road—its headlights blinding—and after passing us, it stops, right where the curvy road takes a sudden turn and disappears around a bend. Technically, soldiers can only pick up other soldiers or reservists, which explains why it stops so far away.

I get up from the curb to approach the Jeep, the first vehicle to arrive within the last hour. There are a limited number of seats available in the car, and by the time I get close, it's clear that I'll be beaten out by the soldiers, a few of whom are already swarming the driver's side window. I have no chance of being picked up. But still, I take a few steps closer, near enough so I can peek into this foreign world.

They're packed in like sardines—all of them with war-painted faces. They are on their way to Lebanon, but they will stop first at one of the neighboring bases up the hill to drop off a few soldiers. I know this because I overhear them chatting in Hebrew. The six soldiers in the back wear green helmets, and one of them shouts something to the Air Force soldier, who runs to the Jeep, opens the door, and then runs back to grab his green duffle bag.

Then the Jeep moves in reverse and stops where I'm standing, still with my index finger raised.

"Where do you want to go?" one of them asks me.

I lower my finger. *Seriously? Will they take me? A volunteer?*

"Kibbutz Malkiyah." I immediately feel self-conscious about my accent. I worry that I sound like a cow chewing its cud, and yet I've never felt the confidence I do right now.

"At Americayit?" he asks. *Are you an American?*

"Ken." *Yes.*

"Me-efo?" *From where?*

"New York City."

"Ah—New York City," the soldier says in a charming accent, as if I've just mentioned the land of his dreams.

New York City. Each time I tell Israelis in Israel where I'm from, their eyes light up like I've just handed them the jewel of the Nile. They are always asking me, "Hey, do you know so and so from Queens?" I didn't understand why in the past, but on this visit I have finally realized that there are many Israelis living in New York City, and the Israelis here think that my corner of the world is like a mini-Israel. I used to think they thought America was a country paved with gold, but now I understand: it's not the riches they're driving at but the need to connect.

I take one step closer to the Jeep, aware of the boundaries between us. I'm a volunteer. They are male soldiers. But I'm not your typical volunteer. First, I'm Jewish; second, I've got an Israeli father; and third, I speak better-than-average Hebrew.

There are sizeable backpacks in the back of the Jeep. Because I backpack everywhere, I can easily see myself squeezing in like another sardine and chatting with the seven soldiers occupying the space. I welcome the physical closeness that my American peers might find off-putting. I find the diversity of their appearances appealing as well. Although dressed uniformly, their facial expressions, hairstyles, and even the way their paint is smeared are all different. One has what appears to be bangs under his helmet, while another has long, stringy hair. One has green eyes and another has brown. (I'll fit in with my hazel eyes and long brown ponytail.)

As the Jeep starts to move, I step closer. Now I'm just a few inches away from the door. One of the soldiers leans out the window and shouts something incoherent in Hebrew. He smiles sheepishly. Pretty soon all seven male soldiers turn to look at me. This little interaction has gathered some attention. Even the volunteers who are sitting a few yards away are now closing in on me, and all I've really said is "Kibbutz Malkiyah."

Air Force soldier leans out of the window and says something, then looks at me closely. For a moment I think he's speaking to me, but then I realize he's carrying on a conversation with his soldier buddies.

"Hey, Shalom, there's not enough room in our Jeep to take her?"

"Shimon, are you crazy?"

I know it's illegal to bring a civilian on board, but I figure it's illegal like not buckling a seatbelt—a soft law. I can feel them sizing me up. I'm not one of those drop-dead gorgeous Swedish volunteers IDF soldiers are known to gravitate toward, and as this thought crosses my mind my confidence suddenly deserts me and I feel terribly self-conscious.

One of the soldiers continues to look at me as the Jeep begins to pull out. This is the closest I've ever been to an IDF soldier. On the kibbutz I see them eating lunch in the dining room after their shifts, but that's about the extent of my exposure to them. I'm in awe of them, and being so close now prompts all sorts of questions: Who are they? Do they go into Lebanon and blast their M16s? Do they blow up houses? How do they attack? I feel so sheltered, and it seems to me that what a soldier goes through is the "real" world.

∽

FROM A YOUNG AGE, MOM PULLED ME AWAY FROM THE news every time Israel was announced on the media. Sometimes she would cover my eyes; other times she physically pulled me away from the television and turned it off. It was clear she hated Israel and was deeply afraid of the terrorists who so desperately wanted to blow it up.

Dad, on the other hand, was hungry to connect with his homeland. News was the only way in. He'd watch with intent as Golda Meir, Israel's first and only female prime minister, bellowed about her big visions for social and political reform for the country while my father steadily commented in a tongue I couldn't yet understand. Years later, I was given a picture of my father, a young Fulbright student, shaking hands with the famous Golda, and I began to understand. She wasn't just this political person on TV. She was someone my father had actually met.

∞

THE SOLDIER COULD BE LOOKING AT ANYTHING—MY pea-sized breasts, my lanky arms, or maybe even the ponytail I'm afraid to release from its everlasting bun. I hear the chorus of a song I've grown to love—"The Weakness in Me," by British singer Joan Armatrading—coming from the speakers in the Jeep. Israelis and volunteers love to sing this song while waving huge cans of beer and knocking heads at our local kibbutz pub.

My mom's fears and worries about Israel make this experience that much more thrilling. Later, when I'm back in New York, I'll start thinking of ways to make up for missed time—to get to know these people that I've always been told are "war monsters." For me, Israelis are far friendlier than Americans. And maybe I'm just naive because I'm just a tourist, but I feel more comfortable, and safer, here than I do in the US. I love how, when we return from our various volunteer trips, the IDF soldiers we pass at the entrance to the kibbutz always raise their hands in a sort of salute before opening the gate for us.

I watch the Air Force soldier squeeze in with the rest of the soldiers and get swallowed up by the sea of uniform green inside. After they talk among themselves for a moment longer, the Jeep moves on, leaving me feeling a jumble of emotions. *I just talked with IDF soldiers!* My hands are shaking. I also wonder if I'll ever get home.

I turn back to the road and stick out my index finger again. I'm hitchhiking in paradise, but now that my soldier friend is gone, I feel alone. In front of me is the majestic Hula Valley, resplendent with fish ponds, and Mount Hermon in the faraway distance. If I were to walk a kilometer up the mountain I would be able to see what this prized area, one of the prettiest in the country, is known for: squares of green and brown patches of farmland.

In a matter of moments, a big white van stops for me, and luckily there's room enough for all five of us. But when I climb in, I discover right away that there are no seatbelts. The Danish and Swedish volunteers immediately prop their knees against the seats in front of them, unworried. *Why aren't they scared?* I think, panicking. *How can I ride in a car without seatbelts?* I take a deep breath and remind myself not to act like my mother.

As we ascend the mountain, we pass apple orchards and fish ponds. Under the early evening sun, the ponds shimmer like diamonds. Soon enough, dense forests, rigidly bunched, take over both sides of the highway, and for a while there's nothing more to see. On a clear day, there's a bird's-eye view all the way to Kiriyat Shmona, the next farthest town, and even to Metulla, known as the last stop *moshava* before hitting Lebanon. But now there's only blackness between me and the rest of this unknown part of Israel—the same blackness I remember from my last trip up this mountain at age twelve.

I find myself leaning out the window, looking for the fish pond in the cozy, carpeted blackness of the night. The Israeli driver makes small talk in broken English, but I'm too nervous to engage. I've never hitchhiked in my life, and as much as I'm trying to ignore the seatbelt problem, it's difficult for me to relax. I grab on to what appears to be a holder above the side window, just like Mom used to do when I was growing up any time she was in the car with Dad. A scene from my childhood comes to mind:

"Drive slower! Can't you drive a bit slower?" Mom shouted loudly over the rickety grating sound our four-door burgundy hatchback made as we crossed the Brooklyn Bridge. She grabbed the holder next to her with two hands. My seatbelt had become unbuckled, but no one noticed. I paid attention to the noises: one long grate and then a *thump* . . . *buh-ump!*

"Avi, PLEASE SLOW DOWN!"

But Dad didn't, and Mom continued to shout.

We reached the end of the bridge, and he finally slowed down.

"Okay, Mimi," he said.

Ignoring him, Mom turned to me and said, "What happened to your seatbelt?" She reached over to fasten it. When it suddenly came apart again minutes later, I didn't bother closing it again.

Now our driver snakes up the mountain and finally onto a straight road offering a multitude of directions. Signs in misspelled English point to various kibbutzim and army bases. Our driver turns right and left and left and right. Each turn brings us closer to Malkiyah, which sits on flat land just a few meters from the Israeli–Lebanese border. I know this because for the last week I've passed by this particular Galilean mountain—one of the higher ranges here. As we curve around the hill, I spy what appears to be a little hut, and a kibbutz member tells me it's an abandoned watchguard tower left over from the 1967 Six-Day War, and not used anymore. It's the same kind of tower I've seen on the other side of the barbed wire fence where my aunt lives, past a lovely expanse of quiet ridged rock and wildflowers that could easily be mistaken for Central Park.

By the time we enter the kibbutz gate, I've opened the window so far and wide that the cold air from the mountains is wrestling with my long brown hair. I fish several strands from my eyeglasses and hold them in one hand to keep them from spinning around me.

Could the Israel Defense Forces really be an option for me? I can't get those IDF soldiers out of my mind. A seed has been planted. This could be my calling.

The van parks outside the dining room, and we walk up a little hill that brings us to a row of one-room volunteer quarters. The cold water I wash up with feels good against my sun-exposed skin. After a full meal of Israeli-style salad and hard-boiled eggs, I continue to entertain the thought of changing the course of my life. I know I won't be able to stay on this kibbutz forever; in fact, I've got only four weeks left until I go back to the States.

From the US, I could see myself as a volunteer on a kibbutz but never as a soldier. But now that I've seen how integral soldiers are to the nation, I'm struck by the fact that young men and women are "born" into service from day one. I've never served or volunteered for anything before this, and even though I have been an Israeli citizen from birth thanks to my father, it was always clear that there was no expectation of my serving in the Israel Defense Forces. Even ignoring her aversion to Israel, Mom always thought volunteering was a crazy waste of one's time. But now I wonder: *Who are these people? What motivates them to serve their country? Will I ever be one of them?*

After dinner, I try falling asleep next to snoring roommates, and instead lie there agonizing over these questions, afraid of what the coming years will bring. I've got this tendency to stick my hand way out into the future instead of just enjoying the moment. For years, friends have told me to stop thinking so far ahead—to be in the here and now.

"Just look at the step in front of you," a wise old friend would say. "Don't look too far ahead. One baby step at a time."

Now, as the pine trees rattle and shake relentlessly outside our window, my own voice says, *Stop agonizing over the questions. Just enjoy the experience, Dorit. You're only in Israel for a short time.*

But I counter myself sharply, *I still have to make a decision. I don't want to be unhappy again for another year at college. No way.*

I find myself quoting poet Rainer Maria Rilke's words to myself. I've memorized them by heart with the help of a note I've kept tacked on my wall all these years:

Be patient toward all that is unsolved in your heart and try to love the questions themselves, like locked rooms . . .

If I were in my New York City loft room, I would simply have acknowledged these words for their beauty. But here, facing the unknown of my future, the words "live the questions" and "do not seek the answers" hold profound personal meaning. I've always thrived on having the answer; I've wanted to do everything right, and to do it in one straight, organized line. To do what's expected. Now that I've deviated from that, I'm on my own. I have a decision to make, and, knowing myself as I do, it's not going to be easy.

2

SHAWNA

I STAY AT THE KIBBUTZ FOR A TOTAL OF EIGHT WEEKS.
Each morning, I walk down the hill and past the barbed-wire
fence that surrounds our kibbutz amid rocks and shrubbery.
It's so quiet up here, with the exception of the times when the
targillim, army exercises, are being performed. There is
shaking, rattling, and booming throughout the area at random
hours each day.

Today, I look for a spot at the Hula Valley below me that I
once observed from my aunt and uncle's terrace, which faces
two hills that come together on either side of a valley. On this
clear morning, the valley shimmers in iridescent greens and
browns.

When I first arrived at the kibbutz, I requested to work in
the kitchen to be with my aunt, who stands on a wooden stool
so she can stir soups with her sturdy, tanned, muscular arms.
Her short brown hair evenly covers both sides of her face as
she moves the tall wooden soup spoon in brisk, circular
motions. After a few rounds she takes a regular soup spoon
and tastes. The two spoon look ridiculously funny next to each
other, their sizes comically disproportionate.

The only time we get to talk is during mealtimes. As founding members of the kibbutz, she and my uncle sit with other first-generation kibbutz members, while I break later with other volunteers. Their group began as a garin, a group of young people belonging to the Nahal, in the early 1950s, which is associated with the Nahal Infantry Brigade of the Israel Defense Forces. Over time, their hopeful settlement turned into a self-sustaining agricultural unit known as a kibbutz, where everybody works for the good of the commune and nobody has more than anyone else. Malkiyah managed to get by with agriculture at first, but they soon realized that if they really wanted to thrive, they would need other sustainable income sources, so they created a factory known as Orda, where they produce educational learning games in Hebrew.

Today, surprisingly, my aunt and I are on break at the same time, and suddenly I feel compelled to sit next to her. I slide my tray onto the table next to hers, and just as I do, one of the kibbutznicks turns to me and asks, "So, you're Maya's niece?"

"Yes."

"From where?"

"New York City."

"This is Avi's daughter," my aunt says in Hebrew, in a tone that announces, "She's part of the family!" Suddenly I feel proud and special. This is the first time she's ever intro-duced me to *anybody*.

Sometime during the first two weeks of my arrival, my aunt and I were watching Israeli news on the only channel in Israel—Channel One—and I asked her what it was like to raise her four now-grown children on the kibbutz. I was hoping she would open up to me, as so far she'd only really shared information when I asked her questions.

She muted the television, looked at me squarely, and said, "We are a very quiet family."

There goes any hope of having a warm and fuzzy relationship with my aunt, I thought. Almost immediately I began to worry about our contrasts. I was the loudmouth, boisterous one with a terribly hearty laugh, whereas she kept mainly to herself, only talking when I asked a question or when she needed to share something important.

When the news came back on, Aunt Maya crossed her legs again and shook them up and down in a nervous sort of way while resting her chin on her hand, listening as the news reporters relayed the latest *pigua*—terrorist attack. There was silence again between us, and for a moment I was back again in my living room in the US, sitting on the carpet, and my mom was shouting, "Dorit, get back! Move back at least nine feet from the television, otherwise you'll get radiation!" It didn't make a difference if the image of the blown-up bus I was seeing on my aunt's television was in Israel or somewhere else in the world. I had no sense of time or place.

At the end of the day, regardless of how things might go with my aunt, I'm an American teenager who prefers keeping to myself. I'm not big on sharing my political opinion on the Middle East conflict because I don't have an informed point of view. I also don't argue with the cashier if I don't get the right amount of change, unlike my father, who quibbles over every penny. When my brother joked about it in front of him, Dad didn't laugh. "Times are hard!" he said. "One day you'll understand."

IF THERE IS ONE THING KIBBUTZNICKS FIND HARD TO accept, it's that they never get to really know a group of volunteers because they are always on the go. I know this because both kibbutz members and the volunteers I've met have shared this with me. The fact I speak Hebrew and have a respected family member on the kibbutz makes it easier to build insider trust. To them, I'm Israeli Dorit, but I also fit right in with the foreign mentality of the volunteers. And the more I fit in, the more excited I am to work. When I started in the kitchen, I found myself volunteering alongside a twenty-eight-year-old Australian volunteer named Shawna who's been working there for the last six months. I was drawn to her warm and generous smile, and ever since she discovered I'm from New York City, she's told me tale after tale about all the American volunteers she's met on the kibbutz.

Shawna's been to the pyramids of Luxor, which I've only ever seen on TV—in Egyptian archeology class at college—and she's worked at a remote Palestinian village school, too, which reminds me of how ignorant I am about the Palestinian–Israeli conflict. Like most Americans, I'm media-influenced when it comes to my view of what's going on in the world. Shawna has also bungeed from a number of high places, including a bridge in the Amazon rain forest. I'm impressed. Besides the fact that I'm afraid of heights, I imagine my mom would have a heart attack if I ever decided to pursue such an extreme sport.

She corners me one day in the kitchen, smiles, and says, "Dorit, tell me about New York City and all the other places you've visited." I find this line of questioning intimidating, considering she's been all over the world.

"I've never been anywhere except New York City and New York State," I blurt out.

This is a lie, and I don't even know why I lie. I've actually been to California and a handful of other states. I remember going to the beach in the summer of 1987. I loved being able to run along a beach with my aunt's golden retriever—something I was never able to do growing up because my mother was deeply afraid of the open sea. She was afraid I would drown and get pulled underwater by currents. Her fear wasn't restricted to water-related injury: When I went on a class trip to Ellis Island and the Statue of Liberty in elementary school, she warned me about the dangers of climbing to the top of the Statue of Liberty: "Just be sure you hold on very tightly, Dorit, because you can fall and crack your head open." That image alone made me stay up for nights.

I don't tell Shawna about the Statue of Liberty and Times Square; instead, I tell her what it feels to bike alongside the Hudson River down to Battery Park, to the point where you can get the closest view of the Statue of Liberty. I also tell her about the Staten Island Ferry.

"It's been free all these years! And it's one of the best things in New York City!" I exclaim. "If you come and visit me in New York City, you'll have to visit me in my loft apartment!"

I describe the wavy fifteen-foot ceilings, and the loft my father crafted by hand for me many years ago. I'm trying to reassure myself that I really am a special volunteer because of my New York City background. This part makes me feel special.

One day in the kitchen, Shawna gives me a hearty pat on the back and says, "I've never met anyone quite like you—you are one of a kind!"

I laugh in response. It feels good to be recognized by Shawna, and I want to get known in the kitchen, and especially by Shawna, for my laugh. Laughing is my way of releasing some of the stress of trying to fit in with this new situation. Back home, as a child, my father often told me to pipe down. "Stop, just stop," he'd say. "You're way too loud!" But I wanted to draw attention to myself and be in the spotlight. I desperately craved attention from my artist parents. So when I discovered I had a hyena-like laugh, I decided to use that to my advantage. At both private and public school, my signature laugh made students and teachers turn their heads. Some kids called me the class clown because I'd laugh and then do something else to continue diverting the teacher's attention, like falling off a chair. Even the teachers themselves would sometimes laugh at my antics.

"There she goes again!" a kitchen worker shouts as I let my laughing fit take me over, and soon enough a crowd of the kitchen workers has gathered around me, and a few are even trying to lift me up.

"Ma Karah?"—*What happened?* My aunt rushes in, her face ashen. When she sees I'm laughing hysterically on the dirty kitchen floor, surrounded by vegetable and fruit peels, she says, "Toda la'el she hacol besder!" *Thank goodness everything is alright.*

Shawna tries to pull me up. "Man, girl, you are a riot. I totally dig your laugh. You are so funny."

I dig Shawna. Unlike anybody else, she makes me feel special. Instead of letting her pull me to my feet, I stay on the floor, laughing as loud and high as I can. The sound echoes all throughout the kitchen.

Shawna gets down on her hands and knees and then plops herself on the ground. "Hey girlie-girl, matey, did you always laugh like this?" She is now laughing too.

"YESSSSSSSSSSS!" Now I'm wheezing between snorts. I puff my chest to sound out the hyena part of the laugh even louder. This way she doesn't have to get to know the real me—

clingy, emotionally dependent, and insecure. She may not like what she sees. I have a high success rate with my laugh. I'll stick with that.

Shawna opens her big brown eyes wide, releases a Cheshire Cat grin, and creeps even closer. I keep laughing. It's my secret weapon. The only way to protect myself.

∞

ONE MORNING, AS I'M THROWING VEGETABLE PEELS IN the garbage on my way to lunch, Shawna grabs me and says excitedly, "Hey Dorit, all finished? Here, let me tell you what you should do now."

It is 12:30 p.m. I have been working since 5:30 a.m., and my shift is over. All the vegetables have been washed and chopped for the rest of the day's meals, and I am heading out to the dining room for my lunch. I am ravenous.

The next thing I know, however, she's pulling me toward the kitchen sewers and ordering me to put on rubber gloves and drag out all the gunk, which is dirt mixed with what appears to be hair. The smell alone makes me want to throw up. Ugh. *Why is she making me do this? And worse, why am I letting her make me do it?*

She watches me and shouts, "Hurry, hurry, Dorit! We're behind schedule. We've got to get the food out for lunch!"

Lunch? Isn't lunch already ready?

Next she's got me hosing down the last of the metal tubs we use for the salads. She rushes me through each task. "Hurry, already! We've got to get moving, Dorit!" she shouts. "No, Dorit! Wash these tubs out like this!"

I obey every request. My work pants are soggy and wet. *Why don't I say something? Why am I letting her control me like this?* Instead of eating the lunch I've earned, I'm getting lunch ready for the first shift of hungry workers who are about to pour into the dining room from the orchards and factories and outside jobs.

Shawna hurries me through cleaning the next vat, tub, and container. I don't even think of wearing gloves. By the time we're finished, I'm wet, smelly, and too shaken up and tired to eat the food I helped prepare. In the dining room, Shawna whizzes by me, pulls a plate from the stacks, and laughs at some faraway joke before patting me on the back and saying, "Thanks, mate."

∞

"OH, THAT SHAWNA. SHE IS TOO MUCH," MY AUNT SAYS quietly after I share with her about Shawna's controlling behavior. My aunt immediately calms me down. Why did I wait three days to tell her? What the heck was I afraid of? I appreciate the fact that Israeli-born people really don't sugar-coat. Still, it's clear that my aunt doesn't realize how emotionally shaken up I am. She's never had the luxury of time to obsess over emotions like I do—to have internal debates about whether people's intentions are genuine or what major she wants to study. She's always been devoted to a higher cause, consistently working for the sake of the common good of this kibbutz. Again, service.

Sabras (pronounced "tsabras") is the term for Jewish people born in Israel—prickly and thorny on the outside, but with a sweet, softer interior. The term goes back to the 1930s and refers to any Jew born in Mandatory Palestine before Israel officially became a state, but today Israelis continue to use the word to refer to any Jew born anywhere in the historical region, which today comprises Israel and the Palestinian territories. My aunt helps explain *sabra* to me by showing me a prickly cactus sitting in a flowerpot in the corner of her modest terrace. After the incident with Shawna, the term finally starts to make sense to me: I can be more assertive, like the exterior of the prickly fruit, or I can be mushy like its inside. In the same vein, I have to get past the prickly exterior of the Israelis around me, including my aunt, in order to taste the "fruit" of the people—who, underneath it all, really are caring.

I suddenly feel as if I have a clearer road of understanding. I can either hang out with my fellow volunteers, speak English, and stay within my comfort zone here, or I can really make an effort to learn more about this "prickly pear" culture so I can determine whether or not I fit in here. And when my aunt says, "Oh that Shawna—she's too much," suddenly, there's a cultural context to understanding the situation. *Sabras* don't have time to waste. In a country like Israel, where there is constant political turmoil and war, there's no time to worry about what another person has said or done. So my aunt would say to my worries and concerns, "Why the heck worry about Shawna and the things she did and said to you?" Relationships here are more direct and less emotional. At home when I've had conflict with friends I've spend hours wondering, *What's wrong with me? Am I such a bad person? What did I do wrong?*—but here in Israel I don't have the time and space to do that.

I have no history here. Everything is new. It's like I'm a plant that's been uprooted and planted somewhere else. I'm not native to this area, not yet a true *sabra*, as my language and cultural mentality are still in transition, but I feel protected by the light of my people. Here I can start fresh.

AFTER A VISIT WITH MY AUNT WHERE SHE EXPLAINS about the Palestinian conflict and the historical context of what it means to be a *sabra*, I walk back to the volunteer quarters elated I've learned something new about my people and heritage. I welcome the afternoon siesta (kibbutznicks tend to nap between two and five in the afternoon) and, deciding to skip dinner, crawl into bed and gratefully surrender to sleep.

What feels like mere moments later, I wake up with a cold sweat forming on my back, side, and face like tears. Someone has closed the window and shutters, enveloping me in the darkness, and there's no ventilation. I'm wrapped up in a scratchy, soggy woolen blue blanket—the kind you use at sleepaway camp. I hear a faint noise that sounds like a siren, and realize that must be what has woken me up.

For a moment, I am back in my aunt's old house, a much smaller place than the one she's in now. I run with my mother, her hand gripping mine, my other hand clutching my baby blanket, past the horses and their silky manes, until we reach a two room bungalow with foamy chairs without frames. It's 1975, two years after the Yom Kippur War. I'm five years old. Mom immediately plants me on a chair and orders me to be quiet. Seconds later, I hear loud booms, the same kinds I'd hear years later as a soldier. "What an insane country," she says. "I knew we shouldn't have come here."

The last thing I remember Mom shouting is, "I don't want to be in this country. I just want to go home."

I didn't know how to react, so I imitated her and cried too.

Funny she once said that because now, at eighteen, I feel at home here on this kibbutz and not in the least bit threatened by any sign of an impending war. If anything, my newfound understanding of the politics involved has strengthened me. There's power in knowledge.

At this point, I think, *I could handle another war more easily than another Shawna outburst.*

Just as I prop myself up, I hear a pounding on the door.

"Hey mate, you there?" a loud voice calls out. "Wanna come to the disco with us tonight?"

It's Shawna.

Ugh.

3

ESCAPING SHAWNA

AFTER EXPERIENCING SHAWNA'S ERRATIC BEHAVIOR, I strategize on getting the hell out of this kitchen. There's just no other choice. I'm fine with the mindless work of chopping vegetables, mixing and spicing soups, and, most recently, making porridge, but now I'm constantly worrying that Shawna will order me around again—that I'll get hurt again by her hot and cold behavior. Whenever I hear her whistle or sing, I think, *That's just a cover-up for the real Shawna who bosses me around.* I consider what other jobs I might take on that will get me away from her.

The small, screened windows provide an expanse just wide enough to view the inconspicuous path of seedlings, forest firs, and wildflowers that meet the apple orchard at the entrance of the kibbutz. It's there that I spy the possibility of peace and quiet—a reprieve from this kitchen drama. I stand on a little stool and stir big pots of chunky, hearty soup, allowing the steam to fog up my glasses and run up my nose.

I hear Shawna's bellowing voice on the other side of the kitchen, and I wince. She triggers fears I've inherited from my mother—mainly her fears of authority and the unknown. She's always been willing to do anything to make sure she remains in good standing, whether that meant keeping her per-diem job as a substitute music teacher with the New York City Board of Education or cooperating with the management of our building to ensure she wouldn't lose our rent-stabilized apartment.

I'm afraid I'll get so pissed off at Shawna that my emotions will get the better of me and I'll tell her exactly how I feel about the way she's been treating me—and that if I do, she'll shut down and give me the silent treatment, or worse. I've never quite learned how to translate emotions into logical thoughts and then words. I simply attack.

Mom's fear of the unknown includes a gamut of wild and uncertain things that aren't on anybody's radar, like her fear of being pushed unto subway tracks late at night, or her fear of contracting cancer from asbestos (she often sent me articles about asbestos when I was at sleepaway camp during the summer; when the articles started to outnumber the care packages, I wrote her back, "Where do you think there's asbestos in a barn? This isn't New York City!"). Eventually, Mom's irrationality rubbed off onto me, and affected how I react around unknown or difficult situations—namely, always leaning toward harsh or negative interpretations of other people's actions. Case in point: Hearing Shawna in this moment, I hunch over the kitchen sink and think, *Shawna's definitely going to attack me—to say something verbally abusive to me. There's going to be chaos. There's going to be a fight. It's going to be terrible.*

When I've mentioned Shawna in my brief phone calls with Mom, she's just said, "Be a happy bug, don't be a worry bug." In fact, she repeats this mantra as if she's captured by some magic spell. It's her way of trying to protect me from the uncertainties of life, but after a while, the mantra numbs me. Her disconnection and ignorance irritate me. Why can't I just *feel* my pain and suffering? Mom is incapable of embodying compassion, understanding, and empathy—all the qualities I have always envied in other mother-daughter relationships. I can already see how working on the kibbutz, not depending on Mom's advice (or lack thereof), is helping me tap into who I am, my own power. I even think it has the possibility of bringing me happiness, though that will come with a price: separating myself from Mom.

I have begun to tiptoe around Shawna, to try to avoid her when I can. This is difficult, since she has appointed herself head of the volunteers. Where can I transfer to so I won't have to see so much of her? A quick brainstorm reveals the possibilities: I can work in the laundry or dining room, or better yet, the glamorous apple orchards, which I've eyed ever since my arrival.

Apples. I yearn to be around them and with them—not just to smell them at a farmer's market. I yearn to get intimate with nature. I've inherited Mom's taste for them, her favorite fruit, and now that I'm far away from her, I want to know what it's like to pick them. Each time we pass the orchards as we leave the kibbutz, I ask myself, *What do they smell like? How do they feel?*

"Dorit!" someone shouts. I turn my head, but it turns out someone is calling for a kibbutz member named Dorit, not me. Shaken from my reverie, I step down from the stool, thinking that I will to speak with the guy in charge of assigning jobs to volunteers today. Maybe I can start in the orchards as soon as tomorrow.

The guzzle of the kitchen mixers, the *woosh-woosh* of saran wrap and aluminum foil, and the *crash-slam-bang* of the huge metal refrigerator door remind me there aren't that many places to escape to in this kitchen. And then, in the midst of this confounding noise, I hear her again: "Do you want me to bring the apples from the big or small refrigerator?"

I know she's talking to my aunt by her tone, which is softer than the one she uses with other volunteers.

Little by little, Shawna approaches the secluded corner where I'm peeling vegetables that never made it into any of Grandma's soups, like parsnips and fennel. Nothing escapes Shawna's beady eyes, and the chances of me escaping are rather slim. I don't want to draw attention to myself by running out the door. So I stay hunched over the two-foot sink, cold water rushing through my fingers. As I shake the lettuce under the stream one final time to rinse the dirt, I think, *Please don't let her notice me. Please don't let me confront her. Please. Please. Please.*

A firm hand grips my shoulder. "Hey, matey. What's up?"

I continue to stay hunched over.

"You know you owe me one."

Oy. "Owe you?" I'm tempted to turn around, but I don't want to see her face.

"For the night at the disco. I was waitin' for ya, matey, at the bomb shelter. Ya never showed up."

For a moment, I feel relieved. No attack. "I know. I was too tired that night. I'm not used to waking up at 5 a.m each day. Next time."

"This is kibbutz life, matey. Better get used to it. This isn't New York City."

Right. You made your point. Now scat. Man, even when she's not ordering me around, she's bossy. I'm trying not to feel intimidated by her, but when I hear her voice, my nerves take over.

"Let's hustle with those vegetables," she says, patting my other shoulder. "Lunch needs to be ready on time today. Okay, matey?"

What's up with all the 'mateys'? I think. The word is Australian lingo for "buddy" or "friend," but it's clear that I'm neither.

This is just Shawna's passive-aggressive way of speaking, and it's starting to tick me off.

"Uh-huh," I say. *Please just leave now.*

"I want to see those salads out at 11:30, not 11:45 like last time," she says.

My adrenaline's now rising, but I don't bother explaining that the fifteen-minute delay wasn't my fault. She seems to expect me to hustle everyone else. But I'm not in charge, and I don't like all this unnecessary pressure.

I'm hoping if that I don't answer, she'll take the hint. But she lingers beside me for a moment more (God knows what she's thinking) before finally walking away.

When she's at the other end of the kitchen I finally step down from the stool. Oh my God. I can breathe. My chest is heaving up and down. I gulp for air as if someone has just punched me. It's a good thing nobody's near me. At least I can cope with this problem without drawing any attention.

I've got to get out of here. Time to get another job.

The apple orchard. Freedom. Open spaces, a place to think without the consternation and worry Shawna creates in me. There's no way I'm going to subject myself to another incident with her in the kitchen.

At dinnertime, my aunt and I approach the small cubicle of an office that belongs to the *sadran avoda*—the person in charge of assigning jobs to all the volunteers and kibbutz members. His name's Avi, and he has a bulging belly. He chats with my aunt at a nearby dining room table, their heads drooping like wilted flowers. He takes out a time-blocking chart full of scribbles, arrows, and notes in Hebrew. He makes a few more notes, looks up at me, and smiles.

"You start tomorrow."

Thank you, God.

∞

I EAGERLY ARRIVE OUTSIDE THE KITCHEN EXIT AT 4 A.M. to report for my new post. I'm first. There's no garbage smell, as there often is later in the day—just the sound of nighttime crickets. The unwavering dotted lights of the settlements and army base in the Galilee Valley greet me only temporarily before the whir of a John Deere tractor and a chorus of laughter from a row of volunteers cut the silence. The driver's got curly black ringlets like my father's; they peek out from under his green work hat. I approach the wagon and perch myself up close to the driver. Others follow. Nobody says a word. Everyone's heads are down. I try to distinguish between kibbutz member faces and volunteer faces, but it's too dark to see.

We're off toward the gate. I'm a kid again, delighted and excited to discover whether the orchards of my memory match up to what I am about to experience. I'm deeply fascinated by the delicate way in which the leaves brush against the tractor as it wobbles, creaks, and moans its way to our destination.

We arrive at the head of the row, and I'm the first one out. I breathe in the lush, fragrant soil.

"Nadav," the driver says by way of introducing himself. "Rak-rega"—*One minute*—he says as he searches for the right apple orchard *sak*, or carrier.

My burly *sak* has a lock on the bottom to keep the apples in place. I strap it over my shoulders and fasten it around my waist, then empty it of brown and green leaves. How long have they been there?

We pick until mid-morning, at which point we break in the shadows of a nearby tree. I bite deeply into an apple and swish the juice in my mouth. Bittersweet. The next one I pick has white blotches on it, and I throw it aside.

Nadav and the other volunteers are somewhere behind me, unaware of how far ahead of the rest of the group I've gotten. In between plucks, bites, and momentary pauses, I turn my attention to the one thing I've managed to avoid thinking about thus far: my departure date. I still have about a month left here, but after that I'll find myself back on an airplane to the States. So much has happened since I've arrived here. I don't really want to go home. If I go back, I'll have to confront Mom again, and she'll try to make me feel like a nobody with her lectures about how important it is to go to college.

I've never been so intimate with nature before, and I figure this is my chance. I sit down, and I'm so busy smelling the fragrant earth that I don't notice that I've sat down right near an irrigation hose until the rear end of my pants become completely soaked. I listen to eighties hits on my Walkman and observe the other volunteers. They work in a scattered, haphazard fashion. Some work while others break. Many are deep in conversation. Nadav inches the John Deere tractor farther down the row as we continue to fill up the huge yellow crates it holds. Life here is unregimented. Like nature. The skies. The trees. There is also no real presence of army life: soldiers do not patrol the warm summer earth here.

Despite this, I know one thing for certain: I'm protected.

At the top of a nearby hill there is an army base that probably houses some of the many soldiers I've observed back at the Koach junction. It can only be an army base, because it has two long poles that come together like an upside down V, with a longish pole on the top like the star of a Christmas tree, only instead of a star there is a long row of red lights. Too narrow to be a watchguard tower, but enough to identify the building as an army building. These army bases seem to be as pervasive as the air I breathe here, and for me they rub out any fear or doubt that I'm living in a "dangerous" country. We're in the "army zone," but that doesn't give rise to fear; on the contrary, the quiet mornings and afternoons here reassure me.

By lunchtime my pants have dried, but my shirt still sticks to my skin. I promise myself I will pay more attention where I sit next time. I relish in the fact that at this moment the issue I'm wrestling with is not which major or university to choose, but rather how to physically manage with a canvas bag full of apples that weighs down on my belly. It's a bit harder to lug my *sak* after the full-course meal of soup, schnitzel, rice, and potatoes topped with homemade peach compote and whipped cream we just ate. We are in the same row we were working before going to the dining room for lunch, but as I fill up my *sak* with more apples, I find myself sinking deeper in the moist ground than before: someone turned on the irrigation system in midday. The sun is now beating down, and I welcome the modest relief the gentle mist of water offers.

As Duran Duran and Suzanne Vega play in my ears, I feel a different kind of freedom—one that opens the doorway to more independence. I start to come up with a bunch of "what-ifs": *What if I don't continue studying at SUNY Albany? What if I challenge that damn status quo? What if I don't get my BA degree at age twenty-one and my MA at age twenty-five and my PhD at age twenty-eight? What will happen? Will I be a "nobody" if I don't follow Mom's voice? The voice of "doing it right"?*

I work alone. I pick another apple. I take a bite. I bite into abundance—into nature. There's a logic to all this picking that surpasses and even defies my expectations. I get a feeling of peace from being alone with my thoughts, and comfort that comes from feeling that way. This is exactly the experience I hoped for. A place I can call my own. My home away from home. Here in these fields, I don't need to prove anything to anybody. There's no Shawna ordering me around, and the closest thing to a person in charge is Nadav, who is a picker like the rest of us. The fact that he's the driver doesn't give him any real authority.

Communing with nature in this foreign world somehow provides me with deeper access to positive thinking, and to faith in my abilities to step outside my comfort zone and experiment with life's offerings instead of shying away from the challenges that usually stress me out. I sprint past the tractor and big yellow crates and go from row to row, trying to see if all the apples look as exquisitely the same as they did on the row I was just on. I breathe in wet soil. I'm connected to Mother Earth in a way that brings me closer to the divine. For the first time in my eighteen years, I am acting on my own intuition, and I feel it is guiding me toward making a decision based on what makes me happy and fills me up with passion rather than on what the "right thing" is—whatever that is. As I crunch through leaves and munch on juicy apples at Kibbutz Malkiyah, I feel a sense of freedom I've never experienced before.

For the next few weeks, I continue to drink in the delicate, fragrant smell of apples, and to breathe in the fresh air, without thinking too many steps ahead. I belong here. Each time we pile into the dining room for the midday meal and grab a hot plate from the dishwasher, we're filling our stomachs so we can replenish the earth and reconnect to its soil and fruit. Despite the monotony of picking apples, I look forward each morning to spending another delectable day in this corner of my protected world. When Shawna approaches me in the dining room, I'm no longer intimidated. I can either take my tray and sit in a far corner of the dining room, happy to be by myself, or join a bunch of volunteers and sip my chicken soup with gusto, even if Shawna sits just a few heads away. Her bellowing voice doesn't rattle me anymore. This experience has empowered me in ways I never could have imagined.

4

TOGA PARTY

ONE AFTERNOON, AFTER RELAXING FROM ANOTHER HARD day's work at the apple orchard, two of my Danish roommates, Emma and Isabella, saunter in. Amidst their Danish, I hear words I understand, like "pub," "vodka," and "toga."

Toga party. Tonight.

I'm trying to bury myself in the pages of Sue Hubbell's *A Country Year: Living the Questions*, which I picked up at a travel store over at the South Street Seaport Museum in New York City before I left. Ever since escaping Shawna, I've been living in paradise. The idea of a toga party does not fit into that pristine, idyllic life. Who needs to get wrapped up like a Greek? I didn't come here to masquerade in a costume.

I lift up my head from my book and try to make small talk, pretending I don't know what's going on. "So, what's happening tonight? Anything special?"

"We're having a toga party," Emma says.

"Toga party? Us? The volunteers?" I give a dumbfounded look.

"Yes. Are you coming?"

If there's one thing I've learned from hanging out with other volunteers, it's that they like to get filthy drunk. This toga party is obviously just another excuse to party recklessly. Not exactly my scene. Growing up in Westbeth in New York City, I saw the ways alcohol affected the artist world. There, children were side dishes and talking about art was the main course—usually accompanied by drinks. Artists would get especially excited when showing their latest "masterpiece" at the building's gallery, and even as a child I'd notice how they would frequently raise their voices or speak out of turn at these events. There was something unpredictable about their mannerisms, and it made me nervous—though it wasn't until I caught whiff of that awful smell wafting from their clothes or beards that I would catch on to what it was I didn't like. They would talk with that smell on their breath, move their arms this way and that, and I felt as if the devil was on his way to whisk me off to his cave of hell. Years later, after my father moved out, I'd come face to face with some of them in the elevator.

In one year alone there were seven suicides relating to depression and alcoholism at Westbeth. I never quite understood the pinnacles of high and lows that the artists surrounding me were subject to. My father, the primary artist in my world, spent his days nestled in his studio on the third floor. Each section of his studio was devoted to a different media of art. Stained glass creations consisting of shards of green, blue, and orange hung from simple chains, too far away from the sun to show even the faintest black lines of the metal holding them together.

This was my familiar artist world. Observing in solitude, as if in prayer or meditation.

If I wasn't observing my father or listening to my mother's Chopin (she played it constantly; perhaps it reminded her of

her Polish roots), I was busy exploring the many hallways and
stairwells with the other Westbeth children. I never knew when
I might bump into one of the drunkards who lingered in the
creepy corners of Westbeth's extensive network of hallways—
usually homeless people who had drifted in from the West Side
Highway—during those ramblings. These people never stayed
for more than twenty-four hours; someone would alert the
security guard and by the next morning they were gone. But I
often came across them in my wanderings, and they were part
of the phatamagoric creepiness of the basement I had in-
vented in my mind, whose hunched creatures could at any
time look up at me with fiery, bloodshot, accusing eyes, making
me feel as if I'd committed some kind of crime.

Artists with alcohol breath and the "creepies" in the
hallways were my earliest exposure to the "drunk" world; but
there was one experience in particular that solidified my fear.

It happened after Dad moved out, in the time when I
spent countless hours roaming the hallways waiting for Mom
to return from her late-night master classes with legendary
Argentinian pianist Arminda Canteros. I was eleven, and one
night—my nervousness in overdrive because Mom wasn't
home yet and it was getting rather late for dinnertime—I
visited a friend a few doors down the hall from us, thinking I
might distract myself by hanging out with her and her mother,
who often invited me over for delicious meals. Not long after I
got there, however, she drove me out of the apartment, screaming, "Get out, Dorit! You think you understand but you have
no idea. Get out!" She sent me off with a fit of jeering laughter
—an eerie memory that shakes me up still today.

Crying, I ran down the hallway to my apartment. I felt
like a wounded animal. This was my best friend's mother, a
woman who I usually enjoyed hanging out with, and who

always seemed to enjoy my company, too. What had just happened? Years later, my friend confessed to me, "She lashed out at you," and explained that she had been drunk. Even today, innocent, loveless me wonders, *Why did she behave that way? What did I do to deserve that?*

Recalling this incident, I shudder inwardly and worry about the party. It will be challenging to find anyone sober there. I want to have engaging conversations about comparative literature, culture, and social justice, but I don't see that happening at a toga party. I never felt at home among the free-spirited artist types at Westbeth; nobody ever seemed to care about how I felt or what I was thinking. Hanging around the other volunteers when they're drunk reminds me of the isolation I felt as a child. Striking up a serious chat is my way of finding my grounding, but a drunken stupor permeates these parties, making serious conversation difficult and in turn triggers deep feelings of loneliness for me.

If I'm going to have fun, I'll need to talk my way through it. But who will I talk to?

∞

JUST AS I'M FRETTING OVER WHETHER I SHOULD GO TO the party for the sake of fitting in, a small-framed British volunteer named Ian with long, luscious locks manages to topple three empty green plastic crates as he sets a stack of them on our kitchen counter. Somehow our room has been chosen as a makeshift storage area for holding all the alcoholic drinks.

Ian has been friendly with Shawna ever since he arrived, and the minute he sees me peering over the pages of my book, he shouts, "Dorit"—he enunciates the second syllable of my name so it sounds like *Dor-EAT*—"I just KNOW you're gonna come to tonight's toga party, right?"

I peer at him from behind my book, and when he doesn't continue talking, I crane my neck even further without saying anything.

"C'mon, Dorit," he says, "it'll be fun!" He starts filling the crates with svelte-looking Coors beer bottles. I toss my book aside and come over to Ian with a smile. I'm still not committed to this whole toga party thing, but Ian exudes warmth and happiness—just what I need right now to calm my jittery nerves.

"That's my girl," he exclaims, giving me a big squeeze on my shoulders and then a big bear hug. The energy of that hug warms me up like a cup of tea on a cold morning. "Believe me, you won't regret it," he adds.

There's a part of me that deeply wants to believe him, but beneath my smile there's a current of fear. I know what's going to happen; I've seen it at previous parties. Ian's great right now, but as the night goes on he'll get drunk and start using words like "bloody bloat" to emphasize his strong antagonistic feelings toward British soccer teams, political parties, and pop figures—subjects that are so culturally removed from my Jewish-artist world that I can't even begin to keep up. And even if I could, when Ian and his buddies begin to slur in their Cockney accents, I can barely understand a word.

I have to accept the fact that I made a choice to work alongside volunteers with whom I have absolutely nothing in common. Perhaps this is a natural step toward adulthood—learning to get along with other cultures and mentalities—but I keep thinking, *If only there were another American volunteer on board here, surely I would feel more at ease.* The reality, though, is that I am far away from Tel-Aviv and Jerusalem—the places where Americans tend to flock in large groups—so it should come as no surprise that I'm the only American volunteer here. The Danes, Swedes, Brits, and Australians all have at least one other person from their home country here, but I have no one, and this makes me feel even more foreign.

Ian and I bump heads as we both reach for the same crate, and I notice that his hair is lopsided.

"Is that . . . a wig?" I say, joking.

He straightens it with a giggle. "Yep! Just for the toga party tonight! So you're coming, right?"

For the last few social events the volunteers have put together, I've opted to stay in my room. And nobody has really paid attention to that fact except for Ian, who always seems to notice. The next day he runs up to me in the dining room or some other public place and shouts, "Where were you?"

I look at him now with deep hesitation. "I'm not sure. It's not exactly my idea of fun."

"You're not scared about Shawna again, are you?"

"No . . . well, not really. I just don't want to be around, well . . . drunk people. It's kind of scary."

Yes! How relieved I feel to finally say what I've been harboring in my soul for the last few weeks.

He looks at me strangely, as if I have just spoken to him in another language. "Scary? What's so scary about it? We Brits just like to have a good time. You can't exactly tell me Americans don't like to have a good time," he says, chuckling.

"Well, they do, but I'm not into drinking. It's not my cup of tea."

"Well, you're my cup of tea," he says, nudging me in my side. It tickles my rib and I let out a giggle. Ian is a flirt, and a damn good one. But I'm just looking for a good friend, and I know better than to take his intentions seriously. Besides, he's not my type and he knows it.

"Well, here's this," he says. "You don't have to stick around if you don't like it. Just come for a little while, and if you don't like it, you can leave."

I nod in agreement. It seems harmless enough. "Okay, sounds like a plan."

∾

A FEW HOURS LATER, IAN HELPS WRAP THE TOGA AROUND me. I stumble with each wrap. He arranges the sheet so that I am only slightly covered on both sides and pulls me toward the mirror.

"What do you think?"

"I look ridiculous. Absolutely ridiculous."

The last time I played dress-up was years ago, when I was a cat in the famous Ralph Lee West Village Halloween parade. Ralph Lee worked with Jim Henson, creator of the famous Muppets, and both were my father's friends. As a child, I would hold the gossamer fabric made to look like floating phantoms propped up with poles and sticks and the googly-eyed fish with larger-than-life scales. When you moved one part of the fish, the scales expanded and moved like a swaying accordion. Magical. Nothing like I imagine this toga party will be.

The party is now going to take place in all the volunteer rooms, not at the pub at a nearby bomb shelter as originally planned, so I grab a zip-up SUNY at Albany sweatshirt and wrap it around my shoulders, then head to the rooms where everyone is gathered.

Groups of volunteers wrapped in togas parade from room to room, filling their mouths with pretzels and guzzling beer and vodka. The men are wearing makeup. Ian has taken out his ponytail for the incessant pictures being taken by some random volunteer. They ask me to join them, but I watch and laugh from a distance. Within thirty minutes, new green crates are brought in. There seems to be an endless supply of beer stashed away in my room.

Shouting and screaming erupts as the night progresses, and I watch in disbelief. What the heck am I doing here? What am I doing hanging out with these hooligans?

For a while Ian lingers, telling me about his upcoming trip to visit Egypt and the pyramids at Giza—a locale I know only from what I learned in Egyptian archeology class at SUNY Albany. He leaves in one week, and won't be coming back to Malkiyah. This upsets me a bit, but then again, I am leaving soon too right after him.

In the end, I rough it out and pretend to have fun. I smile for the camera holding a beer bottle, something I would never do at school, and I laugh when Ian shouts to the volunteer taking the photo, "C'mon, hurry up already—you bloody bloat!" It's clear they're both already drunk. The phrase "bloody bloat" stays in my head, and for the reminder of the evening, I "bloody bloat" this and that as a way to entertain myself. I don't want to look bored or annoyed; the last thing I need is to get on some drunk volunteer's bad side and have him (or her) lash out at me. So I laugh and cheese my way through the evening.

When I get back to my room, I quickly peel off my toga, which reeks of cigarettes and alcohol, and sniff my body. *Ugh,* I think and rush to our tiny shower. I stay there for at least an hour soaping the dirt and the grime from myself. An unexpected barrage of tears falls. The hot water soothes me, but more tears come. When I was a kid waiting for my mom to return from her master classes, I made the unfamiliar familiar by circling the creepiest hallways of Westbeth. Then, I didn't have a choice—I was stuck there—but here I am, far away from my mother's influence, and still I'm overcome with worry and anxiety. At eighteen years old, I've got the same sick feeling I had when I first began those hallway rounds. I feel like there's nowhere for me to go—like I'm stuck here pretending to fit in.

The problem is I have no anchor, no capacity for regulating my thoughts. I just put my foot on the "worry gas" and off I go, spiraling into the world of my mother's fear, drowning in the voices that have controlled me since my childhood, beginning with the articles about lung cancer and alcohol disease that she sent to me for six consecutive summers at sleepaway camp (asbestos wasn't her only concern), exacerbated by her late-night practices.

On those evenings in Westbeth, when it was an hour after Mom's scheduled time to return from her classes uptown, I couldn't help but think of all the dreary possibilities: Mom could be pushed into the subway tracks, someone could whisk her away, her pocketbook could be stolen . . . there was no end to my worry. So I circled the hallways, wanting nothing more than to see a familiar face—my mom's.

When my father still lived with us, the heavy sliding metal door to his studio on one of the roofs stayed open for hours during the day, sawdust carvings wafting out, carried on the breeze to wherever they needed to fly. I would sit and watch him work for hours at a time, wondering if his tiny, precise hand movements really added up to anything and eying the Chock Full o'Nuts cans and Planters peanut jars full of screws and bolts that sat next to him. I kept my distance when Dad powered up the electric cutter saw, and instead of counting how many times he moved the cutter back and forth, I would watch shavings fly everywhere.

The roof at night was a different story. From somewhere up there came the scary churn of an engine, and when I passed the metal-ridged open-air house, I'd get a strong attack of the heebie-jeebies. With the single lightbulb blowing in the wind up there, and no art in the making to distract me, there was too much black space and distance between myself and the other metal objects in and around that long empty frame. With a shiver, I would turn and go back down the black, serpentine stairwell. Somewhere a few flights down, a door would creak then slam. Voices. Laughter. I'd look up at the broken glass of the roof, hoping that whatever was left up there wouldn't suddenly fall, and make my way downstairs even more slowly than before, stretching time so I wouldn't have to face what I'd been dreading all along: an apartment without Mom.

I developed my own system to help cope with my mother's prolonged absence each time she left. If I came back to our apartment and the door was locked, that meant Mom had come home, and I would ring the doorbell. She would zoom down the stairwell, shouting, "Who is it?" I would shout right back, "It's me, Ma!" and that meant I could stop worrying. If the door was unlocked, however, that meant she still hadn't come home, so off I would go again, waiting and hoping to see her suddenly appear from the far end of the hallway in her fake fur coat.

Nobody knew my little system; I made sure of that. I was ashamed. Nobody I knew would go to such lengths worrying about their parents. Mom understood that I was a worrier, but she had no idea how much I catastrophized, imagining the terrible things that might have befallen her between practice and home—to the point I'd make myself sick. She mistook my introvertedness for independence, clueless about how deeply being left alone for long periods of time affected me.

While I wandered Westbeth, my little brother would stay inside the apartment, not knowing where his big sister had disappeared off to. Every so often I'd come back to use the bathroom or get a drink of water, but only briefly. I knew I couldn't stay in that loveless apartment while Mom was out practicing. Worry was in my veins. If I didn't worry about her, I reasoned, nobody else would. Worrying was the only way I knew of to exert some kind of control over the situation. By age twelve, I was in a prison of my own thoughts. I could never find peace.

My father would sometimes call to check in on us, and when he did I usually lied, telling him we had already eaten dinner with Mom and were on our way to bed. I craved what I couldn't put into words, trying to rely on my logical half to help me weather these waves of emotional unpredictability. If I were to voice what I was feeling and say, "I want my Mom to show love and affection," I'd be admitting that I wanted her to change, and I knew that wasn't going to happen. So, since she wasn't capable of becoming the emotional role model I wanted, I lied to protect her.

∞

I END MY TWO-MONTH-LONG VOLUNTEER EXPERIENCE BY taking one-day bus trips to local places like the mystical city of Zefat and the portal city of Acco. I also visit an Israeli cousin in Tel Aviv, and we hang out at the colorful fountain at Dizengoff square. I notice my cousin's Naots—naturally made leather sandals—which everyone in this country seems to wear, and she helps me buy my first pair at a nearby store. I slip them on and twirl in the mirror like a ballerina, just like the days at Westbeth when I wanted to get my Mom's attention while she played her many Chopin etudes. I yelp with joy. I feel like an Israeli.

These trips provide just the right escape from the close-knit existence typical of kibbutz life. But they also help me experience a deeper part of Israeli culture; it's seeping into my skin, my blood. I can feel it.

I have learned so much this summer: the importance of experimenting, of daring to step outside my comfort zone of working, of learning about different cultures and getting to know my Israeli family, and of thinking more positively and not letting the emotional triggers of my childhood get the better of me. But I'm ready to try another year at SUNY at Albany. During these last couple of weeks in Israel, I make a temporary plan: I will return to school for my sophomore year, but if I don't declare a major by the end of it, I'll go home and stay with Mom until I figure out my next steps.

Before I came to Israel, my aunt wrote in one of her letters, "Volunteering on the kibbutz will be a good experience for you. You should do it." She was right—but I'm glad that the experience is behind me. There's a bigger and brighter future waiting for me beyond the perimeter of Kibbutz Mal-kiyah. I can feel it.

I could be debt-free after college; I'd be entitled to receive certain rights, including three years of free higher education— enough to complete a bachelor's degree (BA studies in Israel are only three years); and I would be able to purchase a car without the additional 17% VAT tax I'd have to pay here. As a New Yorker, having a car doesn't really speak to me right now, but maybe I'll want one someday.

At Mom's apartment, unpaid bills are stuck under the piano cover of her 1932 Steinway Grand, revealing the gold plating, red velvet, and black foam covering the keys. Bills for her cosmetology and my braces. Bills for her nose job and her medical bills. More bills for her needs than ours. I have no idea if these bills have been paid or not. But when Julliard School of Music or some library out on Long Island asks her to play a concert gig, she emphatically says "yes" every time. She will never turn down a gig, even if it only pays fifty bucks. (This, too, irritates my dad, because these sums are never enough to pay bills.) When it comes to money, she pretends there are no problems, and as long as Dad keeps paying child support, she doesn't think it's important to take a full-time job.

It takes me until this conversation with my friend to acknowledge the connection between having a fresh start in Israel and money. And a fresh start as far as money is concerned means no bills to pay. No student loans. At the end of the day, in Israel, as an IDF soldier and an immigrant entitled to financial benefits, I'd get to decide how to make, spend, and invest money. The way things are looking now here in the US, I can only look to a future of debt; after college I'll be just as bad off as I am now, living at home with my mom, or even worse. And I definitely do not want to be like my mother, who has no clue about money and finances. She isn't that responsible. By going to Israel, I'll have initiated my own rite of passage—one that will include learning financial responsibility. At my friend's suggestion, I finally make a pro and con list:

Pros to Staying in the USA

- I'm on familiar ground with friends and family here.

- I can stay with Mom while I study in New York City, which means saving on rent money.

- I can continue going to college, even if I don't exactly know what to study (though I may have missed the application deadline).

- Since I'm set on studying in New York City, I'll have a better chance of connecting with fellow New Yorkers.

- New York City has much more to offer than Israel.

Cons to Staying in New York City and Studying at College

- I'll be in debt from my student loans.

- New York City is an expensive place to live.

- I still feel aimless trying to decide on a major.

Cons to Going to Israel

- I'll have to work hard to step outside of my comfort zone.

- I'll have to study some Hebrew, but besides that I don't exactly know what I'll study, if anything.

- If I emigrate to Israel, I'll be locked into studying for my BA there—a three-year commitment—after my service in the IDF, so I'll be in it for the long haul.

Pros to Going to Israel

- Volunteering for the IDF will make me more mature, disciplined, and focused. When I'm done I'll have a much better idea of what I want to study.

- I won't have to pay for my bachelor's degree—the government will pay for my first three years of undergraduate studies—so I won't be in debt.

- I will be away from the constraints Mom places on me.

That last one is pretty appealing.

∞

THREE MONTHS BEFORE THE END OF MY SOPHOMORE year, I show up at Dad's office. My stepmother is there as well. I'm now really pressed to make a decision, because if I'm going to re-enroll for my junior year at SUNY, I have to do it soon. If I decide to leave, I will be joining a *garin*, a group of young people who do the army together by working on kibbutzim, settlements, and army bases as part of the Nahal service, this August.

I swivel on the big wooden stool that once sat in Dad's studio, and now sits in Dad's graphic studio, located in the garment district of Manhattan. I follow him into the adjoining room, a small, dim space containing sketches, orange and gold canvasses, and dried up sea green oils. The same Chock Full o'Nuts can from my childhood is in there, sitting on a collapsing shelf that's twenty years old—older than me.

Dad's face is filled with urgency. He tightens his eyebrows, then exhales as if he's puffing on a cigarette. My stepmother joins us in the windowless room to listen in on our conversation.

"You have a choice," Dad says. "You can either stay in New York City with your mom, or you can emigrate to Israel before us so you can establish residency before we join you."

If I'm going to emigrate to Israel, it's smarter for me to do it before my dad moves there—as a new immigrant, as opposed to a *kitina hozeret*, a returning minor under my parents' authority. That way I'll get the financial benefits a lone soldier (one who does not have parents in Israel) is afforded under the Law of Return, which states that every Jew has the right to return to his or her homeland, and I'll be able to establish both my emotional and economic independence.

As part of a *garin*, I'll be doing a combination of both military service and work on settlements and various kibbutzim. I'll be in uniform most of the time, speaking Hebrew, and I will have a built-in community on a kibbutz, a self-contained unit. I won't have to worry about cooking and paying rent. I'll have my own room, since the IDF pays kibbutzim to host groups of soldiers. The more I think about it, the more I realize that Dad's idea for me to go to Israel is an end-all solution.

"I'm thinking of transferring out of SUNY and studying at one of the city colleges," I hear myself say. I'm trying to drag out time. I'm afraid to step into my own power and really tell my dad how I feel. I'm at a crossroads. "SUNY houses all the students from Long Island. There aren't any New York City kids. It's another world. It's isolating."

I'm hoping he'll understand that as a New York City kid, I can't seem to find my "tribe" among a bunch of students from Long Island. But deeper still, I'm craving acceptance by a different tribe. In high school, I hung out only with the "nerds" and secretly wished I could socialize with my edgy, spunky peers at one of New York City's most prestigious schools, known as the *Fame* school behind Lincoln Center. My intuition tells me that if I give New York City another chance, I may just get a chance to play "catch-up" in some way, to live the life I always wanted to live in high school. I make a mental note to add this to my "pros" list. In college in the city, I'll have a better chance finding my New York City tribe, and maybe make up for those tumultuous high school years.

"But where would you live?" Dad asks.

"With Mom."

"Dorit, if you continue to stay with your mom, you'll turn out to be exactly like her."

Dad has lectured me many times before on this subject, starting with that *New York Times* clipping about Tania Aebi, the girl who sailed around the world. The message? He wants to encourage me to take more risks and think outside of the box. He appeals to my rational and ambitious side—the one that goes against Mom's emotional and irrational world. We both know that Mom's fear and paranoia rub off on me and trigger me to catastrophize.

If Mom had been an emotional role model, able to balance a career as a brilliant classical concert pianist with mothering, I might not have such mixed feelings about leaving, and Dad would not be so worried. But this is not the case, and Dad can see only a fearful Dorit who's stuck in her emotional prison. He can see that moving to Israel will give me emotional independence, but I'm not there yet. I'm too riddled with questions and fears. And then there's the hope I hold out, against my better judgment, for my mom to change. All these years, I've kept thinking she might become that loving and nurturing person who will listen to me as I talk about my insecurities and fears instead of shooing me away and suggesting I see a psychologist. I keep longing for nourishing, home-cooked meals, too, but our refrigerator remains stocked with frozen dinners. I realize I'm fantasizing. This will never, can never, happen.

Dad wanted to go back to Israel as a family when we were young, but Mom resisted moving, mainly due to her fears of Israel. Now, after all these years, he's ready for that fresh start —the one my mother denied him years ago. And this need for a fresh start is particularly important for my brother, five years younger than me, who has been hanging out with the wrong crowd—a group of fifteen-year-olds who think they can rule the world with guns and knives and drugs. It's been getting worse lately, to the point where my mother is almost hysterical; she wants to do whatever she can to make sure he's protected.

"This is New York City," I remind her. "There's nothing you can do to keep him safe."

We both know that living in a major city has its disadvantages. And it was Mom who decided to pull us both out of a private Jewish day school and enroll us in the gang-infested, crime-ridden public school in Chelsea, a neighborhood ten minutes from our home. Israel would probably be a good move for my brother, but I can't broach the subject with her.

I think about all those times I called for her and she continued playing her piano, unresponsive. She wouldn't come unless I made a big deal of something. Finally, I'd shout, "Mom, please . . . come . . . Just *come!*" And then she'd climb those few tiny steps to my loft and say breathlessly, "What's wrong, honey-bunny?"

Once I had her there, she'd obey each of my commands: "Rub me here, it hurts" (often nothing actually hurt; I just wanted her to rub me); or sometimes, "Run your fingers through my hair." I would lie there, breathing in her Estée Lauder perfume, and for a moment my anxieties would subside. What I really wanted to do was talk to her, but I knew that if I started sharing all my worries, she'd back right down those steps, saying, "Dorit, I really don't have time for this. Why don't you go see a psychologist?"

The first time she said this, I thought she was kidding. But she said it enough times in response to my normal childhood needs that over time I became wary of sharing my concerns. Part of me, though, wanted to shout, "But you're my mother! You're supposed to help me with these things—that's your job! Why are you acting like this?" And when I was feeling terribly anxious as a kid, I did shout—I shouted hysterically, hoping Mom would intuit from my voice how I was truly feeling. But she never did. How I suffered from trying, and from knowing that she was only capable of obeying my requests for physical comfort. As I weigh my options for this coming year, I realize those mome

nts were only disguised in the language of hopeful optimism. Neglect was there all along.

Now, standing before my Dad and stepmother, who speak from a place of logic and reason, I say to myself, *Who the fuck are you kidding? Mom's never going to change. She's not capable of changing. Not. Capable. Of. Changing. Start accepting that.*

My stepmother and father see consternation on my face.

"Don't worry," Dad says, misreading my look. "It's just for a year's time. We'll soon join you in Israel. A year will go by fast. And then we'll make a home there. You'll see."

I ponder the concept of a home. If I decide to join them, the experience will stretch to include a completely different definition of "home" than the one I currently have—Westbeth, loneliness, anxiety. This other version of home first presented itself to me when I volunteered in Israel a year ago and tasted the emotional freedom that comes with getting away from my mother. I will be welcomed into Israel, my Jewish homeland. Anti-Semitic discrimination has never a problem for me in New York City, where there is a large Jewish population, and my school experiences here have generally been positive. I don't feel the need to escape persecution that has historically been the impetus for Jews moving to Israel. But still the idea of making my home there calls to me.

"I'll think about it," I say, and rush out of the office. In less than ten minutes, I'm back at the 14th Street subway stop. The minute I reach Bethune Street, closest to the river, the wind almost blows off my beret. I grab it just in time, then cross the street to our apartment. Once on our floor, I hear the music of Chopin. I wait outside for a moment before opening the door; when I do get inside, I head straight for the bathroom. Mom doesn't suspect my plans, and I'm not ready to talk to her. I need to go for a bike ride—to clear my mind and make sure I'm making the decision to move to Israel for the right reasons. I need to know that what I'm doing is right.

∞

PERCHED ON MY BANANA SEAT BIKE, I WHIZ DOWN THE dimly lit hallway to our huge building's West Street entrance. Here is where the wind has always been the strongest and coldest. Mad, too.

Outside, I dismount to run across the street with my bike, then hop back on and bike against the wind, flying *hard*.

There's just one pier on the Hudson River that hasn't gone under. It's full of potholes, but still standing. I've never biked along the pier for fear I might speed too fast and fall off, but this time I decide to detour from my typical "let's-go-down-to-Battery-Park-and-back-in-thirty-minutes" route.

The waves strike against the eddy, bringing salty, dirty

river water over the rotting wood of the pier and close to my feet. Behind me is the façade of our building, now a melting shade of golden brown from the sunset. A couple holding hands pass me, and the guy says something that makes the woman crack up. She looks my way, but I pretend not to notice and brush my hair away from my face.

I bike back to the beginning of the pier and turn right, toward Battery Park. I pass a few abandoned piers fully loaded with garbage. Normally I would bike around the square blocks of our building—Bank, Bethune, Washington, and West Streets—and only go as far as West 11th Street, just a few short city blocks away, to warm up before attempting anything farther away. But I'm heading straight to Battery Park—a longer route that's indicative of the real journey to come.

Each time the wind from the Hudson River tries to knock me down, I push down on the pedals even harder.

Which voice do I listen to now: my mom's, my own, or my father's? Mom has heard about Dad's plans to move to Israel, and, not surprisingly, she's opposed to the move. "Over my dead body you're going there!" she shouts at me whenever the topic comes up, in the same defiant tone she uses when she's resistant to something. It's the same tone I came up against last year when I was getting ready to volunteer on my aunt's kibbutz, and probably the same tone she used when Dad tried to get her to move back to Israel when we were very young. This time, however, she has good reason to be upset about the possibility of my returning to Israel now: she knows that if I go, I may not be back for a while—five and a half years, to be exact, two and a half years of army service and three years of college studies. I could decide to visit during my service, of course. But will I?

The question that keeps nagging at me is this: *If I stay here, will I turn out to be just like her?* My dad thinks so.

I navigate past roadblocks and construction sites to rediscover the bike trail. I end up biking across the street to the 11th Avenue sidewalk. As I ride, I sing Duran Duran's "New Moon on Monday" in a high voice.

You're free, I think. *You can do it. You're meant to follow the beat of your own drum. You have the power.* The more I think about what Israel means to me, the more my father's dream becomes my personal goal. I think of all that Israel has in store for me: freedom from debt, freedom from Mom, discipline, focus, maturity . . . I bike past the empty warehouse lots and their fences, which are practically invisible in the dark. The flickering lights of the Twin Towers are like two giant Shabbat candles—the long, waxy kind I used to light at my grandmother's house in Far Rockaway. They light my way from this point along the West Side Highway.

Just a year ago, when I hiked the Galilean hills with our volunteer group and explored the mystical city of Tsfat—in the Upper Galilee, not too far from my aunt's kibbutz—I got a sense of the freedom that comes with exploring new places, a glimpse of who I could be if I struck out on my own. In my heart, I know that if I truly and authentically want freedom, the right thing to do is to leave Mom. The only place I've successfully experienced that feeling is in Israel. There, I felt less fear, fewer inhibitions. All was possible, and nobody was standing in my way. And I also, for the first time, felt a deep love for where I was and what I was doing—whether sitting under apple trees or intently watching an IDF soldier move his foot in casual fashion while hitchhiking.

At the farthest end of Battery Park, I get off my bike and observe the water. It's darker and murkier here, with bobbling pieces of wood sticking out every which way, trash, and what faintly looks like seaweed. A dark future. An unknown future.

A future tied up in cobwebs and "what-ifs." Everything feels too familiar. I should feel free with the wind blowing in my hair, but I feel claustrophobic. I'm beginning to understand that if I stay here, I'll never leave my comfort zone.

To my left, there's the Brooklyn Bridge; to my right, the Staten Island Ferry—my guideposts in this familiar part of the city. But there's no knowledge gained in navigating the familiar. I have to take risks if I want to change any aspect of my life.

I should feel free right now, here at the farthest tip of the city, but instead the thought of living with my mom on this cosmopolitan island makes me choke.

∽

"OVER MY DEAD BODY YOU'RE GOING TO ISRAEL!" MOM shouts from the bottom of the stairs two days after my bike run to Battery Park.

"I'll do whatever I want!" I shout back at the top of my lungs. "I'm nineteen years old. It's my life. You can't rule me!"

Silence.

Then she shouts the same old Yiddish exclamation from childhood, "Oy Gottenyu!"—*Oh, dear God!*—but this time she is practically hysterical. Her face turns pink as she shouts. Then she spits at me. This is something she used to do all the time in my pre-teen years, but the last time she spat was a few years ago, and I thought her spitting days were over. On the first try, she misses. I restrain myself from spitting back, intending to be the "grown-up." On her second try I don't duck, and her loogie hits me squarely in the face. Her saliva oozes down my face, just like it did when I was younger. In a twisted way I am used to its disgustingness, but still, I am shocked. Why is she doing this to me?

I grab a tissue and wipe my face, understanding that this is her last attempt to regain control—her way of reminding me that I am undermining her power, and she doesn't like it. She is losing control of the war she has fought for years. Her days of controlling my life are now over, and there is absolutely nothing she can do to change that. This frightens her. Spitting is perhaps her last attempt to deal with the fear.

This is the real Mom nobody knows, I think to myself. Not the child musical prodigy, the one who played with Leonard Bernstein in Carnegie Hall in New York City. The Julliard graduate. The world concert pianist who has traveled to six different continents for the love of classical piano.

"I'm going to tell all your friends about the real Mom nobody knows," I scream. "The one who spits. The one who shouts at me. The one I hate. I hate you!"

Her face contorts slightly, as if she's giving in. But instead she turns away and closes the heavy padded door at the bottom of the stairs that lead to her studio.

Two minutes later, I hear muffled Chopin. I leave. Soon, I'll be leaving for good.

6

UP, UP AND AWAY!

I OFFICIALLY WITHDRAW FROM SUNY AT ALBANY AFTER
my sophomore year, and for the next few weeks my life is full
of appointments at the Jewish Agency to jumpstart the immigration process. I come in one day and they have me fill out
every application and form to the best of my ability in Hebrew
and English. For three hours, as the building rumbles and
shakes around me—there's construction going outside on First
Avenue—I work on the forms. I could finish faster, but I don't
want to mess up this once-in-a-lifetime opportunity with silly
mistakes. I feel that I have to get it right. I refuse to use white-
out; each time I make a mistake, I start a new application.

When I'm finished, I go from floor to floor getting my
papers stamped, sealed, and sent. When this is done, I depart
for the office of Avshalom Horowitz, who serves as the liaison
at the central kibbutz Aliyah Desk for American youth who,
like me, want to serve on a kibbutz as part of their army
service. Dad has helped me to get this far, but the paperwork
that remains is all mine, and I commit to the task steadfastly.
The Jewish agency is on the East Side and Avshalom's office is

on the West Side—on 22nd Street between Sixth and Seventh Avenue—so I walk almost twenty city blocks to get there. My decision to go to Israel feels right. I'm consummating a dream that was born when I watched two soldiers hitchhiking at the base of a mountain in the upper Galilee. Walking crosstown to Avshalom's office makes the decision feel real.

When I arrive, he hands me a piece of paper. "That's the voucher for your flight," he says in a heavy accent.

I read the heavy typeset: English words on carbon paper. It's a one-way ticket.

"And here are the papers for the kibbutz where you'll meet the other members of your garin," he says.

I glance at the paper and look up at Avshalom.

"Where's Kibbutz Ze'elim?"

"In the Negev desert."

"Will I be stationed in the desert?"

"If you mean pre-army, when you'll be working on the kibbutz, then yes," Avshalom says.

The kibbutz-type service I've signed up for is known as "Nahal," short for "Noar Halutzi Lohem," or the Pioneer Fighting Unit. It requires three intense months of working on my "home kibbutz" prior to getting officially inducted. This home kibbutz will always be there once I'm inducted, but I'll only go back to it during breaks and weekends; we'll serve once again on the kibbutz for another three months for the post-army part of our service, which will take place a little over two years after I start. This first three-month period will serve as a bonding experience for our garin, many of them lone soldiers like me who opted to serve in the IDF.

"After Ze'elim, you'll be doing settlement work. Ze'elim is one of the more established kibbutzim in the region."

The desert. I turn this over in my mind. I have never even been to the desert. I'm a New Yorker through and through.

The word "established," however, calms me down. There's a difference between a kibbutz that's been around for a long time and a younger one. An older kibbutz brings in more income to support its members, and has more amenities, like a bigger supermarket, bigger houses, and an infirmary. You can't get those things at a young settlement struggling to survive.

Avshalom hands me a promotional pamphlet and points to a picture on it. The palm trees and green lamp posts with white big globes affixed to the top of them are just like the ones at Kibbutz Malkiyah, my aunt's kibbutz. I am reassured by the image's familiarity. I also make out what looks like a dining room, and perhaps a factory, which reminds me of Kibbutz Malkiyah.

"When's my official induction date for the army?"

"September 3rd," he says.

That's immediately after my arrival. I start getting the jitters. I still have many questions, but I figure that I might as well sign the papers or I'll just keep second-guessing myself. So I do.

I sign the paperwork that is required to get me through security once I land in Israel, and which will also speed up the process of obtaining the immigrant card that will entitle me to all rights afforded to immigrants under Israel's Law of Return.

∞

WITH JUST ONE WEEK UNTIL MY FLIGHT, DAD IS lecturing me about not leaving Ben Gurion airport in Israel without my immigrant card.

"It's your ticket to your benefits," he says, emphasizing every word. "Do not leave the airport without it."

I thought I could handle this pressure, and just moments

ago I was calm and confident that getting that card wouldn't, in fact, be a problem—but now I'm tipping off the anxiety scale. I take a deep breath and rehearse what I'm going to say to that government worker at the airport. I'm preparing for a battle—the worst possible scenario. I'm assuming that my steadfast "I-don't-give-a-shit/get-what-you-fucking-want" attitude will do the trick. But I can't help but wonder, *What if it doesn't?*

"So what will happen if I *don't* get my immigrant card at the airport?" I muster the courage to ask Dad.

"Just don't leave that airport without it. Keep asking questions until you get what you need."

∽

EVERYTHING NOW SEEMS REAL. OFFICIAL. I'M STILL ambivalent, but I know in my heart that emigrating to Israel is the right thing to do. The fights with Mom since I announced I'm leaving have left a bad taste in my mouth, but I'm careful not to let her feelings and behavior throw off my future plans. I've got five years of commitment, and the time to take charge of my life is now. At this point she has finally, begrudgingly, accepted my decision, and today she's even offered to help me shop for a suitcase at some of the cheap luggage places at 14th Street and Eighth Avenue. As we shop, she pulls out cash as a peace offering, though clearly she's feeling estranged and distant. I'm old enough by now to know that she's just hurt. She smiles politely but holds her fists tight at her side, as if she's still holding on to something.

"C'mon Dorit. Let's go."

I follow her like a puppy, but my thoughts are elsewhere.

Dad's lecture starts to raise my anxiety level again. What if I'm denied this card, or can't get it for some reason? What will happen to me if I leave the airport without it? I imagine myself crying, screaming, shouting, fist-banging—doing whatever I have to do in front of the airport officials to get what I want.

I recall with some alarm a memory from 1982. I was eleven at the time and my parents, at the edge of getting a divorce, decided that we should all go in for family counseling. Our sessions were videotaped—an innovative concept at the time. The marriage counselor fired off a series of questions, mainly directed to my Mom.

She answered them one by one, curtly, until suddenly she shouted, "I'm not taking this anymore! This is abuse. I'm not answering any of these questions! You can't do this to me!" She shouted and banged her fists on the wooden armchair. She got up to leave, saying again, "You can't do this to me," then hovered there next to the couch, as if deciding whether or not to storm out.

The marriage counselor asked a few more questions and waited a few seconds to see if Mom was really intent on leaving.

Silence on a black-and-white screen.

He asked one more question.

"I'm leaving!" she shouted.

"Wait a second, Mimi!" my father shouted, and now he got up.

Mom paused, and for a second I thought she was going to give the session one more shot—but then she was gone. That poor psychologist didn't stand a chance.

This is one of my earliest memories of witnessing Mom's aggressive side in public. Over the years, she would shout, spit, and shout some more at me whenever she wanted to make sure she got what she wanted. She didn't care about consequences. She'd hold her head high and turn her body far away, as if to broadcast a message to us all: *Don't mess with me. I'm not interested in what you have to say.* I always hoped she'd look at me and see the plea written all over my face: *Please, Mom, don't lash out. It doesn't have to end this way.* But she never did.

∞

"DON'T FORGET TO WEAR A SWEATER!" MY MOTHER cries out. It's just her and me—Dad is back at the office, and Mom has accompanied me to the airport. She seems to have only just now realized that she doesn't have control over me anymore. She is practically flapping the green sweater she's clutching in the security guard's face. Her face is beet red. I can understand why she's behaving this way, but it only makes me want to escape her even more.

"You can't go past the security line, ma'am," the guard says.

She inches closer, as if she hasn't heard.

I slowly scoot forward in line, anxious to get away from a scene that could turn brutal and messy.

"Dorit, Dorit, wait!" she cries. She turns to the guard. "I've got to give my daughter her sweater!"

Who needs a sweater? I think. *I'm going to Israel! Israel! It's blasting hot there!*

"Don't forget the sweater!" she cries again, frantically waving the itchy woolen thing.

I walk full speed ahead in the opposite direction until I get to the metal detectors, my backpack bouncing in every direction. I don't have to go back to her. She can't control me this time.

"Bye Mom," I call back to her—meekly, but there's no regret in my voice.

"Bye, honey-bunny. Don't forget to write!"

I duck slightly so she can't see me after I pass the metal detectors. I'm free. I race to my gate. When I feel I've crossed the point of no return, I turn back to confirm the space between us. Mom is nowhere in sight. I'm on my way.

∞

AT BEN GURION AIRPORT IN TEL AVIV I PASS A newsstand and reach to grab a Snickers bar. It's twice the price it would be at home, and it looks foreign with its Hebrew-covered wrapping, but I buy it anyway. I need and want to feel American right now, to feel connected to where I've just come from. After all, who knows when I'll be back in the States again?

It will be twelve more hours before I reach my final destination: Kibbutz Ze'elim, my dream kibbutz, an established kibbutz that's run by older members and it has all amenities that a younger kibbutz doesn't have, such as a swimming pool, a huge supermarket and a disco. Sarah, a first cousin from my father's side, is supposed to meet me outside the airport. But right now all I can think of is that stupid immigrant card my dad's so obsessed about.

I approach the line at the Ministry of Absorption kiosk. Other immigrants are already squeezing their way to the front of the line. I'm now Dorit in Israel, not Dorit in America. I have to think on my feet. The line that is haphazard, shooting off in all directions. I hear Russian being spoken, and a bunch of what I assume to be new immigrants are trying to either cut the line in front of me or are pushing from behind me.

When my turn finally comes, I plop all the paperwork, along with my Israeli and American passports, down in front of one of the government workers manning the kiosk.

"I'm here for my new immigrant card," I say in clearly enunciated Hebrew. My heart is beating fast.

The white-haired woman opens her mouth to reveal a

front set of gold-plated teeth. She says something in Russian, then catches herself and switches to Hebrew as she grabs my paperwork. She looks up at me as if she's searching for a sign that will tell her I'm not faking my accent. Surrounded by Russian and Ethiopian immigrants, I feel out of place, which triggers my anxiety. But I need to pay extra special attention to what this woman says. The chances of her speaking English is low, since she's clearly been hired to speak with the huge number of Russian immigrants flooding in, and I can't afford to miss out on anything. I've got just one chance to get my immigrant card, and it's right now. Plus, I am here on my own and I feel I have to prove myself. If I don't, I'll lose the battle —not just in this situation but in other situations in which I'll need to assert myself. If I don't stick up for myself here in this foreign country, nobody else will. And it starts now.

There's a pile of papers on each side of the government worker and folders piled high behind her.

"You can't get your immigrant card here," she says in quick Hebrew. You'll have to go to the Tel Aviv office. The main one." She scribbles something on a small piece of paper.

Wha-at? "Why not?" I ask, glued to the counter. I listen attentively, but she doesn't say anything, just continues to look at my papers. This can't be happening! *Don't let her get away with this!* a voice inside my head shouts. *Do something! Say something, idiot! Say something!* Then a more constructive voice says, *Keep asking the same stupid questions until you get what you want. That's the Israeli way.* I can't be the quiet, polite American here.

"I don't understand," I say in perfect Hebrew, still in a calm voice. "I'm volunteering for the Israel Defense Forces. I was told by the kibbutz Aliyah Desk and the Ministry of Absorption office in New York City that I could get my immigration card at the airport."

"When are you getting inducted?" she asks.

"In three weeks."

"Three weeks?"

"Yes."

People start talking in Russian behind me. I have no clue what they're saying. But I don't care. I've just got to get that immigrant card and get out of here. Somewhere past baggage claim, my cousin Sarah is waiting for me. The longer this ordeal takes, the less of a chance she'll be there to greet me. She's a very busy career army officer, and if I don't show up soon, she'll probably leave. And there's no way for me to let her know I've been delayed.

"Then no," the woman says, shaking her head, "you can't get it here. You'll have to go to the Tel Aviv office."

"Why?" *One point for being assertive. Keep it up, Dorit.*

"We don't deal with army cases here. Period. Just non-army immigrants."

I want to die. Collapse. Why didn't someone tell me this earlier? I didn't think of a plan B. What the heck do I do now?

The Russians behind me are slowly closing in, as if my time is up. I thought I would get extra-special treatment because I'm serving in the IDF, but I was clearly wrong.

"If I can't get my immigrant card, can I at least get my taxi voucher?" Something tells me that Sarah has already left the airport. At least I know to ask for my taxi voucher, which is a free pass to go anywhere I want to go in Israel, and I have the comfort of knowing that my grandmother lives close by, and I know her address by heart.

She hands me a small white piece of paper stamped in red.

Will I make it through the first twenty-four hours?

Will I have the tenacity to keep faith in my ability to succeed even if things don't go according to plan?

Will my New York City "smarts" help me survive here?

I'm so tired so I don't even bother trying to figure out the answers to any of these questions. All that matters right now is getting outside as fast as possible. Maybe it's not too late to meet Sarah after all. I quickly formulate my plan B: I'll use my voucher to visit my *savta*—my grandmother. Though I'm exhausted from being in traveling mode for the last twenty-four hours, and part of me just wants to get to the kibbutz and settle in, getting there seems like too much right now. A few hours at my grandmother's will make me feel more at ease in my new surroundings.

❧

WHEN THE TAXI DROPS ME OFF, I LUG MY HEAVY SUITCASE to Savta's second-floor apartment. She opens the door, and before I've had the chance to say "shalom" myself she says, "Shalom, shalom, Dorit from America!" and puts her arms around me.

Her hug is not exactly warm—it's more like a gentle pat on the back. I'm wondering if this is just a cultural thing or if it's my grandmother's personality. I can't remember if she did this when I last visited, which is strange considering it was just over a year ago.

Very quickly I re-familiarize myself with the Israeli residential standards: bare floors, shuttered veranda, storage that is part of a pantry leaning off the side of kitchen containing homemade jars of pickled beets and cabbage, a metal container of homemade sesame cookies with date filling. I know this kitchen well from the visits we made when I was five and twelve, and I resisted eating Savta's hard-boiled eggs. Now I'm wolfing down the food she offers me as she eyes me curiously.

It is quieter here on this side of the apartment without the incessant bus and street noise. With a cup of tea and lemon in one hand, I observe the quiet stability of my grandmother's apartment. I recall the guest room with the sturdy pull-out bed where I once tried to sleep and worked myself into a frenzy complaining of my stomach pain, hoping my parents would hurry home from their Tel Aviv outing and pay attention to me, their love-starved daughter.

On that lonely night in 1982, I whimpered to my grandmother and tried desperately to snuggle next to her cold lanky body, but she soon sat up in bed and cried, "Ma karah?" *What happened?*

I hoped she wouldn't keep asking the annoying "Ma karah?" question. What I wanted was for her to pull me over to her, make me a cup of tea, and stroke my head. But none of that happened. Instead I cried, speaking what limited Hebrew I could manage—"Koav Li Habeten," *my stomach hurts*—and I cried and clutched my stomach just to make sure she could really understand.

When I finally heard my father and stepmother turn the key in the door, I ran to the greet them. Savta followed me.

"Oh my god, oh my god," she blurted to them. "She was crying this whole time. *Ma Yesh La*—what's wrong with her?"

Each moment I sit here brings out even more of what's unfamiliar: I observe just how bare a wall can be without art, and the plainness of her furniture. We chat over the noise of the radio, which is blasting local Israeli news.

I notice a painting I haven't seen before. "Is that Dad's art? Did he paint that?" I speak only in Hebrew with Savta. She doesn't understand any English—just Arabic and Hebrew.

"Yes, he did that when he was studying in Jerusalem and gave it to me."

"Jerusalem," I say. He was born and raised there, and attended the prestigious Bezalel Academy of the Arts from the time he was released from the army until his mid-twenties.

Deep purple, blue, and yellow end in strands of black, forming a tree-lined street, in Dad's painting. I notice how the black almost ruptures the painting. The piece has the same look as the paintings that once hung at my other grandmother's house, my mother's house, in Far Rockaway. Thin trees were always the dominant image of Moshe's paintings, and he and my father are good friends who go back—way back.

When I was young, my father and I walked one day through Washington Square Park to an arts street fair in the West Village where my father was an exhibitor. There we sat in beach chairs close to the sidewalk's edge with Moshe, and they chatted in Hebrew while I looked at Moshe's long, billowy, skinny trees. I finally pointed to one of his paintings and asked, "Where is this place?"

"Jerusalem," he said.

The dark trees. The Hebrew. All foreign. All Mediterranean. My olive-skinned father had grown up there, and spoke this funny-sounding language that I didn't understand. Yet, I felt a sense of pride because I was different, special and unique. We weren't your typical Jewish family. I was part of a different tribe of American Jews: I had an Israeli parent.

Now the shapes my father put on canvas as a young man appeal to my newfound American-Israeli-Zionist mindset. The thin, squiggly tree branches swaying in the wind on what I make out to be the corner of a busy Jerusalem street give me hope. Perhaps my father felt the same thin slivers of hope as he tried to paint his way to his future, struggling over whether to stay in Israel or leave. At the time, he was at the Academy of Rome on a Fulbright, freshly released from the IDF; and now here I am returning to the homeland of his youth as a pioneer.

As my grandmother offers me a cup of cool tea, I'm dying to let my parents know I've arrived, but I don't want to run up her phone bill. *I'll call from the kibbutz.*

"When are you leaving?" my grandmother asks, which immediately turns me off. Why would she already be asking when I'm leaving? I just got here. Over the years, she will continue to ask the same question upon my arrival, and I will learn to accept that it's a way to account for my comings and goings—but in this moment, not knowing that, it feels like she wants me gone before I've even had a chance to settle in.

"Tonight," I tell her.

"Where are you going?" she asks, though I'm sure she knows the answer to the question.

"To the kibbutz, Savtah, as part of my Nahal service with the Israel Defense Forces. I'm going to be inducted in the army in a few weeks."

"The army?"

"Yes, the army. And I'm going to live on a kibbutz just like Aunt Maya lives on Kibbutz Malkiyah." I look at my timeless savta, who at age seventy-one still looks the same as she did in 1975 when I was five. She plants her feet forward. The lines and curves on her brown skin don't move, and her eyes are as solemn as ever. Golden, tangled necklaces that she has worn for as far back as I can remember interlace with one another and blend with the golden browns of her sweater, which she now pulls closer, as if she's about to button it. When she squints here and there, it makes the weathered lines of her forehead protrude even more than they already do, but she still looks healthy and robust, and her eyes are that same deep hazel I'd forgotten until now.

I nervously think of the next three hours of traveling that await me. Since I already used my one-time voucher, I'll have to bus the next leg of travel. I'm anxious to go. I want to get to the kibbutz right away. Since I didn't get my immigrant card, I want to account for my presence on the kibbutz, the home of my new garin. Plus, I'm concerned I may be imposing on my grandmother's hospitality since we aren't particularly "close."

As the warm tea settles in my stomach, I take one more look at the spare room and ask Savta if I can leave my suitcase with her. We agree that I'll come back for it later, once I've settled on the kibbutz, and for now take just enough items for the next few weeks. I have a quick debate with myself about what to do next. Maybe I should stay the night after all? I haven't even figured out the logistics of which bus to take or how to get to the station.

Before I have to make a decision, the phone rings. It's Sarah. She picks us up in her car, and we go to her apartment in Ramat Gan, a neighboring suburb. We walk up to her apartment on the top floor, and my body can barely make it up the five flights of stairs—I'm semi-shaking from tiredness. It's four o'clock now, and I wonder if I have still have a chance to get to the kibbutz by nightfall.

Sarah shows me a video of her marriage, which took place just four months ago, then hands me a glass of water and makes a phone call to find out when the next bus to Kibbutz Ze'elim leaves. There's one leaving in two hours.

"You sure you don't want to spend the night?" Sarah asks.

I nod. A part of me does want to stay with my family, but another part just wants to be on the kibbutz—to start preparing for my service.

Sitting in the back seat of Sarah's white Fiat, I pat the

letters my stepmother and Dad have written, thick wads of paper folded up in my pocket. Their words: "You're doing absolutely the right thing by leaving New York City and your Mom." Rather than indulge in guilt over having left my mom, I allow myself to trust the wisdom of my higher self at that moment.

It's going to be alright. I'm gonna make it.

I'm meant to be here. It's only for a few years, and then I can go home.

I can always go back to the States if I become terribly unhappy here in Israel.

I keep repeating these sentences over again until I've become less jittery.

Sarah, who is still wearing her uniform, zooms to the bus stop and steps out of her small white Fiat. She waves a hearty goodbye and flashes me an authentic smile.

"You're gonna be fine, Dorit. It's okay. Enjoy the ride."

There are just a few civilians sitting on the two thin, rickety slabs of wood serving as a bench. They stare at my cousin with her sea-green eyes and bouncy, wavy brown hair.

"Thanks for everything! I really appreciate it." I blow her a big kiss and offer her a hug, which she returns graciously. I'm already starting to feel a little less anxious.

Part of me wishes she'd linger a bit more so we can chat. After all, I'm just getting to know her and the rest of my family. But I remind myself that this country is small, the size of Rhode Island, and I can always see her again soon.

It's already five o'clock, but the sun is still high in the sky. I inspect my surroundings as Sarah drives away. This old bus station is nothing like Tel Aviv's central station, a modern, five-story building that houses a shopping mall and eatery and is always a madhouse rush of busy Israeli soldiers with their

heavy duffle bags and M16s. This station is completely out-
doors and spread across several side streets, past alleyways and
deserted corners. As I sit on a nondescript, weathered bench, I
wonder if my decision to become an IDF soldier is really going
to change my life in the way I expect it to. Will what I gain
from this experience truly justify my decision to leave my mom
in New York City? I'm still not sure how to answer that
question.

∞

WHEN I ARRIVE AT THE KIBBUTZ BUS STOP, I AM GREETED
by Dov, the representative of the Kibbutz Movement and the
coordinator of this new garin. He's wearing sunglasses and
jeans. He leads me down a meandering path, just like I'd anticipated, until we reach a group of small bungalows. This section
of housing turns out to be well-lit and surrounded by luscious
trees that stand just a few inches higher than the top of the
bungalows. I'm in paradise.

Dov opens the door to one of the bungalows, points out a
room, and tells me to put my bag in it. I obediently comply.
The room is smaller than I imagined it would be, but I don't
say anything about it.

"So," Dov says in an assertive but gentle tone. "You're
Dorit."

"Yes, that's me. Dorit from New York City."

"How was your trip?" he asks, handing me a glass of
water, but before I can respond, he's on the phone, answering
someone's questions.

I gulp the water he just gave me; I'm parched from the
long day of traveling, and my body's still shaky from exhaustion.

"My trip was a bit bouncy," I say when he gets off the phone. "Actually, it was exhausting. Long trip from New York City." I pass him my paperwork, fighting against the tiredness I feel.

"We won't be needing that," he says, handing the paperwork back to me.

"Oh."

Then I notice a confused look on his face.

Tell me there's nothing wrong.

"This garin's filled up," he says.

"Filled up?" I ask. "As in no room? But how can that be? This is where the New York City office told me to go."

"We just got a bunch of new immigrants yesterday. We're filled to maximum capacity. You'll have to go somewhere else."

"But that hardly seems fair!" I barely muster enough energy to say this. What the heck does he mean I'll have to go somewhere else? This was my kibbutz. My DREAM kibbutz. I can feel the tears welling in my eyes, and I wonder if I'm going to lose it. *This can't be happening!*

"I have to . . . leave?" I say, this time in a whisper.

"There's another garin at Kibbutz Ritamin," he says stiffly. "It's not too far away. You can join that one." It's a kibbutz I've never heard before. "It's twenty kilometers south of here—still in the Negev Desert."

When Mom doesn't like something, she screams, cries, does everything in her power to make sure the other side knows how upset she is. But even that wouldn't change things here, it seems. There's nothing I can do to stay here. And besides, I'm supposed to be army material. If I start crying like a baby now, they may not even want me. And I'm so exhausted I can't control my shaking, which makes it look like I'm even more devastated than I am.

Dov offers me another cup of water, but I shake my head. I chew on whatever skin is left around my nails.

This can't be happening.

In Hebrew, I tell him, "I'm here because I'm a Zionist. This is my homeland and this is where I belong." *Maybe if he sees my shaking body, he'll feel sorry for me and let me stay?* "Are you sure there's no way I can stay here? There's really no room?"

He nods his head. He's sure. But his face softens when he sees my tears. Israeli men have always been made out to me to be coarse, abrupt, aggressive, and assertive. I'm afraid to be vulnerable. I've never known the softer side of an Israeli man before. But Dov seems sympathetic.

Tears start choking up my words. I want to speak English to emphasize my deep disappointment, but at this defining moment, I've got to work through my emotions. So I muster the little energy I have left and carry on our conversation in Hebrew.

I can hear a new gentleness in Dov's voice as he responds to my queries, but the facts he offers are still the same as they were five minutes ago: There's no room on this kibbutz. The garin is already too big.

I don't bother trying to fight Dov's decision. To scream and carry on like my mother would only dilute the new fresh start I'm here for. So I tell myself there's no choice but to acclimate. This idea shakes me up until a voice inside me says, "Get used to it, baby! Accept it!"

I first heard this voice when I was in the sixth grade, the first year I attended junior high school in the slums of Chelsea after Mom decided it was too expensive to keep me in private Jewish day school. I'd had a severe anxiety attack from being bullied by some of the neighborhood kids—one that caused such a stomach upset that after three periods of holding in my bowels, I ended up shitting in my pants. I felt ashamed and embarrassed and told no one, and since I couldn't make the twenty minutes walk home to change into fresh underwear, for the rest of the day I wore my tight pinstripe purple pants with zipup legs without underwear. At first it felt itchy; I tried moving the pants this way and that so my crotch wouldn't be centered on the seam, but I just couldn't get comfortable. After a while, though, the sensation faded away and I got used to it.

I think of that day now, and I tell myself to just accept my current situation like I did then. It is what it is. Accept it. For the next twenty-four hours, this logical understanding will fuel me.

To anchor myself further, I decide here and now to concentrate on making "feel-good" connections. I try to let go of the fear I'm feeling. *Trust this man*, I tell myself. *Trust that everything will work out.*

A consummate military man, Dov remains aloof during our conversation, but he sustains eye contact as if to say, *It's okay. Everything's going to be alright. Give it a chance.* I control my hysteria and gradually begin to breathe slower. *Breathe and trust*, I think. *Breathe, accept, and trust.*

My face is as red as a plucked chicken but I'm no longer crying. Dov hands me another cup of water and asks, "So, what are you going to do?"

We both know there's just that other kibbutz, but he's waiting to see if I'm really calm enough to accept that fact.

I look at his olive skin and warm brown eyes. I genuinely feel that this stranger wants me to succeed here. He looks at me with intention as he patiently waits for my response. In the meantime, he tries again to offer me another cup of water.

"No thanks, Dov. I'm good."

I owe it to myself to give this whole experience a chance. It may not be what I expected, but did anybody say it was going to be easy? Nobody told me what an emotional roller coaster giving up my country for another would be, but I'm here now. And everything that will follow from this moment depends on what I decide to do next. I can try to fight his decision, go to Ritamin, or get back on a plane and head back to the States. Only one of those choices feels like a reasonable one.

"Okay, Dov," I say, meeting his eyes. "I'll go to Ritamin."

7

KIBBUTZ RITAMIN

AT 10 P.M., KIBBUTZ RITAMIN IS A GHOST TOWN. DOV and I have just entered through the security gate in his white four-door Subaru. Once we're inside, he calls Elan, the representative from this kibbutz, to come meet us and bring me to my room.

To get to the kibbutz, we drive one kilometer down a road dotted with bushes and short-limbed trees that wave as if to welcome me. In the distance, I can make out just a few houses —and they're nothing like the houses at Kibbutz Malkiyah. They're more like bungalows. This is one of the smallest kibbutzim in the Negev desert; it needs "garin power" to help it blossom into a full-fledged kibbutz. It was established fourteen years earlier, which by settlement standards makes it an infant, and the people here are counting on my garin to build it up so that one day it can become an established and prominent kibbutz like Malkiyah.

Elan hasn't yet arrived when we get to the bus stop, so Dov kindly waits with me. Our small talk is as dry as the desert around us. He puffs on a cigarette, pacing back and forth, sending vapors of smoke circling upward to be absorbed by the cool evening air. He's impatient, it seems, to get back to Ze'elim—to my dream.

He's going back and I'm stuck in this desert crater, I think.

We both turn our heads when we hear someone shout "Dov!"

Elan, a long, lanky man with dark, narrow eyes shaped like hyphens who's probably no more than twenty-five, is walking down the cement path toward us. He gives Dov a hearty *chapcha* on his back before saying "shalom" to me. His job done, Dov hands me his business card and tells me to call if I have any problems, which reassures me a bit, and heads back to the parking lot.

As soon as he's gone I get nervous again. I'm also too tired to chat with Elan, which he seems to sense. He leads me straight to my room, says good night, and leaves me alone. We don't even talk about whether I'll be working the next day, although this has been on my mind and causing me anxiety all day.

∞

AT FOUR O'CLOCK IN THE MORNING, I WRIGGLE IN THE sheets of my new bed—a cast iron frame equipped with a thin foam mattress. My roommate is pulling on her army work clothes. I'm wondering if I should stay in bed or get up and go to work with her.

"What's your name?" I ask in Hebrew, deciding that I should forget sleeping more. Now that there's some light, it's time to connect to people. Since last night I've felt like a ghost—fumbling in the dark, not interacting with anyone. If I sleep in, I'll feel even more like a stranger in no-man's land. Plus, I don't think I *can* sleep in. I feel self-conscious now that my roommate, who I haven't even met yet, is awake and getting ready for her day.

"Karla," she says, her back still turned to me. She pulls the sheets of her bed down tight.

"How long have you been on Ritamin?"

"Almost four weeks."

"Where are you from?"

"Chile," she says.

I remember my five years of Spanish instruction; perhaps that can be a common denominator that binds us. Not a bad start.

Karla wastes no time; by four thirty she is out the door, telling me she's off to work in the field. As she heads out, I don't even bother asking her where to "report for duty," thinking I can figure it out on my own. When she's gone, I look in my closet and find an oversized army work uniform on the top shelf. I put it on and look at myself in the mirror, inspect my baggy appearance.

Yes, I'm a soldier!

I pull on the army boots I also found on the shelf and lace them up. It takes fifteen minutes of walking around the room to get used to how tight they are. I feel like I'm wearing ice skates.

In the small cubicle that is our bathroom, I slick my thin hair back into a ponytail and pull the work hat that is part of my uniform—also far too big for me—over my eyes. One inch to the right and I'm brushing against the shower stall. One inch to the left and I'm against the toilet seat.

I edge out of the bathroom and back into the room. Glancing down, I notice that there is a packet of birth control pills on the circle corner table next to my bed. I look at them with curiosity and wonder about this roommate. Who is she having sex with? By the time my feet touch the brown-and-cream-speckled tiles, however, my mind has moved on to the day ahead of me. I'd better get moving. Being here is a big deal. I need to get adjusted to my garin so I can fully serve. I've got just three weeks before I'm inducted.

My agenda for the next three weeks:

1. Learn my way around the kibbutz (which shouldn't be a problem since it's really small).

2. Reacquaint myself with work. Every kibbutz has a different source of income; from what I understand, I'll be working in the fields here, since agriculture is this kibbutz's main source of income.

3. Bond with members of my garin. This is actually my number one priority. By the time we get inducted, we're supposed to be bonded as a family. Maybe by the end of this three weeks Karla will even feel comfortable enough with me to share about her pills.

I step over my tattered blue suitcase, which is already in complete disarray—the only item in this clean, well-lighted room that isn't tidy and in its place.

I grab the letters from my suitcase from my dad and stepmother and read their encouraging words for the hundredth time: "We will join you in a year's time. Joining the Israeli army is going to make such a big difference in your life."

The only place to look is straight ahead. I know what I look like in the mirror. I don't need to see, but I still look. There's a zombie-faced eighteen-year-old looking back at me. She has bags under her eyes. *Stop worrying so. Don't be a worry bug, be a happy bug.* Mom's words.

I try not to stress out so much. I know that in the end, just like in the Bob Marley song, everything's gonna be alright.

∽

AS SOON AS I STEP OUTSIDE, THE SILENCE OF THE DESERT scares me. It's pitch black, and no one's around. *Am I really going to make it here?* I wonder. I reassure myself with the thought that I can always go back. I try putting my questions aside and focus on this desert crater. It takes just a minute or two to realize how small this settlement really is. To the far right of me is a dining room and a babyhouse (the American version of daycare), only there are no babies in there at this hour. Very quickly the "residential" landscape disappears and I find myself in the middle of nowhere, relying on the few lampposts dotting the settlement behind me to guide me. I have no idea where I'm going or where I need to be. I want to feel purposeful, not insignificant and insecure. I try to listen for voices, but the crickets chirping around me are my only welcoming committee.

I look at my watch, which still reflects Eastern time. It's 11 a.m. EST.

I pass a few more shrubs and bushes and still cannot believe I'm making my way to work somewhere in the fields in the middle of the night. Just twenty-four hours ago, I was at JFK airport.

Clomp, clomp go my boots.

In the far distance, there's a dinky row of trees, a welcome break from this flat, sparse terrain. Suddenly, a strong gust of wind snags the weight of those trees and pulls them into one voluminous bunch. A hiss comes from somewhere near my feet. I look down and make out an irrigation hose in the blackness. Phew. Not a snake.

I follow the sound of voices, which bring me to a clearing. Shadows are hunched over dwarf-sized mango trees. Something metal bangs against a bulky shape that, as I draw closer, resolves itself into a tractor. I feel sick. I want to cry. I want to be back in Greenwich Village.

Is this what I came for? Something tells me I've made a very grave mistake. Postponing my college studies for the sake of volunteering for the Israel Defense Forces—what was I thinking? I listen to the *crunch, crunch* of folding aluminum foil in the early morning, and the silence that follows it. Hats face down. Mouths are shut. Hands work industriously. *Crunch, crackle, crunch*, silence. *Crunch, crackle, crunch*, silence. After a few cycles, the rhythm steadies.

You're here to till the soil and work the land.

I'm just meters away from the group now, and I'm waiting for someone to officially approach me and tell me what to do, but no one seems to have noticed me. Something tells me that if I don't survive this moment, I'll end up getting on a plane back to the US very soon. When I volunteered on Malkiyah last summer, there was no pressure to bond with other volunteers for the sake of the army, we all spoke in English, and we socialized a lot outside of our daily duties. Here the focus is on work—it's the driving ideology behind the concept of the kibbutz—and I attempt to let that notion focus me. But still I'm nervous as hell knowing that I'm going to have to small talk my way into making friends here. It's something that feels completely inauthentic to me but is essential to my surviving and thriving in Israel and within this garin. I take a deep breath.

Back in New York City, Mom small talks as a pastime. She is strategic in her relationships, good at approaching people who could help her in some way. Spanish is her mother tongue —she was born in Valencia, Spain—and when I was a kid, she made small talk with Jacamo, our Spanish security guard, quite a lot. One time, when my Sony mini boombox stopped working, she headed downstairs to ask Jacamo to take a look at it.

Fifteen minutes she came back. "Dorit! It's working!" She laughed in her falsetto trill.

I've always wanted to be able to small talk like Mom; it seems like a good way to feel included. Unfortunately, I've never been good at it. I'm an introvert by nature, insecure. And until now I could get by without being good at making conversation with strangers, but in this foreign place, I realize I have to make some kind of effort. Even if it does not come easy, I know it is the only way in. I am a very private person, and I generally relish in solitude. But staying closed up like a fan will not help me here. I intuitively know I'll end up feeling lonely.

I'm intent on connecting with something familiar—anything will do—but the sights, smells, and sounds here are so vastly different from those in New York City, and even those at Kibbutz Malkiyah. Last summer I had family to support me and I wasn't in the middle of a desert crater.

I push myself forward and approach someone, a complete stranger, in the darkness.

"Shalom, hello. I'm Dorit."

"Yes, hi. You're new to the garin, right?"

"Right."

The person turns out to be Elan, the guy who greeted me late last night.

"This is the kind of work you'll be doing," he tells me. "You need to wrap the mango trees with foil, like this." He quickly demonstrates by taking a small piece of foil and carefully folding it a few times. He looks at me, a shadowed face hovering above trees that are half our height. "Got it?"

"Yes, I think so."

He unwraps the thin-limbed tree and hands the foil to me.

That tree could easily be me, I think. I follow his instructions as he watches closely.

This wrapping routine goes on for two hours, until there's a faint glimmer of light in the sky. After his initial instructions, Elan leaves me to my work. He doesn't offer any more information about what my day will hold. All I know is that I'm supposed to put in a full day's work. I'm guessing that means working until a bit past lunchtime, since it will be too hot to work outside after that, but I'm not sure.

I've been told that breakfast is at eight, but at five minutes to eight no one is even budging. How am I supposed to manage with these people? I am convinced I do not belong here. My stomach is grumbling, the only person I've spoken with is Elan, and I've only wrapped about ten rows of mangoes.

At one point, I'm working side by side with another nameless someone from my garin. "I was the one who arrived late last night," I tell him. "I was supposed to go to Kibbutz Ze'elim."

"Oh, Ze'elim?"

"There was some miscommunication error from the Kibbutz office in New York City. So I was sent here instead."

Silence.

I rub my hands together. "Boy, it's really cold here. I wouldn't expect that from the desert."

"Yes, it is cold here. But it quickly warms up."

Silence again.

I anticipate a long stay at this garin if this first day is any indication of what my interactions with people are going to be like.

❦

THE SHADOWS OF THE NIGHT LIFT SLOWLY, LIKE A FOG, until finally the sky cracks open—first into a greyish purple and then into a bright pink luster swirled with golden rays of light. It's breathtakingly beautiful. Now I'm finally able to see the texture of Elan's curly black hair, which, it turns out, is much like my father's—tight ringlets.

In a matter of minutes, I know, the sun will start to beat upon my head and neck. I pat the letters in my pocket. The written words of my stepmother and dad are a comfort, but they are not enough to help me get through my first full day. I'm still anxious; I want desperately to call them. I make a mental note to do so after breakfast. In the meantime, I repeat to myself the encouragement they offered in their letters: *You can do this. Going to Israel will make such a difference in your life. We love you.*

Around eight fifteen, the tractor pulls in and we climb into the back. I haven't eaten anything since I left my grand-mother's. I know the names of eight members of my new garin now—I overheard enough of them calling each other by name to figure that much out—but still no one has made the effort to initiate conversation with me. I seem to be the only one who cares enough to try.

I again play with the idea of leaving. *Maybe when I call my parents I can tell them I want to come home*, I muse. But I shoot down that possibility immediately. Even entertaining the possibility would suggest giving up on my motivation for coming here. I'm here to get away from my mom. If I tell my parents how unhappy I am and how much I want to come home, I'll be losing out on an opportunity to develop the emotional independence I came here for—the independence my mother has denied me for years.

Maybe I just need to cry.

8

MAKE OR BREAK

FOR THE REST OF THE FIRST PART OF MY FIRST MORNING at Kibbutz Ritamin, I wrap mango trees with aluminum foil. There's twenty of us from the garin, plus a few kibbutz members, doing the work. From the limited conversation I have with the people working near me, I learn that there are sixty of us on this dinky settlement—much less than Ze'elim which has at least three hundred and fifty people, including kibbutz members. Behind me, Elan and his buddies chat about mundane things as they sit on top of ladders.

I work tirelessly for a few hours, but by mid-morning, I'm starting to get antsy. I ask different people the same questions: "Does this tree branch look okay?"; "How many more rows are left?" No one attempts to make me feel welcome. I consider the fact that we are supposed to be together for the next two and a half years and my anxiety wells up. Is this the way it's always going to be? What if nobody ends up talking to me? I realize I can't call my parents when I'm feeling like this or I'll lose any sense of control I have. I need to tough it out on my own these first few days here.

The wooden phone booth I spotted on the way in is one third of a kilometer outside of this kibbutz. In my mind, though, Ritamin doesn't even merit kibbutz status. It's just a settlement. *I'm on a dinky settlement!*

I'm the only American on this desert and in this garin. Nobody here speaks English. I've come to think of these two qualities as special, since Hebrew and English are the two national languages in this country. When I volunteered on my aunt's kibbutz, everyone spoke English, and I can't help but think that this is the difference. There, where I could speak in my native language, I was likeable. I was patient. People sought me out, and it didn't feel as difficult there to connect with people as it does here. Is it really about the shared language? Or was it the fact that when I was volunteering there was no army pressure?

I gave up college life in New York City and said goodbye to my family and friends to devote myself to a few years of military service in a foreign country. My fellow garin members are immigrants too; don't they realize what it's like to be alone in a new country? Don't they know what it feels like to be an outsider?

I feel my self-pity spiraling, so I try to rationalize the situation. Maybe it's because the work is so hard that I'm not getting what I want. I'm being impatient. This is my first morning here.

As I foil-wrap more dwarfy-looking trees, the sun continues to beat against the back of my head, which now feels as hot as an oven. The garin members surrounding me are talking and laughing with each other as if they've known each other all their freaking lives. They've had several weeks on this kibbutz, and many of them have been here in Israel for several months, or even years. They've had a lot of time to adapt to this country. I've got some serious catching up to do. But I try not to stress out about it. *The army is going to help you catch up, Dorit*, I remind myself. And at least I'm not getting inducted with a bunch of native Israelis; the cultural gap would be too overwhelming. I'm not sure I would survive it.

Then again, I'm not sure I'll survive this, either. The other members of this garin have already spent considerable time in this country and on this settlement, so they're emotionally and mentally ready.

I'm not.

I've just got three weeks until induction day. Three freaking weeks. My fear is now manifesting into full-blown anxiety.

I turn to someone next to me and ask a question, desperate for a sense of connection, and again I receive only a curt reply.

A game plan unfolds in my mind. I will not call home today. But I will only give these people twenty-four hours. If, in twenty-four hours, I don't feel more comfortable here, then I am going to have to bail out. *Maybe I made the wrong decision in coming here.*

I can't help but feel my mother is at least partly to blame for how I'm feeling. *Mom*, I think. *It's because of you that I'm having a difficult time. If you were more patient and loving I would have it easier right now.*

I should be more patient with myself and with this situation; if I could do that, I would be able to work with my feelings instead of fighting them. But I won't realize this for some time to come.

∞

ON THE WAY TO LUNCH, I TAKE AN UNPLANNED DETOUR and walk to the telephone booth. I know I've given myself twenty-four hours, but I already know I'm not going to make it. I'm already getting wobbly in the knees.

The wooden phone booth shakes and rattles in the desert wind. Etched in wood under a dim light bulb are Hebrew names and numbers for what appear to be members of previous garins. I rub my finger over the dark letters, some of which are rubbed out completely. Did they, too, feel drawn to the concept of national service? And did they, like me, make a sacrifice to do it, one like leaving their mother country? When I was here volunteering, I felt special because I had an Israeli father; it strengthened my connection to these Israeli soldiers and made the idea of serving in the Israel Defense Forces appealing. But now that I'm here, I feel so adrift.

I hold a bag of tokens. I drop a few down the chute in an attempt to connect with an international operator and make a collect call, but the machine immediately spits them out. I try a few more times and again it spits them out. *What the fuck?* I can feel the heat rising up inside of me. I've got to connect with my folks!

After a few more tries, the phone finally sucks up the tokens and a voice comes through. Success! To hear my dad and stepmother's voices over the line is heaven. A wave of relief washes over me.

"I want to go home. Nobody is talking to me. The garin's no good," I blurt out, and instantly the tears threaten to overwhelm me. I try to hold them back, but then I remember that I'm in the desert—that there's no one to hear or see me anyhow—and I let the tears go. No holding back. It feels good to release of the emotional weight and tension of the last twenty-four hours.

But Dad's only focus is the immigrant card. He seems not to be able to take in my panic. He ignores the crying and asks, "Did you get your immigrant card?"

Through a blanket of tears, I tell him about the ordeal at the airport. "No, I don't have it. Now I have other problems. I can't make it here."

Getting that immigrant card doesn't seem important now that I'm ready to give up on this whole thing altogether.

"I want to come home," I tell him. "I don't want to be here. This garin is too much for me. This country is too much. I'm giving up. I can't stand it." I feel bitterly ashamed.

"Hang on, Dorit," Dad says, finally hearing what I'm telling him. "Hang on. You can do it. Just remember we'll be with you in a year's time."

My thoughts are as scattered as the desert winds, but my dad's words soothe me somewhat. *Calm down, Dorit,* I think. *C'mon, you've only been here for twelve hours. Give yourself a break.* I think of Mom's mantra: "Don't be a worry bug, be a happy bug." For all the times she's used it on me, I've never managed to tap into those happy energies she demanded. How is it possible to be happy when I'm this scared? I've completely jumped off the deep end; I've left my comfort zone far behind. Everything I know is back home.

∽

AFTER A THIRTY-MINUTE PEP TALK, I HANG UP. THEIR voices feel so far away and yet so close. The desert wind fills their place with shakes, rattles, and hums. At least I got to talk with them. I feel calm enough now to give this garin a chance. *Have an open mind,* I command myself. *If you can change your attitude about this settlement and garin, perhaps you'll adjust better.*

I enter the dining room, just three times the size of my loft bedroom at home, and take stock of the layout. There's just one long table surrounded by a number of plastic chairs. The windows are thrown open, and wind is blowing in all directions. Everyone's already eating. Lots of chitchat going on. A few members are already done and filing out. The ones who pass me on their way out don't acknowledge me. Whack goes the door behind me. No one still seated at the table turns their head to look at me.

Because I'm ravenous, I focus on the food. I make myself a quick sandwich by spreading some cream cheese–like spread onto a plain roll, then stuffing in a few sliced cucumbers, tomatoes, and olives. I sit down and eat fast; I lost time speaking to my parents for those thirty minutes, and I'm not sure how much longer I have before we go back out to work in the fields. I barely taste the food as I swallow it.

Back in the fields, I enter into a conversation with myself that goes something like this:

So, you want to still live here? Be a Zionist? Do you really have a clue what that means?

Of course I do—that's why I came! I'm following the Zionist dream of my predecessors, people like Golda Meir and Yitzhak Rabin.

You don't even know who they are. They did much more settlement work than you. You are having it way easier, comparatively speaking. When they came, there was just barren land for kilometers around.

I know, but I wasn't born at that time. This is 1990.

Nevertheless, you have to give of yourself . . . It's called SERVICE for a reason!

But I'm on a dinky little settlement. A SETTLEMENT! There isn't even a TV, and I have to walk half a mile in the desert just to get to the nearest phone.

What did you expect to get here? A five-star hotel?

This move is already challenging my motivation for emigrating here. The religious variety of Zionism supports Jews upholding their Jewish identity in the land of Israel, but I can also be a Zionist simply by serving on a kibbutz. That, too, is considered Zionist since it combines socialism with the principles of work.

To pass the time, I work even more fervently, head down, so the others can see just how engaged I am in this manual labor. Perhaps someone will admire my work ethic and that will inspire them to interact with me. The gawky little transistor radio hanging from the John Deere tractor spits out a *beep-beep-beep* each hour to announce the news, followed by a male voice from Kol Yisroel—"the voice of Israel"—Israel's news station. If I were in Malkiyah, I wouldn't mind this isolation; there I didn't feel the pressure to bond with others. I had no ties to anyone as a volunteer and could leave at any moment. But here, in the desert, I have to show commitment to these people. We're going to be stuck together for a long time.

I look at my watch and it's already two o'clock. I reach for the water jug and let some of the water run down my shirt.

Elan is chatting to some other guy a few trees down to my left.

"How long more to go until we finish?" I ask.

"We've got another hour," he chirps.

"Another hour? It's burning hot out. A person could die of heatstroke out here!"

"Don't worry," he says. "You won't as long as you drink lots of water."

"That's what I'm doing. But I'm not used to this. I come from New York City."

I'm hoping he'll pick up on the New York City bit and be

interested enough to ask me a few questions. But he doesn't say anything—just lifts the Styrofoam water jug and gulps.

"This is really tough work. How does foiling the trees help mangoes?"

I am given only a very curt explanation.

I'm never going to make it in this garin. I guess I just don't get the Israeli way.

I came all the fucking way from New York City to work in a desert with these people, and they won't budge an inch to try to connect with me. No laughter, no jokes, no small talk. Is this the way it's supposed to be? What am I doing here? Even though a full twenty-four hours hasn't passed yet, these people have all failed my test. They are not worthy of my time. The problem is, I'm stuck here. So what the hell do I do now?

∞

LATER THAT AFTERNOON, I AM CONSIDERING MY OPTIONS. I recall my volunteer experience at Kibbutz Malkiyah. When I wanted to escape bossy Shawna, I asked to work somewhere else. Why can't I do that here too? Work in the dining room? I'll have it easier. I'll be calmer. Connect with civilization.

I tolerate the silence and hard work of the fields for a few more days, then approach Elan and ask him if I can switch to working at the dining room—just for a few days. I don't tell him that I need a break from the fields. Mom would have a fit if she saw how red and weatherbeaten my face has become after less than a week here.

To my surprise, Elan agrees, and the next day I begin my new job. The work is still tedious and manual, but at least I'm indoors. I clean out sewers. I hose off tables and chairs. I work the dishwasher. I cut up vegetables and clean toilets. I start to feel better, especially when I stand in front of the air conditioner. It's very hard for me to think and be rational in 95-degree weather.

When Karla and Elan, the only two people I know from this kibbutz, come for breakfast on my first day working in the dining room, they don't even notice me. But nobody, in fact, notices me until the twenty or so garin workers leave the dining room, at which point somebody hands me a hose and a *magav*—a big squeegee that looks like the bottom of a windshield wiper affixed to a two-foot-long wooden pole—and says, "Mop the water into the drain."

He has a bit of a huff in his voice, and from his accent I guess he's from Russia. When I turn around I find myself face to face with a guy with messy black hair and ruby red lips. A cigarette dangles from his mouth.

Mop the water into the drain? Why are you bossing me around? Who is this guy? I wonder.

That night, against the moaning sound of the crickets and the rumble of Karla's snoring, under a dying battery-operated flashlight, I write in my journal, words unfolding rapidly as I zoom in on memories. I think again of Mom—*"Don't be a sad bug, be a happy bug."* I've developed my own new mantra here: "Yes, you can do it."

I'm still homesick, but I'm not as terrified about speaking with other members of my garin now as I was in my first days of arriving here. I've just accepted the fact that this pre-army experience is all about the work. Each morning I make the two-minute walk from my bungalow to the kitchen, listening to the faint chirping of the crickets, a sound that dies with the sunrise—the same sad, singsong melody that used to pop up just as the coolish nights of summer at sleepaway camp in upstate New York came to an end.

I try to keep my focus on work without worrying about making friends. When the transistor radio beeps three times to signal the hourly news, I wait with anticipation for the newscaster's voice, which I find sexy and charming. He's the closest thing I have to a friend here.

9

TRYING TO LOVE THE LAND

"YOU'VE GOT TO GIVE IT TIME," DOV SAYS FOR THE THIRD time in five minutes. I've dialed his Tel Aviv office hoping for some reassurance. I know I have high expectations about how the dynamics should be between myself and the new members of the garin, but I'm concerned it won't change, and I'm not good at waiting things out. I've decided that the best next step is to get transferred.

"You're new, Dorit. How much do you even know about your garin and kibbutz?"

He's right. I really don't know anything about my new garin. But I've made the decision to leave already.

"I can't give them any more chances," I say. I've just used my last *asimon*, or token, to call him, and I have approximately forty-five seconds to get to the point. "Take me out of this garin! I don't want to be here!" Urgency rules. I'm consumed by my emotional and social isolation; I'm buckling under it. I'm terribly homesick. I've been here less than a week and already I've lost weight. My anxiety is at an all-time high.

Years from now, Dov and I will meet at a coffee shop in

the heart of Tel Aviv and laugh about this phone call, but right now I don't know that, and I'm relying on Dov to understand what's at stake for me. I haven't spent enough time in this country to feel relaxed about the army, and I still haven't made any inroads bonding with my fellow garin; they already had so much time together before I got here. I feel if I start with a new group, I'll have a second chance—a better chance.

Dov is the only one who can relocate me to another garin and kibbutz. He can facilitate better communication between Avshalom Horowitz and the United Kibbutz Movement, or the Takam office that put me on this settlement in the first place. *Please, Dov. Make life easy for me. Transfer me out of this garin to an easier kibbutz. I don't want to struggle so much. Do it for me. Please.*

Dov says he will come the next day to see for himself what's going on with the garin. Something tells me my request to leave is more likely to be granted than it would be other cases because I got screwed from the start—starting late and being transferred to another garin—but still, I can't be sure what Dov will decide.

∽

THE NEXT DAY, WHEN DOV ARRIVES AT RITAMIN, HE immediately whips out a cigarette and asks, "Is there a quiet room where we can talk?"

I look at him, dumbfoundedly. Surely I ought to know this dinky settlement by now, but I can't think of a single place.

"Nope, sorry," I say.

"Never mind. I think I remember where to find one. If not, we'll go to the dining room."

He leads me to a quiet, one-room bungalow containing just a table, a few worn-out chairs, and a lamp, which he immediately flicks on. He lights another Noblesse cigarette, the local Israeli brand, and tries to avoid blowing the smoke in my face, but I cough anyway. He keeps what remains of the cigarette in his mouth while smoke curls up at his lips. He doesn't even bother taking off his sunglasses. He pulls out a bunch of papers from his worn-out brown leather briefcase, and a small pad of paper.

"So, what's the story here? What's the problem?" he says —rather harshly, I think. He takes off his sunglasses and slightly lowers his dark head. I'm now face to face with this olive-skinned man, an Erik Estrada lookalike, except without the wide smile and easygoing expression. His penetrating stare tells me that I must answer his questions. All at once, I feel meek, vulnerable, and insignificant against his assertiveness. I will myself not to use the "scream-it-out" tactic favored by my mother to get him to listen to my pleas to leave here.

"Dorit," he begins. "You know you can't just pick up and leave. Joining a garin is a commitment."

This is not starting out like I'd hoped.

I look at my half-bitten, bleeding nails, already thinking of the $586 I'll have to shell out to the Jewish Agency if I do end up going back to the States.

I muster all my strength and launch into it: "I need a break. I didn't grow up on a kibbutz. I didn't grow up in this country. Most Israelis my age have months, even years, to mentally prepare for the army. I only have a few weeks before our induction date, and I don't feel that I got here soon enough to bond with this group. They already know each other. I'm older than most of them. I feel incredibly out of place."

I'm not trying to make excuses for myself, but I realize

that's all it sounds like. I want to tell Dov how hard it's been, and how the other garin members have ignored me since I arrived, but I fear that would suggest to him an unwillingness on my part to adapt to a new culture and environment. I want him to acknowledge that it's not all my fault, but as I talk, I wonder if it *is* all my fault.

He jots a few notes on his pad and looks at me.

"Dorit, you were not born here. You're almost how old?"

"Twenty," I tell him as I pick my nails. Girls serve for two years in the army, usually from ages eighteen to twenty, so I'm borderline.

"*You* decided to volunteer," he reminds me.

Technically I didn't have to volunteer for the IDF, of course, and the army could drop me at any time because of my "old" age, but since I came with paperwork from the States, I've been accepted.

"Everyone here is a new immigrant just like you. Give Ritamin a chance. You're not even a week into *shalat rishon*. Perhaps you just need more time to adjust."

Shalat rishon is the three-month pre-army period of kibbutz work I'm doing now, which exists so that members of a garin can adjust to kibbutz life and bond with each other before getting inducted in the army.

"I understand, Dov," I say, "but I've had less time than the others since I arrived late . . . there's very little time left for me to bond with the others here. We're supposed to get inducted in a few weeks, right? I just don't feel that I've had enough time." Panic starts to rise again.

"That's true. You're right." He bites on his pencil and stares off into space for a moment.

"Still," he says, "you've opted to do the army. Nobody forced you against your will."

It looks like I have no choice now but to tell him about my true feelings—that I'm being ignored. "Dov," I say, "No one's friendly with me here. I know what it's like to be on a friendly kibbutz. I volunteered a summer on Kibbutz Malkiyah and I was able to make friends. People talked to me. Here, no one even acknowledges me. No one talks to me unless I ask them a direct question. How can I spend the next two and a half years of army service with a group of people who won't talk to me?"

That's when a barrage of tears comes. I don't know what Dov's reaction will be, but I can't stop myself. I feel liberated and relieved, however, that I'm still strong enough to use my words (in a foreign language, no less).

Dov rests his cigarette on the armchair and blows smoke to one side, listening. Finally, he looks at me intently.

"If you came from America, and you're already here, what's wrong with giving it a bit more time, like I said? You're too tense and nervous. You won't survive in this country with a mentality like that. You need what I told you earlier: *savlanoot*, patience. We're a small country always under stress. When you're calm, you can think things through."

I start freaking out even more—the exact opposite response I should be having with him sitting there and telling me to calm down. *Oh shit. Now somebody in a foreign country sees me for who I really am.* It sinks in that the problems I'm having with the garin members are mine to deal with. Maybe people here just don't like me. Maybe I *am* the problem. Up until now I was hoping that things would magically work out, and now that it seems Dov is going to make me stay here, I can feel the desperation rising in me.

"I don't want to give this settlement another chance. Nobody is talking to me."

"Give it a chance," he says again, not budging.

I look at him with tear-stained eyes. There's a part of me that wants to tell him everything—about my upbringing in New York City, about my neglectful, anxious mother, about how important this service is to my father—but I'm afraid I'll overwhelm him. I need to be rational, but it's hard. He rests a firm hand on my shoulder for a few seconds. I cry again.

I am in my father's homeland, not mine, trying to find ways to adjust to this country, language, and culture—to make this place a part of my identity. Find my tribe. I have to straddle my two worlds, but I feel as if the odds are against me. There's no one who can help me navigate my own emotional landscape, along with all my anxieties. I have to do it myself. *Maybe this is part of growing up.* I think about the circumstances that led me to this moment and start to get choked up again. I felt so certain that I'd made the right decision, but now I'm definitely not so sure.

Dov eyes me with a kind look. He's right. I need to relax, to stop filling myself up with unnecessary pressure about the garin. Suddenly I remember that for a while now I've been contemplating kibbutz *ulpan*, intensive Hebrew language school, which the government will pay for as part of my immigrant rights. I wonder what Dov would make of a request like this.

"Dorit, this is a very strong garin," Dov says. "They have a strong *giboosh*—social cohesion. Have patience."

Patience has never come easily to me. Here in the middle of the desert, facing its howling, penetrating winds without a familiar face to help, I am constantly forced to give in to the unknown, to trust—which goes against my entire belief system. Because I grew up with emotionally weak role models, I have trouble trusting friends. The only breakthrough I've had in my adult life, really, was when I made the decision to come here, to break away from all of that and to try to see if I can make it on my own.

Trust the unknown. Trust people you don't know. Trust even when you aren't sure you can trust. Trust the desert storms. Trust the winds. Trust Dov. Trust myself. Now that's a biggie.

Dov flares his nostrils; his eyes are bloodshot. He's waiting for me to say something.

"I can't stay here," I say, fidgeting. It's time to listen to my intuition, and my intuition says to do something that's non-army related so I will have a better social experience. Then I can start with a new garin. I know this will delay my induction date, but it doesn't matter. "I want to go to an *ulpan*. I still want to get inducted . . . but at a later date."

I don't know yet which ulpan, as they're throughout the country; I suppose it depends which ulpans have spots available. There are a few things that worry me about this idea—the delay, for one. I'm not getting any younger, after all. But it seems like a good solution, and it feels right. There are hundreds of kibbutz ulpanim all over the country, and I'm hoping for one that's not just about work. Maybe I can find one that offers proximity to arts and culture as well as to a big city. Regardless, going to an ulpan will give me a chance to learn more Hebrew, travel around the country, meet people, and gain more confidence.

For a moment, Dov doesn't say anything. He closes his pad.

"So is it possible to go with the next garin? When's the next induction date?"

He sighs and opens his little black book. "February 12."

"Like next year—1991?" I ask.

"Yes."

It's a while away, but the feeling I get when I think of leaving here is like a tidal wave of relief. I want Dov to help me make this happen.

"So is it possible to get inducted with the next garin?"

He looks again at his book as he cleans his teeth. "Okay," he finally says. "You'll be inducted in the next garin. But that will be your last chance. You can't go any later than that. No more garins. If you start with this new garin, it'll be your third. That's it."

The way he puts it makes me feel like I'm some kind of basket case.

"Don't worry, Dov. I'll stick with the new garin. That's a promise." In November I'll be twenty. I'm already a grandmother by army standards. It's either do it next time or never.

Hurray. I'm out of here!

∽

AFTER DOING SOME RESEARCH, I ASK TO BE PLACED ON a kibbutz ulpan in the north. There's an opening at Kibbutz Yagur, which is situated at the foot of the Carmel Mountains. Haifa, Israel's third-largest city, is twenty minutes away, and Tel Aviv is ninety minutes away. It's a perfect match. For the next three months, I'll be studying advanced Hebrew. After all the stress of Ritamin, Yagur seems like it will be paradise. I'll just need to put in a few hours of study and kibbutz work a day.

Compared to Ritamin, Yagur is like a mini city. It has more than 1,500 kibbutz members, and it's so vast and wide that I have to walk almost a kilometer to get to the main road for a bus (if I don't want to hop on one of the minivans that bring members to the bus stops, that is).

I request to be paired up with an American roommate. She turns out to be twenty-two-year-old, freckle-faced Susan Silver from Watertown, New York. Her hair's never combed

and she wears sunglasses indoors. Her clothes take up just two
shelves of our wooden closet, which is just our height.

On the first day, she is flopping on her bed and kicking off
her sandals as I walk through the door.

"You're Susan, right?"

"Hiya, yeah, that's me!"

"I saw you in the classroom earlier!" I say, closing the door
behind me.

"Yeah, I'm in the intermediate level. My Hebrew's not
good enough. You're probably in the advanced class."

"Well, I need to practice my Hebrew if I'm going to get
inducted in the army."

"Oh wow, the army? What are you doing here if you're
planning to get inducted?"

"Too long of a story," I tell her.

"Oh, okay—for another time, then. What's your name?"

"Dorit, from New York City."

"Oh, a New Yorker—finally I get to meet a New Yorker!"
she says, laughing.

"Yeehaw!" I shout. "New York City!"

She plops a red-grey backpack onto her bed and flops
down next to it, then takes off her sunglasses and looks at me.
She's actually quite pretty, with reddish lips and blue eyes. I've
seen her before, when I first arrived on Yagur: I passed her
while riding camels in the Negev desert, and when our camels
brushed against each other, I waved. She returned the gesture,
but we've never spoken before now, and I've never seen her
without dark sunglasses on.

Now, in the confines of our room, she laughs as I "yeehaw"
this and "yeehaw" that, and suddenly Hebrew homework and
cleaning the floors isn't important anymore, because I've
finally made a friend.

∞

THAT FIRST SATURDAY, SUSAN AND I TAKE THE BUS INTO the port city of Haifa and buy falafel and *knafe*, a cheese-filled pastry. We talk about the exhibit we both managed to see at the Metropolitan Museum of Art before leaving for Israel, and the shops we both enjoy in Greenwich Village.

"You are such a New Yorker," she remarks one day. "You know everything."

I am a New Yorker, just like Mom. "I'll take that as a compliment," I say.

"Seriously, you, like, know everything and you pay attention to everything," she says. "It's remarkable."

This is the first time I've felt acknowledged by someone since I've arrived, and it helps me feel I've made the right choice in coming here. Having a friend makes adjusting to Israel much easier. I'm not so consumed with thoughts of whether I'm going to survive; I'm even having fun.

Eventually, Susan introduces me a friend she works with in the factory: twenty-two-year-old Golan, a second-generation kibbutznick, newly released from the army. We speak only English in Susan's presence, since her Hebrew is not as fluent as mine, but when we're alone I speak to him only in Hebrew for the practice.

"You know Shlomo Artzi?" he asks one day as we sit with our feet propped up on his coffee-stained table. Behind us are paintings covered with white sheets, works-in-progress that he says he hasn't worked on in months. I'm curious to know exactly how he depicts the forest, the sea, and the kibbutz surroundings through his artistic Israeli eyes. Will it be much different from the work my father, who lives outside his home country and has to work harder to translate images from his

youth into works of art, creates? When I ask to see his paintings, Golan shows some to me. He depicts his home country
with patches of red, green, and blue splotched on canvas,
idyllic, nature-like scenes that remind me of the Mediterranean Sea, which is just a short bus ride away.

"Do you get your inspiration from the song 'Ani Hayal'?" I
ask. The title means "I am a soldier," and it's by Shlomi Artzi,
one of Israel's most famous folk songwriters. I love that song,
even more so because the lyrics easily stick in my head.

"Which song is that?" he asks.

I look at him incredulously. "You don't know?" I belt out
the lyrics.

"Oh, that," he says, laughing. "Nobody inspires me," he
says. "I just paint."

Susan, Golan, and I become an art and music trio, re-
flective of our mutual interests, and I'm in heaven. One day
we visit a kibbutz with an art museum, The Museum of Art
Ein Harod. It's about thirty minutes from Yagur and was first
established in the 1930s in a wooden hut. Golan, whose parents
were founding members of Yagur, tells us Ein Harod isn't an
average kibbutz—that it's one founded on the principles of
culture and art as essential components of society. The museum
itself was even built before other essential physical needs of
the kibbutz society were met.

I am relieved to know that not every kibbutz operates only
upon the principles of work that run the engine of the kibbutz.
Compared to Ritamin, this place feels like a cultural mecca. I
feel more at peace today than I thought it was possible to feel
in this foreign land, and that creates a new worry for me:
What it will look like when my time here is up and I have to go
join my new garin?

∞

GOLAN APPRECIATES THE DELICACIES OF NATURE. HE'S
the first Israeli friend I've had since arriving, and I hope I'll
meet more people like him when I join my new garin. He's the
kind of person I can bond with. We like to share bags of
petiburs—Israeli graham crackers—which we spread with
Shachar, the oozing chocolate spread I'm so fond of, and gaze
at the stars from his veranda. Oftentimes Susan joins us, and
all three of us hang out there at Golan's place together.

"So, who is Shlomo Artzi talking to when he sings: "*Al tivki
li yalda*—don't cry for me my little girl? His sister? It's like he's
going back to the army base, no?" I ask.

"Maybe his girlfriend?" Susan suggests.

Golan thinks a bit and says slowly, "I guess it means he's
going back to his army base. But he's not singing to his sister . . ."

"Who, then?" I ask between bites of my petibar.

"His homeland. Because he's going off to war. He's asking
his homeland not to cry for him."

One night during cotton-picking season, after one month
of being on Yagur, Golan and I go for a midnight stroll to the
farthest end of the kibbutz. It's the industrial side, as he calls
it, blocked off for cotton-picking machinery. Metals flash in
the night like ghosts leading the way. We follow the flashes
until we reach a giant bin, at least five stories high. We climb
the huge ladder attached to its side and jump right into huge
piles of freshly picked, odorless cotton that will soon be
transported to another factory for manufacturing. It's as if we
are floating on the backs of stars, about to be carried out into
the clear, open distance.

"This is so awesome," I say. "I've never done anything like
this before."

"It's like heaven," he says in English in his thick accent. "It's beautiful."

∽

PERHAPS IT'S BECAUSE WE'RE SURROUNDED BY LUSCIOUS nature here at the foot of the Carmel Mountains, but none of the work at the ulpan actually feels like work, whether I'm folding sheets at the laundry or cleaning floors. Every morning I make a salad of hard-boiled eggs and freshly picked cucumbers and tomatoes, topped off with olive oil, salt, pepper, and lemon—Israeli style—for the ulpan's 7 a.m. breakfast. Kibbutz members take their salad-chopping very seriously, and it looks as if I've joined the tribe.

My favorite part of the day, however, is cleaning the classrooms. As the person in charge of the weekly cleaning of the buildings that house our classrooms and sleeping quarters, it's my job to take a big bucket of warm, soapy water every morning and throw it from the top steps of the building. What exhilaration! What joy! For the first few days I do it, I feel myself wanting to shout "Whee!" each time. I watch the water cascade as it slowly makes its way to the bottom step, and then I use the same kind of cleaning device, a *magav*, a big squeegee, that I used on Kibbutz Ritamin to clear the dirty water away. Only here, it's just the water and me. There's nobody telling me to clean out drains. Or vats. Or metal containers, like I experienced on Kibbutz Malkiyah. It's liberating.

Being at this kibbutz has allowed me to fully delight in this foreign culture. I feel as if I've made a 180-degree turnabout since my time at Ritamin. I turn up the volume on Shlomo Artzi's "Ani Hayal" so the music blasts and reverberates all throughout the building, and I sing the lyrics while using the pole as a pretend microphone. Even though I'm just a few weeks away from becoming a real soldier, about to be stationed in the Negev Desert with a new garin, I'm not anxious. This experience has made it feel like maybe I'll be all right. I've regained the confidence that had abandoned me during my time at Ritamin. I just need to be myself, and I will find friends among my new garin.

I smile as I clean the classroom floors and belt out my new favorite Israeli songs. I love this strange land, and the realization startles me. I feel emotionally safe. And more important, perhaps, I feel capable of taking on what's next.

∽

THINGS ARE ALREADY HEATING UP IN THE MIDDLE EAST. Talk of the Persian Gulf War is splattered all over the news. Although I understand Israel is under siege, I don't quite understand the technical details of what's going on, or who's against whom, and none of what constantly bombards me on the news really seems to make sense. Saddam Hussein's invasion, the coalition attacks, and the discussions of chemical and biological weapons are like fragmented puzzle pieces. Understanding the news is not the same as understanding conversational Hebrew, and yet I refuse to read any newspapers in English: our teachers have drilled into us that it's important to read, think, and even dream in Hebrew, and I try to adhere to that. I think of this learning mission as getting closer to feeling like a sabra.

The only time I read English is when I get aerograms from Mom. She sends one after another, each one plastered with messages like, "THE US STATE DEPARTMENT IS ASKING ALL AMERICANS TO COME HOME NOW!"

I ignore her until I can't anymore. I finally write a two-sentence postcard:

Dear Mom:
There's really no need to worry. It's safe here. You can come visit me here in Israel, if you want.
Love,
Dorit

After receiving more than twenty aerograms, I use a token to make a collect phone call home. Mom needs to know I'm not getting bombed by the terrorists she's been watching on the Channel 7 news.

I recite my phone number and the international phone operator dials the call for me.

"Dorit, Dorit, is that you? Are you all right?" She is practically breathless on the line, her voice shaking. "I want you home now. It's really dangerous right now in Israel."

Mom has no idea how safe kibbutz life is—how safe the entire country is, really. And I know there's no point in trying to convince her of it. How do you explain to your mother that Israel is much safer than the States when she's crying over the phone about the biggest bomb threat in the history of the city of Jerusalem, or about how several terrorists, as well as Israeli civilians and soldiers, have died? How do I convince her that Israel has the toughest army in the world—that the security of this country is so high that I feel more protected here than I ever have in the States?

"You've got to come home now, no questions asked!" she shouts.

"I'm definitely NOT coming home."

There's a moment of heavy silence.

There's no way she's going to ruin my life, I think. *She's not going to make me suffer. I've suffered enough.*

We argue back and forth for a few more minutes. I hear a *click*—the indicator that I'm running low on time. I look at the narrow plastic tube where I dropped my token in to make this call. The token has been swallowed by the machine. Our conversation will soon end, but for now her voice still rattles through the receiver.

"Ma, Israel is really not the scary country you make it out to be. It's safe here."

"I don't care. I want you home, now!"

"Ma, it's safe enough to stay here."

I don't know what's worse, the silence or the static on the line. It's as if someone just gave her a death sentence. She's lost the battle, but she doesn't know it. She has been here before, so she knows how idyllic kibbutz life is, far from the city, which is where all the terrorist attacks usually take place. I'm hoping that fact will help her calm down a bit and come to her senses. I haven't told her yet that I'll be leaving Yagur in November 1990 to enter a new garin. She wouldn't under-stand what I've been through so far, nor would she appreciate how I took my fate into my own hands to make a better situation for myself here. In the past three months I feel as if I've become a different person altogether. I wonder if she would even recognize me. I'm ready to face what lies ahead, and I don't have space for her anxiety. I have never felt so sure about my path.

"Ma, I've got to go now. I still have Hebrew homework. I'll call you soon. Try not to worry about Israel. It really is okay here." I dash through the last few sentences so she gets the hint.

"Okay, but call me soon. I want to know what's happening. The things we see on the news about Israel aren't very good."

"Okay, Ma."

"One more thing, Dorit . . ."

"Yes, Ma."

"I love you."

"I love you, too."

10

NEW HOME

ONE THING THAT I FIND COMFORTING ABOUT KIBBUTZ Sufa, the kibbutz of my new garin, located minutes away from the occupied territories in Gaza—the West Bank—is that it's not a dinky little settlement like Ritamin was. I don't feel overcome by fear and anxiety when my bus pulls up next to the wooden bus stop. I'm more relaxed and up to the challenge. I'm looking forward to getting to know everyone, including Orna, our garin "mother," whose job is to help us acclimate to our new kibbutz. And the flat loneliness of the Negev desert no longer makes me want to fly off the handle; now it orchestrates a different melody, telling me I will survive. It's not so bad, really, even on a hot fall day like today.

I feel like a different person from the young woman I was when I arrived at Ritamin. I hope I'll have an easier time bonding now that I've spent some time studying advanced Hebrew at a kibbutz ulpan. I also know that at least part of the reason for my poor experience at Ritamin was my own attitude, and I'm happy that I feel ready to fully enter this new garin—ready to be a joiner.

I'm given a two-bedroom, one-bath beige bungalow with a

Spanish-style ceramic tile roof, typically reserved for small families, located at the farthest side of Sufa, closest to the back entrance. There are a lot of these bungalows, and they are bunched closer together, which I find comforting because the proximity reminds me of life in New York City. At Ritamin, these kinds of rooms were scarce, but here nearly all the soon-to-be inductees in my garin are given one. On the first day, I learn I'll be sharing this bungalow with the five other girls in my garin. Since I got here first, I get to pick the better of the two rooms, which I'll share with just one roommate instead of two—although it's smaller, it has a built-in closet and mirror on the inside closet door, which the other does not. The other four girls will stay in the adjacent, slightly bigger room.

I marvel at all the empty space in our bungalow. There's a sixth girl who will be on a different kibbutz until we're inducted; apparently she's been on it for a number of years and doesn't want to relocate. The assumption, I guess, is that because she has been in the country for a while, she will be able to catch up and bond with us later.

What luxury! An entire home! But it is especially remote and lonely here; we have no neighbors, just the barbed wire fence, a tractor, the security Jeep that patrols around the borders, and pinwheels of dust that blow at random points during the day. I stand in my new backyard, which consists of a large square cement block surrounded by grass and weeds, and I play Duran Duran's lush ballad "Save a Prayer" over and over again. Instantly I am back in Greenwich Village, pretending I'm an actress in some MTV video from 1982. In my fantasy, I'm walking down the cobblestone streets of Greenwich Village, New York, singing the lyrics, tears running down my cheeks. In my real life, the desert wind just tousles my hair, and there's nothing romantic about walking down the paved road singing lyrics in English when just a few kilometers away there are IDF army bases and occupied Arab territories that, as I understand it, have the power to blow us up.

On my second evening at Sufa, Orna confirms that my roommates will be coming in a few days. I have already gotten used to having my own space again, a nice break after sharing a room with Karla at Ritamin and with Susan at Yagur. A surge of anxiety wells up. How will we manage all five of us in a two-room bungalow? Will we be able to get along?

I remind myself I'm on a kibbutz, and that I've committed to being pleasant, to making friends, to bonding with these people I'll be spending the next two and a half years with. I play more Duran Duran on my Walkman, turning the volume up high. These lyrics don't add up to much in the literal sense, but the ghostly melody does evoke a mood that fits my surroundings. I fall in love again with the way Simon LeBon croons his lyrics, his lascivious voice backed up by a purely electronic soundscape composed of icy synthesizers and throbbing drum machines.

I open the sliding door and step out onto my unfenced terrace, which faces the entire desert. It's as if I'm watching on the set of a movie, or inside one of my own fantasies. I note the difference in how I interpret the lyrics to this song here versus at home. In New York, it always made me think about how trapped I felt, but here it just lends familiarity in a foreign setting, and makes me feel more fully alive. I belt out the chorus as I look out past the grass and the IDF Jeep making its patrols. Then I walk until I reach the dining room, where the elementary school kids who have just gotten off the school bus are running inside for lunch.

I am relieved not to feel my body convulsing from an anxiety attack as I detour from the perimeter of the kibbutz and cut straight into the residential landscape, making my way to the center. Unlike Westbeth, the empty apartment I will return to after my wanderings will not ignite any catastrophizing. When I waited for Mom to return to our apartment as a child, I feared for her safety, but on this kibbutz I'm learning how to survive and thrive on my own—developing my own emotional independence so I don't have to live the rest of my life trapped in fear.

I remind myself that I have made it. I'm still here. I'm starting over on my own terms. I'm in my own element, testing my resilience and power.

I'm on my way.

∞

MY BUNGALOW WILL BE MY HOME AWAY FROM THE various army bases I will serve on for the next two and a half years, so it's time to get settled. The small brown door to the left of the entrance opens into a closet. I look in and find an assortment of wires, dead leaves, branches, and twigs. On a shelf in the back, there's a black hunk of something. I reach in. It's a pair of canvas work shoes the kibbutz typically gives its workers, its laces tied up with thistles from the previous owner.

For the next few days, in preparation for my roommates and to make the space my own, I swish warm soapy water over the floor to wash away excess layers of dirt and dry it with a soft linen cloth. I even throw water from a small bucket into the closet and use the cleaning items the kibbutz has provided for us, including a magav, cleaning fluids like bleach, and soft white square rags that you drape over the magav to dry the floor, to tidy it up.

To reward myself for my hard work, I buy an expensive

(twenty-five-shekel) bright pink–and-gold-rimmed bottle of Pnina Rosenblum spray deodorant from my own personal soldier budget: one hundred and fifty shekels per month, the equivalent of forty American dollars.

When Geraldine and Karine, who are from France, and Eina, Svetlana, and Vered, who are from the former Soviet Union, show up the next day to join our garin, our house is nearly completely furnished: it has a big bear throw rug, a wide open sofa and throw pillows, and in my room there are various knick-knacks and decorations, including an Indian-style scarf I've draped over our window as a makeshift curtain —items I've managed to find by asking other kibbutz members. Lots of what I've scraped together are secondhand, salvaged from empty bungalows nearby. I've already started to feel a bit more at home.

My five roommates show up on the doorstep with an array of suitcases and duffel bags. I show them the big room, which consists of two metal bunk beds, and my room. Karine decides to room with me. Once that's settled, she and Geraldine start chirping back and forth in French, while the other three girls squawk to one another in Russian. All of a sudden, I'm not feeling so comfortable anymore. I'm now a bit overwhelmed.

❧

A WEEK AFTER THE GIRLS' ARRIVAL, SVETLANA PLAYFULLY takes pictures of me wearing a low-cut two-piece dress that sashays and swishes like a ballroom dress. The sassy array of flowers on the skirt complements the smart matching bolero that I've borrowed from Geraldine. This moment reminds me of a time, many years ago, alongside the West Side Highway in New York City, when I kicked my legs up Marilyn Monroe-style to reveal pink ballet shoes and white pantyhose while Mom snapped picture after picture. It was prom night. My stepmother made me a pink ballroom dress out of taffeta with puffed sleeves fit for a Disney princess. I felt so free and beautiful that night, and it was a moment that stayed with me, since feeling free and beautiful was something I so seldom experienced growing up.

"That dress looks so beautiful on you," Geraldine exclaims. She is from Deauville, France, a place known for its upper-class society. Her kind words instantly soften my initial impression of her, which is that she is a bit difficult. Ever since she arrived, she has been making a big deal about the smallest things. "Girls," she'll say in a demeaning tone, tossing her wavy, dyed-blond hair, "this bathroom isn't clean enough. We have to scrub it more." Or, another time, "Who keeps leaving the screen door open? There's a hole in the screen! C'mon, let's patch it up. Now!" And one day she told our Russian roommates that it's prohibited to speak a foreign language, saying, "We must talk in Hebrew! We'll need to when we're inducted, so we'd better get used to it." I agree with her on that one, but I catch her speaking French with Karine all the time, which makes her a hypocrite.

All these incidents added together have made me feel like Geraldine's a bitch. But I can't afford to mess things up at this garin—it's my last chance. So I avoid confrontations at all costs. It's important for me to get along with these girls.

Soft-spoken and introverted Karine, who is from Paris and has rosy red cheeks and a small frame, keeps to herself at first. I wonder if it's because she doesn't like Americans, or maybe because she doesn't like the garin. It's clear she's doesn't care about getting work done the way the rest of us do. She becomes so engrossed in her French conversations with Geraldine that she often forgets to work. Svetlana calls her "ditzy" and "lazy," but to me Karine is delicate and unassuming, and I like her despite her work ethic, or lack thereof.

At night, in our room, I ask, "What made you want to volunteer for the army?" She's sketching with a charcoal pencil under the dim reading light and doesn't seem to hear me at first. I wait patiently for a few moments. She looks up at me.

"Our country doesn't like Jews. It's a very anti-Semitic country, and the situation's getting worse," she says still sketching. "Israel is my home now."

I listen attentively, not immediately responding. I have no idea what it feels like to suffer from persecution, since New York City is not only home to many Jews, it's a mecca for diversity in general.

"So you're a Zionist?" I ask.

Up until now, she's never made direct eye contact, but now she locks her eyes with mine and says, "Yes, I'm a Zionist."

"Are you a *hayal boded*, a lone soldier? Do you have any parents in the country?" I ask.

"My parents are still in Paris. They don't want to come. But the anti-Semitic attacks are getting stronger every day. One of my friends was killed, the victim of a hate crime, on the way home from school."

Her brown eyes are now glossy. There are tears welling up in her eyes. She fingers the two gold Hebrew letters of her necklace, which spell, *chai*—"for life."

"I'm a Zionist, too," I say. I'm not sure if it's comforting, but it's all I can think to say.

She blinks away the tears and hunches over her pad again.

∽

SVETLANA AND I HAVE FUN THE SECOND WEEK SETTING
up photo shoots. She steps over to the untended, weeded area
of our yard, lifts her leg up, and turns it to the right, striking a
pose while I photograph her. She's totally enjoying the attention, and we're both having fun acting silly. Svetlana is the
direct opposite of Eina, who curls up on the futon with a
Russian newspaper while we play with the camera, her dyed,
greyish-blonde hair covering most of her face. Most of the
time, she'll have nothing to do with either of us. Vered, meanwhile, tall and broadly built, stands outside with us smoking a
cigarette and ordering Svetlana around in Russian about what
she should do physically to accentuate her body.

I'm having fun with the girls, finally, and I'm relieved to
be enough at ease with them to goof around. We're having a
great time acting like we're high-paid models. Svetlana turns
her puffy, dyed-brown hair this way and that.

"Photograph me now!" she says.

I snap the photo.

She exclaims again, "Now, photograph me like this!
Wait . . . wait a minute!" She repositions herself by dragging
one leg over the other, and then she lies down in a patch of
weeds. "Oy," she says in a seductive voice that makes me giggle.

Svetlana arrived in Ashqelon, a fairly large city in the
south of Israel, in 1989 during a massive wave of Russian
immigration. The government efforts of Perestroika to abolish
Communism were futile and resulted in unprecedented numbers
of Russians coming to Israel—which subsequently caused
major resentment among native-born Israelis, primarily because
of the sudden lack of jobs that coincided with their arrival.

Along with her parents and older sister, Svetlana settled in
a cramped two-bedroom apartment in Ashqelon, which is two
and a half hours away from the kibbutz by bus. With the other

two Russians, Vered and Eina, Svetlana speaks her mother tongue. Geraldine rails against it, and privately I agree with her; for me especially it can be alienating and isolating to be living in a house with five people who all have at least one person to speak in their native tongue with. I understand it, though. I imagine if there was another American here I would be hard-pressed to speak to her in Hebrew. But with these girls, I speak only Hebrew, which is a big change having lived with Susan for the past three months.

Fresh from my ulpan experience, I am more confident taking language risks, especially with soon-to-be inductees from other countries. I feel pressure to make an effort to bond with these girls, past the point where I stopped at Ritamin. But already I'm making huge strides in connecting with them, which has made my experience here so much more positive than the one I had at Ritamin. I'm building good relationships with all the girls. I'm relieved.

∞

OUT OF ALL THE GIRLS AND GUYS IN OUR GARIN, ANDY, thin and tall as a telephone pole, is emotionally the most mature, though I don't recognize this quality in him right away. But others do, including Orna, who suggests that he become our fearless garin leader. The expectation, though, is for us to self-select leadership roles within our garin, and to figure out for ourselves how we should all bond. Orna and Dov want us to figure it out on our own.

We do elect Andy as our leader, but Svetlana and I don't take him seriously. We find his limp funny for some reason, and in the beginning we make fun of him for it—until we discover it's an injury he'd sustained from serving in the British army. I enjoy making fun of stuff in general—it's how I relieve stress and pass the time—and I pull Svetlana along with me. I'm desperate to make friends, and it doesn't occur to me how immature I might be perceived to be as a result of my actions. For now, it's all about having fun with Svetlana. Even after we learn about his limp, we find other things to make fun of. I move my bottom jaw and speak Hebrew way Andy does, which we perceive as snobby. I even lift my head and brush my index finger against my nostrils to exaggerate his pretentiousness.

Svetlana giggles, egging me on.

Andy's job is to help us resolve any problems that may come up during our weekly meetings. We won't have these meetings once we're inducted, so we need to make sure we're on track as a garin, that we're bonding without any problems. There is no direction for these meetings, and neither Dov nor Orna usually attend, but today they are here to explain the timetable of our army service: three months of working on Sufa, then army ulpan, followed by six grueling weeks of basic training that culminates with an eighteen-kilometer march around the camp. Then it's a toss-up where we'll serve: some of us will go to an army base, while others will end up serving on a settlement or kibbutz. After it's all over, we'll all return to Sufa for the last three months of work, and then we're home free. All in all, two and a half years of service for the girls; the guys can put in more army time if they choose to.

We listen with excitement and purpose. The room is silent, and I can feel my anxiety dissipating. A soldier—I'm really going to be a soldier! Finally! The basic training aspect brings up a ton of questions from Darren, the other British guy in our garin besides Andy. He wants to know exactly what basic training entails for the guys. I notice that he stands up each time he asks a question, and looks at us girls with disdain.

Geraldine catches on to this, too, and throws me a look that reads, *Who the fuck is this dude? What's his problem?*

Our intuition is spot-on: we soon learn that Darren sees himself as the Alpha Male and doesn't think that girls should be in a garin at all. Later he will flat-out confess that he has no tolerance for girls in the garin because he thinks we aren't cut out for serving in the IDF. Unfortunately, he's not the only one. Many guys I come across think that women should serve in secretarial and other non-combat jobs if they're going to serve in the IDF at all. Darren's attitude reflects the state of affairs for women in the early 1990s, which slowly, thankfully, will change with time.

Darren makes me nervous, and I worry about his attitude. He's clearly looking to pick a fight with one of us girls, and I start to notice him eyeing me in the dining room each night as he lays his tray on the metal counter across from the dishwasher area where Svetlana and I work.

"Cut out the laughing, Dorit," he shouts one evening, dropping his tray in the dishwasher area. "Get back to work. Laughing on the job isn't allowed!" He shouts this in English, presumably to berate me so that Svetlana can't understand. I shoot him a look that says, *Yeah, right—just make me stop.* I know I'm being bullied, but I can't yet find the words to tell my enemy off.

He's just jealous because we're having too much fun, I tell myself. *What an asshole.*

Nobody has ever expressed a problem with my laugh before, but it seems to drive Darren crazy, and he starts calling me out more and more as time goes on. I'm used to being somewhat anonymous, as I always was at home, but here I've established a reputation already as the "goofy American," and my very existence seems to piss Darren off.

Late one night, after Karine has fallen asleep, I wake up with anxiety. What is this animosity from Darren all about? Why does this guy have to get in my face? I'm devastated that he's singled me out. I'm already hypersensitive to being an outsider, and Darren triggers all of my fears in that area. I worry that he's going to unravel all of my hard-earned confidence.

∽

DARREN IMMEDIATELY DESIGNATES HIMSELF AS THE spokesperson for our weekly meetings, and one of the first things he brings up is that there are major problems between the girls and guys.

Problems? Between the girls and the guys? I think confusedly. *Since when?*

He speaks in perfect Hebrew, but with a thick British accent. I have an accent too, of course, but his is stronger. It's not his accent that gets to me, however—it's the defiant tone in his voice that's upsetting to me from the very beginning. And unlike me, he has no problem asserting himself.

"You girls are constantly having fun," Darren says to me one day. "It's especially you"—he points a stubby finger at me—"you, Dorit. You're dragging Svetlana into your world. You're making her stop working. I can see it."

"What? That's totally untrue." I can feel my adrenaline rising. "We get the job done every time, and nobody has a problem except you!"

"We'll see about that. I'm gonna raise this exact issue at our next meeting," he says threateningly.

He's won. I'm terrified.

At our next weekly meeting, as promised, Darren stands up and shouts, "I want to throw Dorit out of the garin. Like, right now!" He looks straight at me, and I tense. If we can't get our act together now, how can we possibly serve together in the Israeli army? He pounds on the table in front of him with his fist. Israelis by nature are demonstrative with their body language and facial expressions, so Darren fits right in with the "sabra tribe"—he pouts, screams, yells, and often stands up to emphasize his points.

Andy turns to Darren and says, "Now, hush. This is getting totally out of control. You've got to stop this!"

"Well, look at her. She does nothing but laugh at your limp, and now you're defending her!"

Up until now, as far as I know, Andy hasn't exactly known why Svetlana and I always giggle in his presence, but now the cat is out of the bag. I'm a bit embarrassed and nervous. What must he think of me now? It dawns on me this might be the main reason Darren doesn't like me, but I can't understand how it could escalate to throwing me out of the garin. I suspect Andy is ruffled enough from Darren's reaction, but he purses his lips even tighter and nods—which confirms his gentle and understanding demeanor, which I seem to be lacking.

This guy who I hardly know is escalating all my insecurities about serving in the IDF. He's pushing all my buttons, making my stomach churn. Fire burns in his eyes as if he's on some kind of mission. My eyes threaten to overflow with tears. Words stick in my throat. Luckily, Geraldine stands up and speaks up for me.

"Who are you to start throwing girls out of the garin just because you feel like it? *Ein D'var Kahzeh*—there's no such thing!" she shouts. Everyone is paying attention.

For the first time, Darren is silent—but not for long.

I finally find my voice. "Darren's been calling me lazy." I feel like a tattletale, but I've got to let everyone know my side of things. "He claims I'm pulling Svetlana away from work with my jokes and laughing. This is a lie!" I'm boiling. My body's shaking, but I've got to set this jerk straight. I continue, "I work in the dining room and in the fields just as hard as everyone else, Darren! You're just looking for a reason to throw me out!"

I sit back down. I can't get my body to recalibrate. Svetlana rubs my back in sympathy.

"Still, she needs to leave!" he shouts in Hebrew, ignoring everything I've just said. It's as if I'm not there.

"Oh hush, Darren," Andy says to Darren in English. "This is absolutely stupid where this is going."

From behind Karine, I peek at Darren's face, and see that it has softened a bit. *Andy knows how to talk with this bozo.*

Once Geraldine sits down, she turns to me and says quietly, "Okay, Dorit, you know better than to laugh at Andy. That's not exactly very nice." I nod in agreement, even though I don't like being told how to behave by someone else. If anything, I am the "grandmother" here—I'm two years older than Darren, and at least a year older than everyone else. I should be the one telling people what to do. But I've sacrificed my potential leadership in order to have fun. I like being the goofy one, but now I realize I'll also need to be a positive role model so I don't elicit negative attention from garin members like Darren. I may have to let go of my goofiness so I can get along better with other garin members.

Historically, Nahal garins have never consisted of just men. But Darren has already called our garin "his" garin. He calls the Russians "good-for-nothing whiners" because they sometimes complain about work. He calls the two French girls bossy and annoying.

And yet he doesn't want to throw them out. Only me.

∞

THE PROBLEMS WITH DARREN ESCALATE. AT OUR NEXT weekly meeting, one month into our time on the garin, he stands up and shouts, "I WANT TO THROW THE GIRLS OUT OF THIS GARIN!" Again he looks straight at me. I want to cringe. Or better yet, get up and leave. At this point, I believe he has the power to throw us out. Or at least me. None of the guys say anything to contradict him, which gives me the impression that they, too, want us out of the garin.

Geraldine stands up and screams, "This is absolutely ridiculous! You don't have the power to throw anyone out of this garin—*mi ata bichlal,* who the heck are you?" She punctuates her statement with an upturned sweep of her hand that Israelis are notorious for using in order to emphasize a certain point.

Take that, you asshole.

Raul, Geraldine's boyfriend from South Africa, stands up and turns to Darren. "This is not something we should be doing. We're supposed to be a garin. If you guys continue to behave like this, there won't be a garin!"

This is the first time someone besides Andy has stood up for us girls.

Darren now looks stupid with his puffed out face and googly eyeballs like a toad's. Still, he fights it out, not intimidated by Raul or Geraldine, who is taller and has a bigger build than most of the guys. "Girls shouldn't be on a garin. There's no use for them here," he argues.

"Man, like who are you to decide?" Raul shoots back.

"*Eize chutzpah*—what chutzpah!" Geraldine jumps in. "You can't just throw out whoever you want. It doesn't work that way. How would you feel if we decided to throw you out—all of us, girls and guys combined?"

"There *are* problems between the guys and the girls!" Darren protests.

"So what? That's life!" says Geraldine.

"Darren," Andy says calmly. "Just what *kind* of problems are you referring to?"

"The girls who work in the kitchen, like Svetlana and Eina, work too slowly; they don't know how to work at all!"

Now Eina and Svetlana stand up. "*Eize chutzpah!* How dare you tell us we're bad kitchen workers! You're a terrible field worker!" they shout.

"Ha! And how would *you* know?" Darren says with disdain. "You don't know anything. All you two do is speak Russian all day long." He laughs.

"Darren, that's enough," Andy says, lightly placing a hand on his shoulder.

The entire meeting room is in an uproar. Just a few of us, myself included, have remained silent during this entire time. Everything ends in confusion.

As I leave the meeting, I breathe a sigh of relief that I wasn't the subject of any more accusations, but I'm reeling from the confrontation. It takes me right back to middle school, when Brenda, a Puerto Rican classmate, threatened to fight me at a nearby schoolyard after school. I had no experience dealing with bullies before her, and I didn't know what to do, so I ran for home as fast as I could. The same feeling of panic I felt that day rises in me now. I'm supposed to stand up for myself, but what do I say? I know if I speak I will start crying, and then it will seem as if I'm overreacting.

I'm disappointed in my garin's inability to come together. Here, on Sufa, instead of cultivating good leadership, we follow the path of a silly Brit who believes he's the leader. It's so obvious we lack the tools to do this right—we stand out as immigrants. So far all we do is follow those in our garin who speak assertively, regardless of what they say. Andy is trying to live up to the role of leader, but Darren pulls him in all directions, and all Andy can do is try to appease him. If things keep going this way, this garin will be a failure.

∞

ONE NIGHT, I DREAM OF DARREN TERRORIZING ME. FROM the dust, his face emerges. "I want to throw all the girls out of the garin!" he shouts, looking at me the whole time.

The next morning at breakfast, I march up to Andy.

"Darren is a terrorizing menace. He even appears in my dreams. I'm getting sick," I tell him. There's something about Andy that makes me trust and respect him. I know I can tell him this without repercussions.

"He can't throw anybody out," Andy reassures me. "He doesn't have the authority!" He pulls out a cigarette from a corner pocket. "Look, if you must know, Darren's just really childish. He's filthy rich. He comes from the upper class. When he doesn't get what he wants, he becomes spoiled and nasty. He's never had to work for anything."

"So, basically, he's now on a roll and nobody can stop him, all because of the fact that he's rich? Not even you guys?" My eyes tear up as we head down the steps and into the dry desert air.

"Just don't get worked up by him and you'll be fine; he's not worth it."

"That's easy for you to say, Andy," I cry.

Andy shrugs helplessly. He doesn't know what to do. And the harassing at the meetings continues. Each time Darren points his finger in our direction, I want to retreat to a dark hole. He won't let go; every time, the words come back: "I want to throw Dorit out of the garin."

Am I the only one taking Darren's threats seriously?

To help myself get some perspective, I take a long walk in the Negev desert one evening, just before the sun goes down. I circle the kibbutz again and again, always coming back to the same starting point, where just a barbed wire fence separates me from the empty terrain beyond my porch. Army Jeeps are the only entertaining images in this vast desert crater, driven by soldiers who have an obligation to this land, and at the moment there aren't any—just boring, tired sand. I watch how the wind scoops up and twirls the tannish sand, which is so smooth and silky it could easily be beach sand. All at once, the spirals brush away the tire tracks made a few hours before.

I start kicking up dust with my heels. "Kick it, kick it, kick it!" I shout. My little sandstorm shakes up the earth, leaving a small cloud of dust that penetrates the air.

I look across layers of sand to a row of yellow lights, first in rows of twos and then threes. We won't know for some time which army bases we will be assigned to. Will serving in the Gaza Strip be in the cards for us? The thought scares me, but on the other hand, I do look forward to serving as a soldier in a uniform—no more of this pre-army, agrarian-type framework. There's an entire world out there I'm not yet privy to, and all I can do is focus on the fact that once I'm inducted into the army, I'll have less contact with Darren. I do wonder how many others will share Darren's opinion of women serving in the IDF. The fact that he has so much authority here—that he has not been completely shut down by the other guys—makes me nervous about what lies ahead.

∽

As the coordinator of all the garins in Israel, Dov has no choice but to make the trek from his Tel Aviv office after Andy phones him asking for counsel on how to deal with Darren. Terrorists are blowing up buses all over the country and we are lining up to get our gas masks due to the impending Persian Gulf War, and yet our garin cannot seem to solve its own petty issues, which have now turned into big, unsolvable confrontations.

At approximately five o'clock the next day, just an hour before dinnertime, Dov pulls into the parking lot adjacent to the meeting room in his white Subaru and Andy, who's been eyeing the parking lot for the last fifteen minutes, runs out to greet him.

"So what's the problem?" Dov asks as he pulls off his Erik Estrada sunglasses. "What is this nonsense about guys throwing out the girls? I've never heard such a thing."

Bit by bit, the story of how we cannot get along spills out. The two Brits serenade Dov with their versions: one simple, represented by Andy, and one lengthier and much more complicated, represented by Darren. I want to stand up and tell Dov how Darren has been terrorizing me—in fact, I want to cry to Dov and tell him the way Darren's behavior would never happen in an Israeli garin, but since we are an immigrant garin, there are far more cultural problems. But I remain silent.

The meeting ends with an ultimatum from Dov: no more threats, and do your best as a garin to get along with each other.

"You have absolutely no idea how badly you will need each other when you're inducted into the army," he says. "Right now, you're in a summer camp. Trust me."

I want Dov to know the real truth behind Darren's behavior. I want him to know about his bullying and that he wants me in particular out. So I run after him as he exits the meeting, and walk alongside him until we reach the parking lot.

"Dov," I pipe up as we draw closer to his car, "Darren claims there are problems between the girls and the guys, but there aren't. And that's the truth." I spill out the same version of the story I told Orna a week ago. It bothers me we are giving the Nahal such a bad name and we aren't even in the thick of our military service yet. We aren't fighting to protect the kibbutz and other settlement borders—we're fighting amongst ourselves.

"Thanks," he says in friendly tone. "It's just what I figured. Darren is just a ball of hot air. I've seen this kind of stuff before. Just try to find a way to work together, okay? This is a complete waste of a garin's energy. Good luck to you in this garin." He pats me on the back. "You can manage this. You don't need me. You have the answers."

What I really want him to do is put Darren in his place. But he doesn't. This is something we're going to have to work out on our own. I'm stuck here. *Try and find a way to work together. Try and find a way to work together.* It will be my new mantra. At Ritamin, I was unwilling to give the garin a chance because I was so focused on myself and my misery. Now that I've spent a few months in this country, however, I know I'm capable of building relationships based on values of communication, trust, and respect. But will that be possible with Darren?

∞

DURING MY DAILY DESERT WALKS, I IMAGINE WHIZZING down the street in New York City on my bike singing "New Moon on Monday." Here I try to tap into that, but I just kick up more sand. It's harder to evoke the level of wistful sentiment this song holds for me when I'm in a desert crater, just kilometers away from the Gaza Strip, rather than biking alongside the West Side Highway. No matter how many times I pull the loose strands of hair that keep escaping from my ponytail, there are always a few that keep getting in my face, reminding me of the times I used to spend by the Hudson River, when life was a bit more carefree.

We've now been at Sufa for almost a month, and we have one week left before we leave our "home base" for a special army ulpan that will combine intensive Hebrew learning with military tactics. Before we go, I manage to get the key to the secretary's office from Orna so I can call Mom. Something tells me it'll be the last time I'll be able to call her for some time. Instead of talking about the IDF, I tell her about Darren. It's safer territory, and honestly, it's weighing more heavily on my mind than my upcoming induction date: February 12, 1991, which is less than two months away.

"There's this guy here, Darren, and he's a real *mishuga*—a crazy person," I say. I follow that with something that surprises me: "He's really scary."

Predictably, Mom's reaction is the same as always: "Oh, honey bunny, don't be a worry bug; be a happy bug." It's never helped me before, and it doesn't help now. "It's okay," she goes on, "you can do it. You're a big girl."

I'm always looking for a deeper connection with my mother, but this kind of reaction pushes me to just tell the story, without getting too deep into any emotions.

"Yes, Mom," I say, "I'm trying to be a happy bug," not knowing what that really means right now.

We talk for over an hour and a half about random things. I decide not to worry about the phone bill. She responds over and over with "Don't be a worry bug."

I get off the phone feeling deeply dissatisfied and more disconnected from Mom than ever.

∞

TWO MONTHS LATER, I BUMP INTO DARREN AS HE'S SERVING himself a salad from the breakfast bar in the dining room. He's the last person I want to see. We're getting picked up later that day by a special bus that will take us to the *Bakum* —induction center—in Tel Aviv.

When he notices me, Darren hits the metal tray of the bar with his spoon and shouts, "You and Svetlana! What a dumb-ass Russian-American pair! Ha!" He says this in English and then chuckles to himself.

I want to tell him to go to hell. To shut the fuck up. That he knows nothing about Svetlana, and that there is no room for inappropriate name-calling. But I say nothing.

With a completely nerve-racked stomach, I, along with the other girls from our garin, drag my army duffel bag down the narrow path to the stop where the bus just arrived. We wait. Some of the other guys mingle with us.

Then something strange happens. As if they've practiced it, they join into a single-file line. It's as if they've been pulled into a trance. Darren brings up the rear.

"*Kadima, kadima*—forward, forward!" he shouts.

Oh, good lord. Who does he think he is?

Now the real test of our bonding begins. And now I'm thinking the absolute worst about what might happen at army ulpan as I shove my duffel bag into the bottom compartment of the bus. But then I catch myself. I'll be in the military now, with a different kind of pressure. We'll be learning military tactics; it'll be less about the "social" stuff. Plus, Andy's on my side. I allow these thoughts to uplift me.

Onward.

11

ESHBAL

THE BUS SNAKES UP THE MOUNTAIN ON THE WAY TO OUR language school. We've just gotten inducted, clad in our freshly pressed uniforms, and are on our way to Eshbal, a settlement-type military camp where we'll spend the next six weeks perfecting our Hebrew under a military framework. We're now Nahal soldiers, a special division of the army dedicated to working on settlements and kibbutzim in conjunction with military service. We don't have our signature green berets and unit tags yet—that will come after basic training, when the six of us girls complete an eighteen-kilometer march.

Trees and lush vegetation line the narrow road. The bus's engine throbs as we turn unto the long, twisty road to the settlement—the final stretch. I am wearing my travel uniform. My new black army bag sits comfortably on my lap, yellow fluorescent striping around the shoulder strap. I play with the zippers of the two front pockets. I've been given a sewing kit with a broken needle and "gaz madmia," tear gas, in case I get abducted, and a small first aid kit. When one of the commanding officers at the induction center learned I was American, he said, "You and all of us soldiers get this stuff because your country paid for it." I don't exactly know how I'm supposed to feel about that.

In addition to my black bag, I've been issued a new green duffel bag stuffed with green soldier gear, including a thick, itchy sweater, the kind my mom would have me wear. This is the *madim aleph* uniform intended for traveling between bases. We're given a long- and short-sleeve shirt, a skirt, three pairs of unhemmed pants, a thick jacket, a black traveling handbag, and a pair of black sandals, but the most important possession I've received is my new army number: 3866256. I finger the numbers on my dog tag and recite the numbers in my head, first in English, then in Hebrew. After a few times, the number is already ingrained in my memory.

It's hard to believe I'm finally a soldier. I'm filled with nervous anticipation and anxiety, mainly because I've delayed the onset of my service by three months by joining a later garin. Will we be able to work together under pressure? It's hard to have *savlanoot*, patience, when you're challenged by the dynamics of different foreign mentalities. The impatient part of me wants to know what it's like to fire a gun or wake up at 4:30 a.m. for inspections, and I know many of the guys share this feeling as well. I guess it's just a matter of time before we have our chance. How different will my new life as an IDF soldier be from what I've imagined it to be? My only reference for military life is what I've seen in American movies. What part of my work will depend on other garin members, and what part can I do well on my own? Somehow, this pressed travel uniform I'm wearing indicates to me that there will be serious lessons that will test the limits of my courage, faith, and endurance beyond random kibbutz work. Looking now at the green silhouette of myself in the window, my former college life seems insignificant, as if I was never that person to begin with.

All my life I've done one "right" thing after another, fulfilling my "good daughter" duty: picking up after my mother's slack at home; leaving a private, nurturing Jewish school for a crime-infested public school with no complaints; and fulfilling my mother's desire for me to go to college. Each of these tasks was riddled with anxiety, fear, and self-doubt. I don't expect my uniform to magically turn me into a leader, but I'm looking to this period of my service to help me to respond to difficult situations from a place of peace, emotional security, and rationality. This will be a major challenge. Something also tells me our garin is behind the curve, and some of us will need to outperform others in the area of leadership. Even so, in this moment I'm more motivated than I've been since I arrived in Israel. I'm ready to become the soldier I came here to be.

During the three-hour bus ride, I watch as the majestic beaches of the Mediterranean Sea turn into Arab villages and the high rises of Tel Aviv finally disappear altogether. The guys in our garin cannot stop talking about basic training. They can't wait to do their forty-kilometer march, a test of their physical endurance that they are anxious to prove themselves at.

At this ulpan, in addition to learning Hebrew, we'll be shooting on a shooting range, taking orders from our officers, getting up at 4:30 a.m. for inspections, and cleaning our guns every day. From the back of the bus I can hear Jake from Canada, who joined our garin as a *misupach*—a soldier in our garin but from another kibbutz—right before our induction date, shouting in English, "We're gonna kill those motherfucking Arabs! We're gonna shoot their motherfucking asses off!"

At his words, all of the guys break into a thunderous round of laughter, including Robin from England and Daniel from Uruguay. Only Luis, a Spaniard and also a *misupach*, asks, "Jake, are you serious?"

I'm taken aback by this sudden aggression and I'm deeply concerned about Jake's attitude. Does he really mean what he says, or is he just trying to elicit a reaction? Either way, I feel leery of him now.

I turn to Svetlana, who rolls her eyes and says, "*Eize idiot ha Jake ha zeh*—What an idiot Jake is." I nod in agreement, but keep my thoughts inside. Jake and I hung out a bit when he came to visit Robin on Sufa. I was flattered by the attention he gave me, referring to me as a "New York City girl." I rolled my eyes when he called me that, but I was also taken with his bravado in some ways, and the fact that he was Canadian gave us a certain common ground in this environment where I often found myself so desperate for connection.

The guys, including Daniel from Uruguay, break into the chorus of a well-known Israeli song, "Two Fingers from Sidon," as if they've sung the words all their lives. My room-mate, Eina, joins in too, but she's the only girl singing. The last three months on Sufa have been exceedingly difficult for us as a garin, and singing is a place of common ground for us. I want things to improve, though, so halfway through the song I join in, singing at the top of my lungs. Despite our troubles, I'm hopeful that we'll still be able to bond now that we'll be operating under a military framework.

We're down now to six girls including Dalia, the girl from the other kibbutz who joined us at our induction. Karine left Sufa after a few weeks, claiming she wasn't cut out for army life. Svetlana says Karine was flaky and couldn't stand up for herself. The rest of us girls have come a long way in three short months, and I'm confident of our abilities to deal with the pressure we'll face, but I'm still not over the interactions I had with Darren at Sufa. I'm concerned about how we'll continue to fare together, but I refuse to let myself wallow in those thoughts. Whenever I'm tempted to veer into anxiety over our group dynamics, I remind myself, *We've got to make it work. We've got to make it work.*

Now, as I listen to my fellow soldiers belting out the words to this song about a nineteen-year-old soldier serving in Lebanon, I wonder about the anguish and pain the Israeli singer who originally recorded this song must have tapped into. Like us, he sacrificed the years of his youth to serve. Each time the chorus rings out, I can see the "broken" soldier in me hoping and wishing for something better. If Mom were the type of mom who could grab my duffel bag full of dirty work uniforms and lead me to the table for a home-cooked meal, and if only she urged me to share my stories, perhaps I would feel a little less broken.

When the song is over, the driver raises the volume so we can all listen to Kol Israel. Song time is over. It's time to listen to the news of Israel.

WHEN WE PASS THROUGH THE BARBED WIRE GATES OF the ulpan, I look around. There's not much to see—just empty mountains around us for kilometers, and not even a firing range in sight. I immediately notice two bunkers at the bottom of the hills with grey walls that can only be described as "wavy," as they remind me of rolling ocean waves in their shape and design. An Israeli flagpole surrounded by a circle of small stones in the ground separates the two buildings.

We retrieve our green canvas duffel bags from the luggage compartment and, just as the last of us seizes theirs, the commander of this "farm" appears and, after introducing himself as Officer Dror, tells us in quick Hebrew, "Everyone! Listen up! Drop your bags off in your bunks and stand on opposite ends of the flagpole—girls on the lower side and guys on the upper side. Everyone must dress the same. If you choose to wear a sweater, then everyone must wear a sweater. The same goes for a coat. Everyone must be dressed identically. Be out there in ten minutes. On the dot! No questions asked. Okay? Now go! *Zooz*—move!"

I dart downhill in the direction the officer is pointing toward, noting a few offices to my right and a small dining hall to my left along the way. My boots can't run fast enough. The hill is steeper than I realized. Dalia from Denmark is way ahead of me even though we're not even going very far. I manage to speed up, however, and in a few seconds I'm so close I can almost touch the brown curls escaping from her army work hat.

Dalia is the girl who worked on another kibbutz while we were all at Sufa. Like Jake, she joined our garin once we were inducted. Her father's also Israeli, and she has an Israeli name, and we're both go-getters, but she's aloof. I'm hoping that she will warm up and we will become friends. I'm drawn to her because she's calm, focused, and rational—leader-worthy qualities.

Ten short minutes later, our whole group is standing on opposite sides of the flagpole. Eina notices it first. The guys are dressed differently. "Wait! Some of you are wearing sweaters and some of you are wearing jackets!" she calls out. From the lower side of the flagpole, the girls shout in Hebrew,

"*Im sweater*—with a sweater!" while the guys shout out, "*Bli sweater*—without a sweater!"

This continues for what feels like way too long. I want to shout, "C'mon, people! We don't have time for this—let's go!" But I stay silent. I don't want to become the subject of negative attention.

The girls and guys fight it out. Daniel from Uruguay continues to protest even after the shouts die down. He's got a health profile of 97, which is the highest medical rating and determines one's suitability for fighting, but he chose to serve in the Nahal Brigade because of his socialist principles. He's a sight to behold. Standing just over five feet tall, he's half-bald, with a shining head you can practically see yourself in, and when he grins, he reveals two buck teeth. Even when he's wearing a neatly pressed going-home uniform, his shirt is perennially hanging loose and his bootlaces are untied. He reminds me of Elmer Fudd. He's flirted with all of the girls, trying to get at least one of us into bed, but his comical appearance does not attract any of us.

"*Nu, banot*, girls! It's not cold. Why do we have to wear jackets?" he says. "Those things are too thick!"

In the end we give in to Daniel, not because he's right but because we're tired. Just moments after the decision to wear sweaters is finally made, I see two of the officers making their way down the hill.

Urgency flows from my voice. "People, *hem ba'im*! They're coming! They're coming! Let's go!"

We rush into two straight rows parallel to each other on either sides of the flagpole. The air whips at us from both sides. The cold, mountainy air finds its way into the thick, itchy seams of my green sweater. Just as I entertain the thought that we're in good shape and ready to go, I notice that

Igal, the slow-moving Russian, is still wearing a jacket. But there's nothing any of us can do now. Hissing over to Igal at this point would draw suspicion. We crane our necks upward position. Andy buckles his hands behind his back and shouts in his very courteous-sounding British accent: "*Hamachleka titen hachshev la'mifakedim—shtayim, shalosh, hachev!*" The platoon will now pay attention to the commanding officers—two, three, attention!"

Silence.

Officer Dror now stands in front of us, accompanied by a female officer. They look at us intently. Under her army work cap, the female officer is just an adolescent; I am older than her by almost a year. She stares ahead as Officer Dror talks. His stout appearance is weighted down by his M16 and the rows of magazines belted around his waist. He looks like a buffoon.

"Soldiers!" Officer Dror shouts. "Good! You made it on time. But Officer Dorit and I are disappointed. One of you isn't wearing a sweater. Why is that? I told you that everyone needed to dress identically."

I want to speak up, say that we did the best we could and that perhaps Igal didn't understand what was going on, but again I say nothing. I feel as if I've lost my voice; I wait for someone else to speak up.

Akiva, the other Russian, moves closer to Igal. Akiva is bulky and has broad shoulders. He's what Israelis would typically call a "sociomat": he only cares about eating and making sure he's first for any special privileges. He couldn't care less about Igal, as far as I've been able to tell, but perhaps he realizes that maybe we won't get to dinner on time if this situation doesn't get fixed.

"Soldier!" Dror shouts. He's so close to Igal now, he's

practically breathing on him. I hope he won't bop him over the head with a gun or something.

"Yes, Officer," says Igal.

"Tell me, why aren't you wearing a sweater?" Dror asks.

At Sufa, Igal acted like my big brother, encouraging me to be strong in the face of Darren's masochistic attitude. I feel compelled to stick up for him. I can hear the slight quiver in his nasal-sounding voice as he says, "I wasn't paying attention, officer."

"Well, you put your garin in jeopardy. This is a serious issue. Today it's a sweater issue and tomorrow it's making sure each soldier is accounted for when you're in Lebanon. Who's not communicating here?" He surveys us and then looks back at Igal.

"Who's not communicating?" he asks again.

"Yes, Officer!" Igal shouts. He's still as a statue.

"No, you tell me!"

"We are, Officer. We're not communicating."

"That's right. Now, you have to find a way to work together here on Eshbal. Understand?"

A sheep bleats in the distance. No one dares to look in its direction. There's an intensity in Officer Dror's eyes, and Officer Dorit looks steadily at us. Their caps are pulled intentionally down, making it impossible to see the whites of their eyes.

The female officer, Officer Dorit, reminds me of myself as she sits back and observes. I wonder how this officer with a porcelain-looking face and small-framed body can have so much power. I'm intrigued by her, perhaps because of her age, or because we share a name. She's got a short, jet-black ponytail that reminds me of my former college roommate, Surelle. A smile curls at the edges of her mouth. My intuition tells me she's never been out of the country and is very connected to her family and friends on the kibbutz—just like Surelle and her small group of Jewish friends from the Bronx were.

Growing up, I sang the well-worn chorus, *"bichal dor v'dor hayav adam lirot—et atzmo kielo hu yatzah m'metzrahim*—all people, in every generation, should see themselves as having experienced the Exodus from Egypt," at my Aunt Frieda's and Uncle Isaac's house in Far Rockaway at their annual Passover seder. Here in Israel, I have to work to give voice to my journey as an American Jewish girl who's left Egypt—or, in my case, New York City. I also have to work to think of myself as part of a team. It's always been hard for me to give of myself without thinking about what I might get in return. But in this moment, Igal's mess-up is my mess-up—just as it is everyone else's. Aren't I partly to blame for not helping him? Maybe he's experiencing a deeper cultural or language issue than I am. During my time here, I've learned that Russians who serve in the IDF often face emotional challenges because of their communist history. Svetlana herself has told me she never wanted to serve in the IDF, but she's a minor who immigrated to Israel with her parents, so she has to be here.

Standing in front of these native Israeli-born officers, I am more conscious than ever of the difference between the American and Israeli mentalities. The only real exposure I ever had with Israelis growing up, aside from my father, was watching the occasional news commentaries in Hebrew on our big black-and-white TV. I remember watching Golda Meir, Israel's first and only female prime minister, bellow out her big visions for her country as my father unleashed a steady stream of commentary I couldn't understand. From this I learned that to be Israeli meant to speak aggressively and assertively. So far, my officers are living up to this image.

"Does everyone here understand?" Officer Dror says.

"Yes, Officer!" we shout.

"It's going to be tough, but you can do it. Some of you aren't used to working together like this. This is going to be a new thing for you. You're going to have to learn very fast."

"Yes, Officer!" we shout again.

"Remember, *work together*. This is a warning. Next time, there'll be consequences. Got it?"

"Yes, officer!" we all shout.

As our officers ascend the hill, I look at my watch. Seven o'clock. Everyone's already running toward the dining room. My stomach's a rumbling mountain of nerves. I wonder how I'll get through the rest of the day.

∞

ON DAY TWO WE ARE AWOKEN BY A FEMALE VOICE THAT says, "*Boker Tov Hevreh*—good morning, everyone!" It's Galit, one of our Hebrew teachers. "You girls up?"

"Yes, we're up!" Eina says from under the cover.

Svetlana says something in Russian to Eina in the darkness. It takes a few moments for the glow-in-the-dark numbers of my watch to come into view: 4:30 a.m. Ugh. I am on a top bunk in a tiny room that's housing all five of us girls. It takes a few moments to process that it's our first morning here. We have just twenty minutes to dress in full uniform and get outside in front of the flagpoles. I sit up and unlock the Uzi that's strapped to my bed. All night long, the long firing part of the gun poked and prodded my leg until I finally realized it was my gun and sat up in disbelief, thinking, *What the . . . ? Phew. No bullets.*

The morning Muslim prayer of a nearby mosque wails. I

lie in the dark and listen to undulating, singsong Arabic. I try to imagine what Arabs do when they listen to it since I've never seen anyone do their five-times-a-day prayer before.

I consider an interesting fact: I'm now army property. Number 3866256. I finger my dog tag and think about the fact that if I lose my gun, I'll go to jail for seven years. That thought scares me silly. Eina, Vered, and Svetlana are already chirping in Russian as they dress quickly in their work uniforms. The bathroom consists of three holes in the floor and a bunch of swarming flies. A cracked mirror and dim lights accentuate the bare army look. As I look at the holes in the floor and then stare up at my face in the mirror, I think, *Do you know what the fuck you're doing, Dorit?*

Ten minutes later we're at the flagpole again. A few of the guys are wearing sweaters and some are wearing coats. Geraldine's the first to shout, "You guys better hurry. We're all wearing coats. You're not! And you've got exactly two minutes!" I count the coats. Fifteen of them. Shouldn't there be sixteen? I ask Svetlana, who nudges Geraldine.

"Where's Igal?" Geraldine shouts.

One of the boys turns to Akiva, Igal's bunkmate. "Hey Akiva, where's Igal?"

"I don't know," he says, shrugging his shoulders like a little kid. "We were just smoking a cigarette just a few minutes ago. I don't know where he went."

"C'mon, let's find him!" Andy shouts. I've never heard him speak with such urgency before.

"Igal . . . *Igal!*" the guys all shout as we look on with uneasiness.

Finally, a short, stout figure appears from one of the bunks. It's Igal.

But Officer Dorit has already arrived, and now there's no

time to lose. We scramble into two straight rows opposite the flagpole.

"The platoon will now pay attention to the commanding officer—two, three, attention!"

We all crane our necks, and I look up at the sky. Stars are scattered everywhere. They remind me of us and the way we're haphazardly handling this new army life.

Igal rushes into position. He's without a coat. I pray Officer Dorit won't notice, but I doubt that's going to happen.

"Oh my god," Svetlana whispers. "Now we're gonna get it."

"Uh-huh. I know."

"Good morning, *mahlekah*."

"Good morning, Officer!"

"I see you're all wearing the same clothes today. Good. You made the effort."

"Yes, Officer."

Will she say something about Igal not arriving on time? I hold my breath. She turns around to face the guys and then faces us again.

"Unfortunately, however, you didn't all stand on time. This is a fuck."

A "fuck"? What's that?

"If one soldier isn't here, then that soldier isn't accounted for. If your gun's like your girlfriend or boyfriend, then your fellow soldier is like your bodyguard."

As punishment for our "fuck," Officer Dorit has us run down and up the hill at the farthest side of the base twenty times. We start by first jogging to the opposite side of the base, where sheep and goats are grazing. At five in the morning, this hilly mountain is a shadowy, peaceful mound—but it's steeper than it looks, and running up and down it requires focused physical effort. Once we've done our twenty laps, she sends us running around the camp numerous times—too many to count.

"*Oy, oy, ze kasha*—this is so difficult!" Svetlana suddenly cries, and after drinking a few sips, she stops and spits out the water. "I can't hold the water. My stomach."

"You can do it, Svetlana. C'mon." I try to pull her along. "We just have a little bit more to go!"

She doesn't budge.

I wonder if I should ask the officers for help. Vered is also spitting out water from her canteen. Between spits, they talk in Russian.

I decide to catch up with Dalia, who's running with Eina. Dalia doesn't exhibit a single sign of weakness. She's a war machine!

We finish by doing one hundred push-ups and sit-ups combined, after which we're ordered to drink a full canteen's worth of water. It's 6 a.m. by the time we finish. The canteen water is warm and tasteless, but I welcome it gratefully. What I really want is a cup of hot chocolate, but that's not going to happen. As soon as the thought surfaces, I push it away.

Just as we finish up our punishment, before we line up again by the flagpole, Andy runs up to Igal.

"What the hell happened, Igal?" he shouts between pants. "Look what you did; you got us into some major trouble!"

"I was trying to unlock my gun," Igal says. "It somehow got stuck. It was the key!"

"You can't delay the garin like that!" Andy says fiercely.

I want to tell Andy to go easy on him—that Igal's slow to pick up on things and may not always understand. Everyone assumes that Igal understands, because he gives the impression that he does with his nasal-sounding *ken* ("yes"), but I know he doesn't. Because I'm afraid of being singled out, though, I don't stand up for him as much as I probably should. After all,

I'm trying to change. I don't want to draw attention to myself as the "goofy American" anymore. But so far what this means is I just stay silent, which I hate. Why am I holding back? Am I afraid of being associated with a nerd like Igal because I hung out with nerds back in high school and I don't want to go back to that? Am I being selfish?

Igal is laughed at constantly by the guys for his awkward behavior and nasally voice. No one is particularly sensitive to his plight, and the other four Russians barely interact with him. The only time they offer help is when they are forced to translate military content into Russian for him.

When we finally regroup in our two rows opposite the flagpole, I notice I'm next to Dalia instead of Svetlana. Dalia's chest is heaving from all the running we just did. I wonder what she thinks about this situation. Her face is unwavering. Should I consult her about Igal's behavior? Something tells me not to bother and to just be the best soldier I can be. I stare at the sky and say nothing.

THE SAME ROUTINE CONTINUES FOR THE NEXT THREE weeks. We get up at the crack of dawn for early-morning inspections, then separate our Uzis into their various parts and pieces, laying them out side by side as if we're selling wares at some county fair.

At first I am a bit scared that my gun will fire off by accident. It's not lost on me that I am assembling a fighting machine; each gold-colored tip of the twenty-five-magazine pack has the power to shoot and kill. But everywhere I go, I see soldiers with guns, and I start getting used to always having mine by my side. Soon I have no problem cleaning and firing it. But I still don't ever want to use it outside the firing range.

The easy part is cleaning the tarnish and rust from the gun with cotton flannel known in Hebrew as *flannelit*. The hardest part is figuring out how to reassemble the gun once it's clean. Since I get confused by this process all the time, I watch Dalia, who executes with perfection every time.

Dalia disassembles her gun and lays out each piece, including the *kane*, the shooter, which happens also to be the longest part of the gun, along with the spring mechanisms and the cover. She carefully unscrews each part. Her deft fingers carefully separate the holder part from the gun's body without upsetting all the other little pieces, making sure that nothing gets misplaced. She carefully releases the *machsanit*, the part of the gun that holds the bullets, and uses the special metal stick with a slit in the top that we've all been given so we can push the flannel cloth down into the hole to clean all the rust and dirt that accumulates there. Dalia continues to aggressively push until the rust is gone. Somehow my kane is always rustier than hers.

Dalia is also always the first to finish cleaning the parts and reassemble her gun. One day, watching her quick, precise movements, I whisper to Svetlana, "What do you think about Dalia? Is she a good soldier?"

What I really want to know is if Svetlana agrees with me that Dalia has leadership potential.

Eina looks at us warningly and says, "*Banot*, girls," as if she knows where this conversation is going to end up. When Dalia leaves for the bathroom, she tells us quickly that Dalia's father killed himself and Dalia found him hung from the ceiling by a rope at their home in Denmark.

Wow. Maybe that's why she keeps to herself.

"*Eize miskena*—poor thing," Svetlana says.

I don't say anything more. When Dalia comes back, I want to tell her how sorry I am for her loss, but I can't without betraying Eina's confidence. The fact that Dalia's a very private person makes it hard to connect with her. As much as I want to be her friend, she doesn't seem to want to get close to anyone except Eina.

Usually the time after early-morning inspections and gun cleaning is the quietest part of the day. In a few days we'll be going for our first target shooting practice—our first time shooting our guns. I am excited and nervous. During today's break, I circle the base, amazed by how tiny it is against the mountainous expanse. In the far distance I make out what appears to be some kind of clearing; its lighter color stands out against the rest of the mountain's darker green.

I follow a small path that arches down the mountain, wondering why I haven't noticed it before. To my right are signs that indicate land mines. *Land mines in this pristine place?* I walk down, past a dirt road lined by barbed wire, leaving my fellow garin members behind me. Thirty seconds later, I hear someone call out to me, "Where are you going, Dorit? That's land mine territory. Get out of there!"

Before I even have the chance to respond, Geraldine shouts at me like a mother hen, "Dorit! You're not supposed to be there!"

Clearly they're concerned not only for my safety but also about the entire garin getting into trouble. We can't afford suffering through another "fuck." (A fuck, I have now learned, is the army's lingo for a "bad mishap." There are various levels of "fucks," and each results in a different consequence.)

The adolescent part of me wants to resist them. I feel like they're ganging up on me. *What's the big deal?* I think. *It's quiet here. It's all good. There are no land mines on this path. Everyone needs to relax!* I want to be the free spirit I got to be back in Greenwich Village, left alone to explore. But Geraldine is yelling at me again.

"Dorit! You're not this stupid. Why didn't you look where you were going?"

Raul, her boyfriend, makes a "duh" face at me while making circular motions with his fingers by his head. I want to die.

"I didn't know," I say. If you don't know something in the IDF, it's not always great to admit it, especially if you're a girl —but it's better than the alternative in this case: admitting I know what I was doing and did it anyway.

"Seriously, Dorit," Geraldine says.

Really? Is exploring an unknown path so deplorable? They don't really care about me and whether I get blown up or not; they're just upset about whatever punishment might ensue. Tears burn under my eyelids. My throat gets tighter. I struggle to breathe. I'm angry, specifically at Geraldine for drawing such unwanted attention to me. Why is it that I'm constantly looked at as a goofball or an incompetent soldier and never seen for my good intentions?

Years later, I will come to understand how self-absorbed I was and how even simple acts of ignorance or curiosity like this one could have jeopardized me and my garin. We didn't pay for my blunder in this case—in fact, no one even mentioned it again. But the incident stood out for me because all I wanted was to be liked and respected, and instead, in this moment, I felt wholly misunderstood. I felt stuck in a limbo between not wanting to be known as the goofy American and holding back so much that I wasn't allowing myself to be seen or understood by my garin members.

∞

THE SERGEANT TAKES US TO THE OUTDOOR FIRING range beyond the base on the day of shooting practice. When it's our group's turn, I step forward with the others, take a wide stance, and wait for the first command.

"Magazines in!"

Along with everyone else, I repeat "Magazines in!" as I place the magazine inside the opening at the bottom of my weapon.

The sergeant tells us how to aim and shoot our weapons. I was hoping to fire the lighter M16, but we're shooting with the much bulkier Uzis. Having not quite gotten used to handling my Uzi, I feel a bit anxious. After all, the gun is almost as long as my arm.

Once I begin shooting, however, I am exhilarated by the thrusting motion of the Uzi and how it shakes once the bullet is released. As I keep my aim on the target, shells fall on the ground next to me. I manage to hold the weapon steadily, look through the sights, and focus on my target.

Halfway through the magazine, one of the commanding female officers bends down and adjusts my gun so it doesn't weigh down my arm so much. I have never handled a weapon before—I was brought up to be afraid of everything, including firearms. But I do not approach this shooting exercise with the echo of my mother's fears. Quite the opposite, in fact: I feel the power of the weapon, and I enjoy it. *If I told Mom about this, she would send aerogram after aerogram until she convinced me to leave the army and Israel for good*, I think.

After that first day, we have shooting practice every day. I am always the first to target shoot at the yellow bull's-eye of each cardboard cutout, giving myself the chance to learn from my mistakes while the other girls wait and watch. I imagine the weapon has the power to transform me into a soldier of an elite combat unit. I want to embody everything I've observed in other IDF soldiers I've admired. I want to be confident and competent. At times, the female commanding officers come and help me reposition the gun, and once I get the hang of how to aim better, I hold the gun steadily. I lift my Uzi close to my ear and feel my entire body rattling again with every shot. I pull the trigger. Release. Pull the trigger. Release. Pow. Pow. One, two, three. Bullets pop out like candy.

On the shooting range, I am safe. I feel the plastic ridges of the Uzi's body against my skin. Superior officers stop coming to help once they see I can manage. I'm now on my own. This accomplishment fills me with pride.

I settle even more into my prone position and scoot forward. There is no distance between the dusty ground and my uniform. Every worry I have about the garin disappears in these moments like the smoke from my gun as it evaporates in the air. At times I forget to breathe, and it's a struggle to keep my eyes open, too. Even with the yellow foamy earplugs, the noise of each shot is deafening, making the impulse to close them almost impossible to resist.

Just as I start feeling comfortable shooting my Uzi (I'm now calling it "*my* Uzi," affectionately, as if it's my boyfriend, just as the officer suggested it would start to feel), the magazine runs out of bullets, and I have to get up and give my space to another soldier. I always relinquish my position with reluctance.

On one of these occasions I look behind me and see a girl who's not part of our garin—a perfect stranger who's biting her nails. I look at her tags. She's newly inducted. Probably got inducted around the same time as me. She looks nervous.

"Don't worry," I say. "You'll get the hang of it. It'll be okay."

My hands feel extremely tired and heavy, and I feel spent, but I also feel satisfied. It's becoming clear that I take to shooting more than most of the other girls. I am far better at shooting than I expected to be.

Just a few weeks into our stay on Eshbal, and I start to talk like a gun pro. I've acquired a lot of Hebrew and army lingo about shooting; I know all the parts of my gun and I know how to shoot it—accurately. Now I really do feel it's my girlfriend or boyfriend. I'm not in the least intimidated by it anymore. How did I suddenly start to feel so confident about a war machine?

Thirty minutes after practice is over, my body rattles from the physical sensation of shooting. I love it. Shooting has secured my faith that I can handle IDF service. I'm serious about what I'm doing here. I feel in my element.

∽

TOWARD THE END OF OUR SIX-WEEK ULPAN TRAINING, we are instructed to stand at the farthest side of the camp at 5 a.m. for our last early morning inspection before we move on to the next part of our service—our six-week basic training, which is the longest for Nahal soldiers. Our officers know they can now trust us to follow basic military commands both in and outside the classroom.

I'm still concerned about my ability to work with the rest of the garin—a concern I voice to Svetlana. All she says in response is, "*Lo yoda'at*—I don't know."

At this inspection, we stand in our two straight rows opposite each other, as if there's an invisible flagpole there between us, and stand straight as matches as we wait for our officers to appear.

Suddenly, from the near distance, a group of sheep starts to bleat. First one. Then another. Then, a chorus of high and low vocals. *Baa, baa, baa.* On and on they go. Some of us can't keep from smiling. The minute our officers appear front and center, we stop, and I try to keep a serious face, but I'm still thinking about the sounds the sheep were just making, and I find it ridiculously funny.

Svetlana senses that I'm starting to get out of control. *"Nu tafsick kvar*—C'mon, stop it already!" she hisses, accompanying her statement with a look of warning. Although we've kept a healthy track record since our earlier days at Eshbal—we haven't gotten any punishments in a long time—but there is pressure on us to make it through to the very end. I've got to be careful, as I'm still considered to be the goofy one.

"The platoon will now pay attention to the commanding officers—two, three, attention!" Darren shouts.

Silence.

"Congratulations for almost getting to the end, *maklakah*," Officer Dror tells us. "This has been a very long and difficult journey for you, and you've all proven yourselves."

No sooner has Officer Dror finished, all the sheep bleat in unison as if to congratulate us on our job well done. I laugh hysterically for just a second, thinking others will follow suit, but apparently nobody else thinks it's funny. Especially not Officer Dror.

Svetlana jabs my side.

Uh-oh.

We know we'll get some sort of punishment for my laughing fit, but we're not sure what it's going to be. As we enter the dining room for breakfast, Eina, Vered, and Dalia do not say a word to me. Clearly, they're pissed off.

"Let's just hope we don't have to stay our last weekend on

this base, Dorit," Geraldine says. "That would be totally unfair!"

I let the girls file in before me to avoid any further interaction with them. Svetlana pinches my arm on her way in, and I'm not sure if she's doing this to be funny or to show her frustration, but either way I'm feeling like the "odd soldier out." I didn't feel that I was that out of line, but my blunders are getting costly.

I enter a conversation with myself that goes like this:

Stop resisting these people. You've got to work with them. If you don't, you're going to set yourself up for more trouble for the rest of your service. And that's a long time. Do you really want to spend the next two years with these people suffering because you've alienated them all?

But all I did was laugh at a bunch of sheep.

It doesn't matter. Stop fighting these people; stop expecting them to change and laugh along with you. It's just like you and Mom back in New York City. You wanted her to change. You expected her to be a loving, nurturing mom she just couldn't be. Don't make the same mistake here. Stop expecting people to change. Stop trying to make them change.

I'll try.

Right after breakfast, Officer Dror has us run down and up the hill about twenty times; then we run around the camp numerous times—too many to count; and then we do one hundred push-ups and sit-ups combined. After all that, we are instructed to drink the water from our *mimias* within a minute as both officers watch. Then we fill up our canteens and drink again. Svetlana has problems holding her water down and says "*oy, oy*" between sips and laughs as the rest of us gulp fast. Eventually, Svetlana and Eina stop drinking altogether and laugh, whispering in Russian. Immediately I think, *Man, like why don't they take this kind of stuff seriously? Why do they always laugh? Don't they know they're in the army? Is this their way of resisting authority because they grew up in a communist country?*

"Drink faster!" shouts Officer Dror, who's now practically standing next to us.

As usual, I am the first to finish. Eina and Svetlana talk in Russian. Officer Dror stays silent.

We start running again. We break first into a trot and then a run. Five minutes into it and the gaps between us are wide. The morning sky cracks open into strawberry pink and orange swirls.

When she runs, Dalia's Uzi hardly moves, even though it appears she isn't even holding onto it. Mine, meanwhile, moves every which way, jabbing into my back and sides. Halfway into the run, I try to tighten the strap and reposition my gun so it rests comfortably, but nothing seems to help. She is the only one of us who was given one of the newer, sleeker Uzis, which has a black collapsible handle as opposed to the wooden body and frame that makes my Uzi look more like a rifle than a submachine gun. Maybe she got it because she was the only one who figured out how to disassemble and reassemble it so quickly.

Finally, Dror gives us the "okay." We can stop now. Our punishment is behind us. And we won't have to stay here our last weekend. Phew.

∞

ON THE DAY WE'RE LEAVING ESHBAL, OUR COMMANDING officers take us into a small room at the far end of the base. There are a few commanding officers I haven't yet gotten to know who are in charge of other soldiers who aren't part of a Nahal garin. Officers Dror and Dorit take off their caps, and for the first time they seem human to me, not like menacing army officers. Dror even has bald spots.

Dror is the first one to speak, and even though the distance between us has been softened by our completion of this phase of training, he puts hands on his hips. "As you know, you guys are almost finished with your army ulpan, and soon you'll be graduating from here. Unfortunately, the IDF has decided that your basic training will be delayed by four months. You'll do your six-week basic training with a large platoon in August with other newly inducted Nahal soldiers. Until then, you'll be going to serve on a settlement in the Arava desert."

What the fuck? Working on the settlement in the desert? You gotta be kidding! Everyone, including me, groans at this news.

Many of the guys in our garin never wanted to join the army ulpan but accepted it as part of the Nahal setup. What they really want is to taste the real pressures of army life, the part of training that will culminate in their forty-kilometer march around the basic training camp. I suspect the girls are upset for the same reason I am: they don't want to be stuck in a desert.

"What the fuck?" shouts Jake. "What kind of army is this?"

Andy, Darren, Larry and a few others try to calm Jake down while the officers look at us with uneasiness, but there is nothing anyone can do to rectify the situation. I am with Jake, feeling that maybe the IDF isn't living up to its reputation as one of the best armies in the world. How could they screw up like this, sending us all to a settlement prior to finishing our marches?

Though I'm disappointed, this situation also gives me a chance to stop feeling anxious about my position within my garin. I'm not the problem on everyone's minds anymore. Everyone's worried now about what will happen next. They're apparently sending us to a settlement where we're supposed to relax, but how can we relax if we haven't completed the part of our service that gives us the validation that we've achieved what we came here to do? It works against the natural order of progression in the IDF: you prove yourself during basic training, and *then* you relax at a settlement—because you've earned it. For an American college student like me, being pulled out of basic training before we've completed it feels like skipping the SAT after months of prepping for it. Also, I'm not excited about hanging out with Jake and Darren. The military framework on the settlement won't be as rigorous, so our social dynamics will be much looser and more unpredictable.

Before leaving, I decide to use my rights as a lone soldier to phone my parents. I am feeling homesick. I wonder if I should call my stepmother and Dad, or use my call to talk to Mom. I follow the pebbly walkway, and only when I'm inches away from the door do I make my decision: I'll call my stepmother and Dad. If I call Mom, she'll just worry over how I'm faring in the army. My Dad and stepmom are much more logical and rational.

I enter the cubicle of an office, where I come face to face with our platoon commander, Idit. Her flaming red curls rest along the sides of her neck and bubble outward. Hands crossed over the desk, she smiles at me, asks for my personal army number, and finds my name in an oversized book. After she makes a few marks there, she hands me the heavy black iron receiver.

The air-conditioner blows cold air full-blast—weird, considering it's only February—but I'm grateful for the noise it makes. It's obvious that Idit will stay in the office until I finish with my call, and I just hope the fan will drown out my voice so she can't understand me.

As I dial the international dialing code, she asks, "Where are you from, Dorit?"

"New York. Manhattan."

"Ah yes, Manhattan." I wonder if she's been there but I don't ask. Her cheerfulness lessens my homesickness. When I connect with my parents I feel a sort of bravado when I tell them that everything is all right. I've come far since the first few days on Ritamin, they tell me. I convince them that I am making great progress, and perhaps I convince myself too. After all, considering everything, I'm doing well, especially with shooting. I'm taken aback to realize that I'm actually looking forward to the next chapter of our service. I hang up the phone and smile at Idit. I made it through ulpan. I'm still here.

1 2

SHITIM

ON THE FIVE-HOUR BUS RIDE TO SHITIM, THE SETTLEMENT in the middle of the Arava desert where we've been placed, I take comfort in the fact that we've just passed the Dead Sea, a place I've always wanted to visit, and that Shitim is just an hour north of Eilat, a tourist hotspot that borders Egypt. Very few of my fellow female garin members are on the bus with me, though—the IDF has sent the majority of our group on a weeklong vacation known as a *regila*—so of all the girls, it's just me and Dalia who are heading to Shitim today.

My ears plug up as we pass the Dead Sea, the lowest point on earth. Our bus rumbles along the serpentine road for hours. Dalia and I sit in silence.

Before we left Eshbal, our commanding officers gave us the official timeline for the rest of our service. I pull it from my pocket now and study it closely.

- March–July 1991: Settlement work at Shitim

- August 1991: Six-week basic training

- September 1991–April 1992: Work on various army bases scattered throughout Israel

- May–November 1992: Work on a kibbutz
- November 1992–January 1993: *Shalat Aharon*—return to our home kibbutz at Sufa to finish service

As I understand it, there's one big problem with our basic training coming *after* serving on a settlement: without the fundamentals of basic training, we are vulnerable. If anyone attacks our settlement, we will be unprepared to deal with it. But the IDF has made its decision, and there's nothing I can do about it.

Finally, we arrive. All I see is an unpaved road with no signs or markers, so long that it seems to go on forever. Eventually the bus makes a full stop and pulls up to a familiar sight: a flagpole. We're ordered to gather around it with our duffel bags. Through the curtain of dust, I take a good look around; I make out just a few bungalows in the distance, and that's about it. To my right is the flagpole, which flies a single ripped Israeli flag, and a few buildings with noticeable bullet holes in their walls.

"*Elohim*," I say, "Good lord. What a place." Thankfully no one hears me.

Dalia has already stepped into the small semi-circle being formed by our platoon commanders—Menny, a tall, clean-shaven Israeli with soft brown eyes and thin hair, and Sarah, whose smile reveals a huge gap in her front teeth, along with one black tooth. When Sarah turns to face the other side of the circle, I catch a glimpse of the messy ponytail shooting out from the hole in the back of her green cap.

Sarah informs us that we will be sharing this settlement with some members of another garin comprised of native Israelis, many of whom are also on a regila. All in all, we're about forty soldiers and a handful of officers.

Even Ritamin had more bungalows than this place does—and a paved road and a gate. I was being dramatic when I referred to Ritamin as a settlement, but Shitim really is one. There is almost nothing here, and we seem to be in the middle of nowhere.

Sarah hands Dalia and me two M16s, which we sling over our shoulders, and leads us down a narrow walkway to our bungalow. In front of me is a melange of brown, rocky, dusty mountains. Since we're in a section of the Jordan Rift Valley, past the Dead Sea and close to the Israel–Jordan border, I deduce that those mountains must be on the Jordanian side. Here and there, kalaniyot sprout out of the ground. The tulip-like flowers break the monotony of this landscape, but they are outnumbered, just like we are, by shrubs.

We enter a bungalow, and I almost have a heart attack when I see the inside: the walls are painted with a thick coat of black paint, and over that are painted three white figures dressed in green uniforms who look as if their heads are detached and floating in outer space. It reminds me of an exhibit I saw once at the Museum of Modern Art in New York City, but in a very weird and disturbing way.

"Oops, wrong one," Sarah says, and I heave a huge sigh of relief. She hurries us out the door, back into the 100-degree heat, and leads us to our actual bungalow, which happens to be the farthest one out. There are only ten total, and it's not lost on me that forty soldiers are supposed to fit into ten bungalows. But as it turns out it, our bungalow is two attached rooms—similar in size to the bunks at Eshbal. I choose the room closest to the entrance, and Dalia chooses the one farther back. In my room, there's a small metal closet next to the sink and three beds set up in a U-shape. I look up. *Air conditioners—thank God!*

I plop my duffel bag down and attach my guns to the foot side of my metal bed right away, and then I flick on the air conditioner and let the cool stream of air run through my sweaty hair. I sit on my tired-looking mattress and gather my bearings.

Sarah chats with Dalia in the other room and then, soon enough, pops into my room.

"Everything okay here?" she asks with a smile.

"Yes, everything's okay," I mutter. *She has no idea what hell we've been through. If only she understood.* Sarah seems to think we're ready for this experience, but I know we're not. We haven't even gone through basic training. Wait until the rest of our garin gets here and starts to act bitter about it—then she'll understand.

After Sarah leaves, Dalia and I start putting our clothes in our metal closets. Within ten minutes, I'm done. It's still much too soon to head out for dinner.

"*Elohim*—good lord," I say again, leaning against the doorway of Dalia's room and watching her unpack her uniforms. "I can't believe we're here." Ever since our officers at Eshbal broke the news that our basic training start date would be delayed, all of us have been venting to one another. Dalia usually keeps to herself, but now that most of our group is on their regila and Dalia and I are here together, I'm hoping we will talk more. I need to express how robbed I feel by this experience.

Dalia remains level-headed, but she's also perturbed. "Yes, it's really annoying," she says.

It feels good to be able to share this experience with her, and to know we're on the same page. I continue to watch her put her uniforms away, very conscious of the fact that I'm intruding on her personal space but not really ready to do something else. After the last of her uniforms are neatly put away, Dalia wastes no time: she starts disassembling her gun. After she lays each piece neatly on the floor, she cuts a long piece of cotton flannel, pulls it through the hole of the special iron stick we use to clean the barrels, and gets to work.

"We just locked our guns," I say. "Why are you cleaning yours?"

"Gotta kill time somehow, right?"

She pushes the iron stick down through the barrel then pulls it quickly out. The flannel is completely clean.

For the past few weeks, loneliness has come in and out for me like ocean waves. Right now, it's so acute that I fear it won't ever go away. I can't even find the words to express what I'm feeling. I feel trapped—like I'm shut up in a hot oven, completely cut off from civilization and life, and there's no freaking way out. But these are the cards I have been dealt. *This is it*, I think. *This is all I've got. This moment.*

I unlock my gun and bring it into Dalia's room with my cleaning supplies. "What a serious fuck the IDF did by postponing our basic training with our garin. Major fuck."

"Yes, I know," Dalia says, now proceeding to clean other parts of her gun.

We both know this kind of thing never happens—perhaps not ever before in the history of the Nahal. Yet nobody outside our garin is even talking about it or questioning whether it's a serious problem or not. Even Dalia doesn't seem too interested in having a conversation about it, but I'm not ready to let the subject drop.

"Why did they have to do this to us?" I persist. "Why? I don't get it."

"I guess this is how things work in the IDF," she says. "I don't know the reason, Dorit. But complaining about it isn't really going to help bring us to basic training. We just have to move on."

We just have to move on. Really? That's it?

There's no way I'll get the kind of response I want from Dalia. I withdraw into myself and stop trying to make conversation, feeling lonelier than ever. How am I supposed to protect this barren earth when I can't even help myself?

∾

ON DAY 2 OF WHAT DALIA AND I ARE NOW CALLING OUR own regila, since we won't be assigned any jobs till the others come back, we are left to figure out Shitim on our own. My brief exchanges with Dalia don't help me to accept this new situation more peacefully. For the next few days, I count the hours until the girls show up.

Five more days until the rest of the girls return from their vacation.

Four more days until the rest of the girls return from their vacation.

Before heading out for breakfast, I'll usually ask Dalia, "Do you want to use the bathroom first?" and she'll respond with, "Do you need to shower?" Often I'll let her shower first to see if she'll warm up to my politeness, but nothing happens.

Just when I think I can't handle our dynamics anymore, on the fifth day Dalia finds some paint, and our inner artists emerge in both of us. Dalia outlines palm trees on the small metal closets that hold our toiletries, uniforms, and civilian clothes, and I fill them in with whimsical colors—first with sea green, then hot pink and magenta. I'm suddenly a castaway on some magical island.

When we're finished with the closets, Dalia motions to the left with her paintbrush.

"Are you serious? The entire wall? Isn't this army property?"

"Don't you remember the other bungalow we entered by mistake?" Her tone is sardonic, but this is the closest she's been to friendly with me.

I nod. "I guess you're right . . ."

"Remember, Dorit, this is our regila," she says, chuckling.

I laugh along with her, and I feel peace for the first time in days.

Holding a thick black marker, Dalia climbs on the bed opposite me and proceeds to outline what appears to be beginning shapes of a mountain. We add trees in baby blue and green; they offer a soothing visual in the otherwise colorless room.

At the end of the day, we stand back to admire our handiwork. What I really want right now is to climb those mountains. In fact, I would love to be anywhere but here right now. Like Malkiyah, where my family would welcome me with open arms. But right now Dalia is the closest thing I have to family. I've got to make our interaction count for something.

"Wow, Dalia, I had no idea you were such a gifted artist."

She ekes out a smile but doesn't say anything.

"You didn't expect this mountain to turn out quite like this, did you?"

"What do you mean?" she asks.

"I mean, I feel as if I can practically climb it. I didn't expect it to turn out so beautiful. Or that it would break some of the . . ." Here I pause. I am almost driven to insert the word "loneliness," but that will reveal my weakness, and I don't think Dalia will respond well to that.

"I agree. It doesn't look so bad," she says. "But the mountains . . . they could use more color."

Dalia is perennially hard to please. Either that, or she's just plain unhappy. No matter what I try to say or do, I can't seem to make her relax.

For the rest of the week, I sit below our mountains each time I feel lonely and dejected and imagine I'm back at Malkiyah, eating a delicious Shabbat meal at my aunt and uncle's home. Though we're still nowhere near to being close friends—our conversations never last more than five minutes or so—things do feel a bit easier with Dalia after that day of painting. For now, I'll settle for that. And for the fact that we've created something lovely together.

◦◦◦

TO LIFT MY SPIRITS DURING OUR REGILA, ONE DUSTY morning I visit Luis, the twenty-eight-year-old Spaniard and oldest guy in our garin, and Akiva, the older Russian guy. Today it's their turn guarding at the *butkeh*—guard's quarters—which is slightly off the main road. I'm feeling that familiar sense of urgency to connect with the others from my garin, and the fact that so many of our fellow garin members are on regila presents an opportunity for me to get to know Luis and Akiva better.

I walk down the unpaved road with my M16 strapped behind me, carrying a blue plastic dish loaded down with tea and chocolate sandwiches that are melting in the 100-degree heat. I feel like I'm embarking on a camping trip. The only thing missing is my pack.

When Luis and Akiva see me approaching, their faces light up, and instead of calling me the crazy or goofy American, they step outside and wave excitedly. Before I even get a chance to enter the three-by-three-foot space, each of them grabs a sandwich.

Akiva paces as he eats, but he eventually stops and moves his hands from their resting position on his M16 to grab another sandwich. "*Arzot Habrit, Ma la'asot? At mishuga'at aval at*

177

besder gamoor, USA—What can one do? You are crazy, but you are alright, USA," he says. "USA" has become my nickname among some of my fellow garin members.

I know that a lot of my garin members haven't seen me as a serious soldier, so I take Akiva's words as a compliment. From the beginning, the Russians have always taken a particular interest in the fact I'm American, and it's always bothered me that the "goofy American" label has stuck, even though I know I brought it upon myself. Now it's up to me whether I want to put that goofiness behind me. If I don't put it behind me, I realize, I will not give myself the chance to become more fully a part of the group. And I'm beginning to see that the goofiness was a way to evade my responsibilities in some way. I'm ready to be seen by my fellow garin members in a way that elicits their respect and not their disdain. Akiva's comment makes me feel like I belong, like I'm finally part of the crew.

I take a bite of my burning hot sandwich and pull off my work hat, smiling. I did the right thing by coming here.

Luis unstraps his gun, pulls out his guitar, seemingly out of nowhere, and begins to sing Ladino music in Hebrew. I love the lyrics, and his voice. I observe that only three cars have passed in the last fifteen minutes of their watch. Sitting here with them, I'm no longer bothered by the silence and the whooshing desert winds that feel as if they are caving in on me —in fact, I've grown to like it. I'm beginning to feel settled in this unfamiliar world. Dalia's art and Luis's music are bringing me back to myself.

∞

IT'S SUNDAY MORNING AND WE'VE BEEN HERE A FULL week now. In Israel, Sunday is the first day of a new work week; this week, it also means the end of our "regila." By 10 a.m., a bus from Eilat has arrived with a fresh batch of Israeli Nahal soldiers—some from our garin, and some from the other garin of native Israelis that we'll be here with—and the settlement is awash with activity.

At the first sight of Andy, I give him a big bear hug. He high-fives Akiva and Luis and asks, "How'd it go? What was it like to guard here the entire time? Shitty?"

Akiva and Luis glance back at me and we exchange smiles.

"No, we had fun," Akiva says. "Right, USA?" He high-fives me.

"Right!" I smile back and give him my own high five.

Just before we gather around the flagpole, Andy quietly pulls me aside and whispers, "I have some good news for you!"

I am already giddy with excitement that he's back, but all I can think is that he might have a care package for me.

"What is it?" I whisper back. "Tell me!"

"It's Darren," Andy whispers back fiercely. "He's leaving the garin. He's actually leaving the army for good. He won't be bothering you ever again."

"Woo-hoo!" I exclaim, and give Andy a hug. Darren hasn't been bothering me since Eshbal; I've come far from those early Sufa days when I woke up in the middle of the night in a cold sweat with images of Darren terrorizing me. Quite far. But I'm thrilled he'll be out of my life. And I'm sure Andy is relieved as well: as our garin leader, he has spent his fair share of time trying to minimize Darren's antagonism, and it hasn't been very easy for him.

At the main gathering area, we are asked to separate into our two different garins so our officers can start assigning us the various jobs we'll start tomorrow. The sun is still very high in the sky, and I'm grateful for the extra afternoon off. I've been wearing a T-shirt and my army pants the entire time I've been here, but tomorrow I'll have to don the full work uniform. Just the thought of doing so in this heat is unbearable.

Here we go again.

✌

THE JOB I'VE BEEN ASSIGNED IS TO CLEAR THE FIELDS half a kilometer away from Shitim and get them ready for the planting season. As I understand it, I'll be doing this tedious labor for the rest of the week.

I exit my bungalow at 4:30 a.m. on my first day of work, and immediately hear footsteps behind me.

"Luis? Is that you?" I ask. I can tell from his walk.

"Yes, my darling."

"Wait a minute . . . are you serious? You've also been assigned to the fields too? Cool!"

We walk to the fields together, and get to work immediately. We start by pulling plastic wrapping almost one kilometer long from what we were told are rotten tomato fields. Luis is on one end and I'm on the other, pulling plastic wrapping across a field that's one-third the length of a football field. I'm ecstatic I get to work with Luis; he's so easygoing. As we work industriously, he sings in Spanish and Hebrew.

"*Hola, qué pasa?*" I ask him once we are close enough to talk and I hand him my side of the wrapping. I laugh at my own rudimentary Spanish, but Luis is gracious and plays along as he grabs his end of the plastic and makes his way to the far side of the field.

"*Muy bien, y usted?*"

"*Yo estoy muy guapo*"—I am very handsome—I respond,

laughing. I know full well what I said, but it's practically the only Spanish I know, and I'm grateful when Luis laughs too. Being with him makes the harsh physical labor a little more tolerable. I can be myself, and he has a good sense of humor. Having to pick all these rotten tomatoes suddenly doesn't seem so bad.

As the sun rises off the horizon and begins to penetrate through my T-shirt and army work pants, Luis sings more Ladino and Hebrew songs. I don't quite understand the words, but his calm voice travels well in the desert. While he sings, I imagine him strumming on some Spanish guitar.

I pull on the wrapping with all my might, and hot beads of water trickle downward, making the inside part of the wrapping filmy. Once the wrapping is lifted, I glance down at the grounds. Tomatoes—ripe ones! There are tons of them. I bend down and curiously turn a few around. They're perfect.

"Hey, Luis! These tomatoes are not rotten!" I shout with excitement, but he doesn't hear me, so I run toward him holding the tomato and grinning ear-to-ear.

"I know," he says when I show him. "What did you think we were getting from the ground? Bread crumbs?"

"No, but someone said that all the tomatoes in the fields were rotten."

"No, we just throw out any rotten ones. As you can see, most of them are ready to eat!"

"That's great! I thought they were all going to be rotten."

"That would be gross," he says, smiling at me again.

Together, we keep working. There are six beds that we need to pull the wrapping off of, and I want us to get it done fast. Each time I give the wrapping a tug, I think, "I love this land! I love this land!" I figure if I say it enough I'll eventually start to believe it. It's a new mantra. After the first two rounds of thinking it, I start saying it out loud. I will myself to believe that a mundane chore like pulling plastic wrapping can make me love this land.

Luis and I develop a routine: we meet in the middle, I hand him my plastic wrapping, and he bunches it together and whisks it away. It reminds me of sleepaway camp, when my friend Tammy and I would fold our scratchy blankets once, twice, and then meet together for a fold up and down, laughing.

When breakfast rolls around at eight thirty, I fill up on boiled eggs, freshly cut cucumbers, and the tomatoes we've picked, which I lightly sprinkle with salt and pepper; soft and hard cheeses; chocolate spread; and all different sizes of pickles and olives. I also slurp down two or three *Danees*, a pink yogurt that goes down smooth and creamy. I feel the satisfying food slowly fill the hollow space in my insides, and I close my eyes in satisfaction, knowing I earned this hearty breakfast. I'm content enough to barely notice the flies swarming around me, or the heat coming in through the windows, which don't quite shut.

After breakfast, Luis and I head back to the empty fields and begin the arduous task of emptying the fields. First, we gather lumpy tomatoes and place them in red buckets filled with water. I inhale the smell. I've been holding my breath, though I didn't even realize it until now. The smell is strangely tantalizing. Getting deep, learning to love this strange corner of the earth in a foreign land called Israel, shouting back and forth with Luis, digging my hands into the ground until my fingernails are black and grimy—the moment seems perfect now. Each time I say my mantra, "I love the land," I embrace what I'm doing with all its imperfection, even the fuck the IDF made in sending us here. This is my country, my homeland; my service is bringing me peace and making me feel whole. I belong here, and the work I'm doing now proves it.

By the end of the first day, my knees are shaking and I've

got splinters in my hands. My clothes are sticking to my body. But I'm happy. My mantra efforts are working. Each time I wince in pain or start to complain about the unbearable heat or that I'm stuck here without having gone through basic training, I cut myself off and say, *I'm loving this land!* Luis and I have been assigned to the fields for the entire week, and I find I'm actually looking forward to the next day. I sleep the rest of the afternoon with the air conditioner blasting and wake up in a stupor to a knock at the door. I look around to see that I'm alone. All of the other girls are out.

Luis is at the door when I answer.

"Did you rest?" I ask. "You look exhausted!"

"I have a royal headache," he says, and walks right in. "Come, keep me company."

No one in our garin, has ever asked me to keep them company. When he asks for a pain reliever, I jump up from my bed and try to open my toilet bag to find the bottle without showing him what else is in there, doing my best to hide my pads and panty liners from view.

"Got it! Here you go!" I exclaim, handing him two pills, which he takes gratefully, along with the warm cup of water I've just poured from the sink in my room. He sits on Svetlana's lumpy bed, directly across from mine, and inspects our painted mountains.

"Thanks so much, Dorit," Luis says. "Now, it's time for me to guard. Thanks for the company." His exhaustion makes the ridges of his forehead sink even deeper into his weather-beaten skin, making him look older than his twenty-eight years. He gives me a look of gratitude, and I open my mouth to say something, but he's already out the door. I try to process what just happened. Luis sat down in my room to get a pain-killer and we hardly talked and now he's leaving!

I watch Luis walk down the path in the direction of the guard's quarters until he disappears from view. Thank god for Akiva and Luis. Now there are two garin members who know me for me, who don't just see me as the goofy American. After weeks of worry, I've finally made a connection with someone. I'm not just a goof; I have it in me to make friends here.

∞

ON SHITIM, ONE HAS THE ADVANTAGE OF SWITCHING JOBS every so often—as opposed to the kibbutz, where I was assigned to one job for the whole summer, and was only able to change to something else because I insisted. For my second week on Shitim, I request to work in the small factory there, where it is my job to put together small plastic electric outlets that will be shipped to some other factory in the North of Israel. For my third week, I request to work at the date factory on a nearby kibbutz called Ketura, which seems to be the most popular job.

Once I begin my work at the date factory, Sagiv, I understand its popularity right away. On the first day of this new job, Eina, Vered, Svetlana, and I wait for the minivan the kibbutz sends to pick us up. We hop in excitedly when it arrives, and when we get to Sagiv we get right to work on the assembly line, packaging dates according to size and type. On our breaks we dip dates in honey, and even have date fights.

Jake and his friend Robin are among those who enjoy working at the date factory, and though I had my reservations about him before we came to Shitim, our social dynamics have improved a lot here. Jake has turned out to be funnier than I thought—even pleasant to be around. There is a part of me that is drawn to his warmth; I still crave connection, and he pays attention to me. At the date factory, he throws dates at me, and I have enough experience with guys to know that flirting often takes the form of teasing.

One day he shouts "Duck!" just as he throws another date at me, and when I duck under the conveyor belt to escape, he crawls under from the other side, grabs me, and kisses me. News travels fast in our garin, and even though no one actually saw the kiss, rumor soon has it that I'm Jake's girlfriend. We keep having fun at work in the factory, but when our day is over and we head back to Shitim, Jake changes. Once the van doors shut, the contours of his face harden, and he grabs his M16 tightly—no more fun-loving Jake. I try not to take his sour attitude personally, though. After all, we are still new soldiers trying to navigate our way in the IDF.

We begin a short course on army code and language, which fills me with purpose and pulls my mind away from Jake's unpredictable behavior. Soon my notebooks are filled with copious notes in English. I quickly learn that "flowers" in Hebrew means "guns" and "a slanty situation" means "sleeping." I find these things funny, which makes it easier for me to learn this new code.

I soon get the chance to apply my new knowledge at our small communications room. For hours no one talks, and the only sound in the room is that of the flies swarming under the bright lights. Finally, though, there's a voice:

"*Kod-kod, kod-kod* . . . come in please."

I grab the receiver in nervous anticipation. It's my first time communicating in army code.

"Yes, this is *Kod-kod*," I say, pushing a small button on the right-hand side of the bulky receiver I'm holding. My voice rings strongly on the system. It's me—American Dorit from Greenwich Village, New York City—speaking on an army radio. I can hardly believe it.

There's a raspy Israeli voice on the other end. "How many 'flowers' do you need?"

I pause. I remember a commanding officer of the Nahal brigade at Eshbal who once said, "You can endanger your army base if you reveal too much information or if the information is inaccurate." I haven't been instructed on how to answer this question, so I need to find someone who knows the answer.

"One minute," I respond, and I put the heavy black receiver down, turn the volume button down on the main system, and eagerly run out to find someone with the authority to answer this question.

The only soldiers I see nearby are Dalia and Menny, one of the male officers. Both of them are rocking on a swingset I haven't noticed before. I run over to them.

"Can someone help me? They're asking me how many 'flowers' we need over at the communications room, and I've no idea how to answer."

Officer Menny gets up from the swing and rushes past me toward the room I just came from. Dalia and I tag right behind. Menny picks up the receiver and responds with the right answer.

"You misunderstood the question," says Dalia, turning to me. "They didn't need *flowers*. 'Flowers' means guns!"

"I know that. But I didn't know how many guns! How am I supposed to know that?"

I feel I did the right thing. There are times when Dalia is such a know-it-all. I'm sure she would have also run to find the right answer if she had been the one on the radio. There's no shame in asking for help.

A WEEK LATER, OFFICER MENNY APPROACHES ME IN THE dining room.

"Congratulations, Dorit! You've been selected as one of the few to attend a course in Eshbal."

"A course? In Eshbal?" My heart beats fast. Eshbal is less than an hour away from my Aunt Maya and Yosi. I long to be in a non-army environment with their home-cooked meals. It's been months since I've seen them. But then again, I'm just getting comfortable here.

"It starts tomorrow," he says nonchalantly.

"Tomorrow? So soon? I just got here."

"You lucky thing," Svetlana whispers, and she nudges me in the side as if to say, *Take it and get out of this place.*

"It's only a three-week course," Officer Menny says. "Then you'll be back."

"Can I ask why?" I ask.

"Why what?"

"Why are they sending me to a course?"

"Didn't your officers explain this to you?"

"No. No one did."

"Well, based on previous officers' recommendations, we select a few soldiers from each garin to participate in a number of courses during their service on the settlement."

Officer Menny explains that when a soldier is sent to a "trade course," she or he learns skills that they are then expected to come back and teach to the other members of their garin so everyone can implement the knowledge at their kibbutz.

I mull this over. *Me? A college dropout from SUNY at Albany teaching others? Are you kidding me?*

Then I think of the course's proximity to Kibbutz Malkiyah. *It won't be so bad.*

"So what kind of course are we talking about?" I ask.

"Agriculture," Officer Menny says. "An agriculture course specifically designed for learning how to nurture life in the desert."

An agriculture course? It strikes me as ironic that a girl from Manhattan would be charged with helping Israeli soldiers learn how to tend to plant life in the desert. I want to tell Officer Menny that I'm not equipped for this kind of course. That I don't have enough Hebrew, or the right skills. I feel like there are a thousand and one reasons why I shouldn't go. But opting out would make me look like a wimp, and also indicate that I'm not serious about my service. Plus, the fact that I was recommended by my former officers has to count for something, right?

I see a different me, standing in front of a group of male Nahal soldiers, explaining agriculture and water systems to them. I like that image.

Now my test of loving the land officially begins.

1 3

NEW COURSE

THE VERY NEXT MORNING, I HEAD TO JERUSALEM ON THE 6 a.m. bus. I arrived at Shitim from Eshbal just a month ago, and now I'm returning to Eshbal alone.

After all we've been through as a garin, it feels weird to be on my own. But it doesn't take long before I find myself mesmerized by the peach-colored mountains across the Jordan Rift Valley. This brings me immediate peace.

Since becoming part of a garin, my concept of privacy has changed. I am rarely alone. Work seems to define us as a group, and working together is a test as to how well we will face challenges together. Succeeding at this new course will showcase my ability to function on my own. I feel myself gearing up for the challenge.

When the sun rises fully above the mountains in the distance and lights up the inside of the bus, I pull the blinds down and try to take a nap. I've got four and a half hours to go till Eshbal. But I can't relax. As the bus descends toward the Dead Sea and my ears become plugged once again, I feel an accompanying pressure to perform. What if I can't follow the information? What if the content becomes too technical?

By the time we reach the Dead Sea, I'm filled with so much anticipatory anxiety that I decide to jot down a list of pros and cons about my attending this course:

PROS

- I'll have a break from my garin for the next three weeks.

- I'll be able to visit my aunt and uncle at Malkiyah every weekend.

- I'll be studying at one of my favorite places in the country—the Upper Galilee.

- I'll get a chance to improve my knowledge of specialized vocabulary.

- This experience will give me a greater chance to step into a leadership role.

I'm surprised I'm able to list five positive points about going to Eshbal, a place that was so challenging for me when I was there; I also recognize immediately that the cons I am about to list—"I will have to leave my comfort zone" and "I'll probably have to ask other people for help"—don't really qualify as cons for me anymore. It feels good to know that I'm not the same soldier I was just a few months ago. I can only surmise that the course at Eshbal will be much harder than ulpan, but I feel hopeful that I will find my way.

I look at the vast sea to my right. Just a few people float on its salty waters at this early hour, and a few others are sunbathing. The mountains are no longer peach-colored but a buttery brown. *Look at the pros, Dorit. You can do this. Look how far you've come already.*

I reach up and turn the dial of the air conditioner a full click to the right so the cool air blows directly on me. I'm nearly alone on the bus, with just a few other passengers, all civilians. I look at my watch. We're not even halfway there. I lean back and prop my feet against the seat in front of me and fold the handle of my M16 inward so I can let it rest on the plastic holder on the seat in front of me without having it bang around.

Two hours later, about thirty minutes outside of Eshbal, I awake to music and a full bus. A well-known song by popular Israeli folk singer Leah Shabbat, "Only the life," is blasting on the radio. Just as the chorus begins, our bus passes a memorial site wrapped in wreaths that commemorate the memory of those who perished in a recent terrorist attack. I consider the words of the song, and turn the lyrics into questions for myself: Which life is taking me? Which life is worrying me? The one I live now as a soldier, or the one I have in general?

Up the circuitous road we go, past the mountainous expanse of Jerusalem, which seems to go on forever, higher and higher, until the walls of the highway seem to cave in on us. Then the bus comes to an abrupt stop, and the driver stands up and walks off, followed by everyone else on the bus. I'm not sure what's happening, but I follow suit: I grab my gun and head down the stairs.

Sirens are being broadcasted from national radio—a sound loud enough to penetrate my heart and every cell of my body. I quickly look around: everywhere I look, buses and cars are stopped and people are standing in the middle of the highway. *It's Holocaust Remembrance Day*, I suddenly remember. I'm surrounded on either side by male soldiers from the Golani Brigade.

The siren continues blasting its strong, steady ring for

three minutes. At first I'm a bit squeamish—my hands are fidgeting, and my heart is beating fast. But eventually I let my hands drop, I stand straight, and suddenly my heart knows what to do. The images of beaten and starved Jews from the concentration camps that I saw during our recent trip to Yad-V'shem museum in Jerusalem, also known as "The Hand of God," float into my mind. I stand tall along with the others, looking into the distance. It doesn't matter that I'm American or that I'm insecure about the agricultural course I'm traveling toward. This moment binds me to everyone who's standing alongside me here: We're one big family. We share the same history.

As the siren dies down, my body still hums from this experience. Where would one stand up in the States in this way to honor the six million Jews who perished in the concentration camps?

Back in the US, the Holocaust barely even made its way into my history classes. There was no human face to what it was, just that it happened. To stop your car on the highway in the States on Holocaust Remembrance Day would be ludicrous. But here it's expected, and this experience of standing up for those six million Jews touches me profoundly. In this moment, I feel an acute sense of personal responsibility. I've got a tribe of Jewish people who've got my back here in Israel. The smell of war is around me, but it too is a part of me. I'm a soldier in the Israeli army. I have a space to claim here. These are my people. My roots. I am home.

Once I'm back aboard the bus I take another look at my pros and cons list. There's one last "pro" to add: I'll be able to apply the knowledge I've learned to help build Shitim—make it a better place.

There's something about this land that grounds me, and

this is becoming more apparent every day. I feel a sense of security knowing that the soldiers I see have my back, even if I don't know them. I feel safe, protected. In this moment, it feels like every person in this country is my big brother or sister.

∞

MY AGRICULTURAL COURSE STARTS THE MORNING AFTER I arrive. There's no time to waste. I'm up at 5 a.m. again, and I trudge up the small hill in my polished black army boots. Halfway up, I look down. Why the heck am I wearing these? There's not going to be an inspection. I can be comfortable here. I rush back to my room—where I sleep alone, since there are no other girls in the course—and change into my black sports shoes.

The other soldiers in the course have completed basic training, so while the atmosphere in the dining room is relaxed and easygoing, I'm also aware of being the odd person out since all my fellow classmates wear their beret and tags, while I still have not been officially inducted.

After a hearty breakfast of zesty Israeli salad and my usual feta cheese sandwich, we head straight for the classrooms. Since there's no ulpan, there is no Hebrew teacher to raise our heads for *hakshev*—attention—and no one here is a new immigrant.

We start the class by sitting in a U-shape and introducing ourselves and the garin and kibbutz we're from. My classmates are from every kibbutz imaginable—from Eilat to the Golan. As soon as the initial wave of excitement dies down, the head instructor, Danny, tells us how we'll be spending our days: half of the time we'll be in the classroom, and half of the time we'll be applying our newly acquired knowledge by working in the fields.

Very quickly, it occurs to me that there's nobody to report to. I'm on my own and responsible for my own learning. I take copious notes. There's lots of technical jargon. Learning Hebrew this way will be complicated, and it takes me a while to learn trade words like *ma'arechet hamisoefet*—"an extensive system." I wonder just how many other "systems" there are.

For the rest of the first day, I fill my notebooks with many words relating to plant descriptions. There are also tons of words I don't understand, and they fly past me without being recorded.

Halfway through our first day, Danny explains how in rural, isolated areas like Eshbal and Shitim, it's necessary to know how to work the land, especially in a country like Israel, which has few natural resources. Coming from America, rich in natural resources, this concept of limited resources surprises me, though I realize it shouldn't when I consider the desert terrain I've been subjected to these past months.

On the second day, we go on a *tiul*—a trip—to the Israeli-Jordanian border to visit school centers and *moshavim*, a unique type of farming cooperative, to see what kinds of plants live under certain conditions and how they survive. Danny digs his hands in the ground for a long black tube attached to another clear tube. When he lifts it higher, water starts gushing out. He explains how various water systems have been important for automating the transport of water into the region. Each time I hear the word "system," I confuse it with the other systems we've discussed. Which "system" are we referring to?

By the end of the first week, I'm overwhelmed, which turns into restlessness for me. I speak with the commanding officer to see if I can switch to a "sewing course" (I'm not really into sewing, but at least I won't be responsible for applying any sewing knowledge back on Shitim), but she refuses, saying it's too late.

There's no use in protesting, Dorit. You've got to do the best you can here.

I try to make friends with my classmates, but I have nothing in common with anyone here. They know the material, ask questions, and can easily talk about what they've learned. No one else here is an immigrant. I feel like an outsider. I did not grow up in this country, and will never be one of them.

Just when I'm feeling at my lowest and most hopeless, I speak for the first time during break to a classmate named Shai Tachimi. He's from a settlement called Kelay Golan in the Golan Heights, which borders Syria.

I tell Shai I'm a lone soldier in the Nahal brigade and that my parents are abroad.

"Wow, you're really brave to come here to serve in the army," he says, smiling, as he brushes his light brown hair out of his eyes.

I think of Tania Aebi, who left New York City on a small sailboat to prove to her father that she could sail around the world. Like Tania, I have something to prove to my dad—that I will not turn out like Mom, anxious and self-centered. But right now I feel the consequences of having given in to his pressures. I feel alone and guideless, like a ship adrift at sea. I'm truly unsure of my next course of action. The only thing I can do is just keep talking—anything to get myself out of my own head.

"I don't know if it's bravery or just plain stupidity," I remark.

Shai laughs as he plants his gun straight up and down in front of him. "I respect any immigrant who comes here. I wouldn't be able to pick up and leave my country and serve in the United States Army."

I smile at him, grateful that he can see how difficult this must be for someone like me. "I think I visited your settlement when our garin took a trip to the Golan Heights," I say.

"Oh yeah?"

"Isn't Kelay Golan that settlement with a small bunch of houses on a hill surrounded by kalaniyot?"

He rubs his fingers through his hair. "Well, that sounds like a number of settlements in that area—but it very well could be."

I fill him in with more details, and indeed we are talking about the same place.

"Wow, you guys work at one of the most beautiful settlements in the entire country," I exclaim in a whisper. "It doesn't even look like a settlement, it looks like a kibbutz."

He's encouraging and patient with me as I tell him about my garin, and share with him how the IDF sent us to Shitim instead of to basic training.

"I've never heard of such a thing," he says. "That is so weird, not like the army at all."

"Go ahead, make me feel bad," I say, laughing. "It sounds completely crazy. And it is."

"Hey, look on the bright side. At least you're in the Arava desert, the Jordan Valley, the Moab mountains, everything . . ." he says. "Our garin served on a settlement in the Negev Desert. The deserts in Israel are one of the most beautiful pieces of countryside."

"I guess you're right. When I first got here I felt a bit more scared about the desert. Now I think I'm in love."

He chuckles. "I love that. You're in love with the desert."

"Dorit in the desert," I say, laughing.

I am falling in love with the desert's character, and with how it looks at certain times of day—with how the mountains magically turn from peach to cinnamon depending on the angle of the sun.

"It's ironic," I tell him. "You see, I'm a New York City girl through and through."

"I'm from the city, too. Rishon Le'Zion. We city people get around," Shai says, his bright green eyes shining. "But sometimes I get homesick for Rishon."

"At least you can just get on a bus. I'd have to get on a bloody plane and cross the Atlantic Ocean if I wanted to see New York City."

"I don't have a problem getting on a plane. New York City's my first stop after finishing the army."

"Cool. Meet you there?"

We laugh all the way back to the classroom.

∞

BY THE SECOND WEEK OF CLASS, I'M NOT TAKING ANY of the learning material very seriously. I figure that since I don't understand most of it anyway, there's not much point. Part of me wants to just give up. I pay less attention to what's going on and more attention to passing notes with Shai.

Me: "I didn't sleep very well last night."

Shai: "Forget all the worries and problems of the night and enter a new day."

Me: "Why do you have a gun that is not your typical M16 like mine?"

Shai: "It is an M203, a M16-type launcher."

Shai writes "launcher" in English, which makes the rest of the sentence look foreign. *His written English isn't bad.* For the next ten minutes, we pass notes in English and Hebrew. Then, for a while, I start paying attention to Danny, who's talking about preparing the land for seeding, and I take notes in English to retain the information, translating the information as I go—*Plants always need to be surrounded by water; Find sources of water, provide for plants; Local soil is always better*—but soon enough, I find myself bored and restless again. I write to Shai:

Me: "Is there any end to all these plants?"

Shai: "I wish there was an end to it."

Me: "Isn't Danny tired? I'm tired."

Shai: "He's in euphoria."

I stifle a giggle. *Euphoria.*

Danny is a tall officer with large, wide-rimmed spectacles who definitely seems a little nerdy, like he can't get enough of the plants. He has dark circles under his eyes, and yet he chirps as he jumps from discussing plants to soil and back again.

I sigh.

Shai loves plants and agriculture, and even if he didn't, he's not one to complain. He lets me be myself when I'm around him. But how am I going to explain to everyone on Shitim how to apply this knowledge if I don't learn anything here? *I guess I'd better start paying attention.*

I quickly scribble the many trees and roots Danny is drawing up at the front of the class. He begins to speak about water filters and the configurations of plastic faucets, and suddenly something clicks. *That's why I was picked for this course,* I think. *I'm supposed to build roots in this foreign land in the same way I'm supposed to learn about roots in an agricultural context!* Everything is clear to me now: These three weeks are an opportunity to learn not just about pipes and water pressure, but also a new vocabulary, among other things. I'm always learning new things here in Israel; this is simply my latest challenge. And the concept of personal responsibility has stayed with me since my experience on the highway on Holocaust Remembrance Day. I'm aware of being an individual in the world, but also part of a greater whole. I must do things for myself, but also for my people. Building roots means activating my knowledge—doing something that makes me feel like an Israeli rather than an immigrant. I'm not just an automaton taking orders from the officer or learning Hebrew at an ulpan; I *want* to be here.

I take notes with a renewed enthusiasm for what Danny is saying. *Tichnoon gan hanoy* means "planning the landscape." It also means "to replenish the land and preserve it for the future," or "aesthetic appreciation for the art to preserve the beauty of the environment."

The first part of that second definition catches my attention right away—"replenish the land and preserve it for the future." Isn't that what I've been doing? When Luis and I released all that plastic wrap from that smelly tomato field, we were making it possible to reuse that land. This country was founded by idealists who believed in the state of Israel—people like me. I may not be an officer or garin leader, but I am laying down roots, just like my predecessors. Just like former Prime Minister Golda Meir, who came from Milwaukee as a new immigrant, and believed enough in the state of Israel to build roots and lead the country toward democracy.

∞

THE NEXT DAY, SHAI AND I WORK TOGETHER TO PREPARE our own plot of land along with our fellow students. This is the first time I've ever worked with a native Israeli soldier. I remember that day—so long ago, it seems—when I eyed that Air Force soldier back in the summer of 1989 as I was trying to hitchhike my way back to my aunt's kibbutz. I've come far since then. Quite far.

We've been given a small challenge: prepare our small area for planting.

"What exactly are we supposed to do?" I ask, dumbfounded.

"We're supposed to see if this plot of land is ready for us to plant."

"You mean like examining things like sewage and water?" I ask, bending down, careful not to let my gun jab me in my side.

"Well, not really. I think he wants us to examine the quality of soil and how fertile it is."

"How are we supposed to do that?"

"Like this," he says, scooping up a pile of dirt. "We need to analyze it for dryness, rock sediments, and other qualities that Danny's been talking about."

"Oh, I get it."

He holds forth the pile he has just scooped up, and together we examine it, applying the criteria of what makes soil fertile to what we see. It feels weird to crouch down upon this dry earth and check for soil fertility as the metal of my gun presses into my leg. But I try to focus, and Shai is incredibly patient as he explains the rock and soil qualities to me in great detail. I ask question after question, and he answers them all to the best of his knowledge. I take notes about our findings in Hebrew while Shai dictates them.

After two hours of examining, writing, and more examining, my work pants are stained and my foot has fallen asleep.

"That wasn't that bad. I think I'm getting the hang of this. Thanks, Shai!" I give him an enthusiastic high five. "I wouldn't have been able to do this without you."

"I know," he says with a smile.

We head back to the classroom for the last few lessons of the day, which Danny describes as "An Intake of Needs," which really means things to look out and plan for when trying to build a settlement.

I start writing:

1. The number of people at the settlement—this way we can plan what kind of gardening is required
2. Games
3. Relaxation spots
4. Shade

Now it's all starting to make sense! The skills we learn in this course aren't just about farming—they're hugely important to the quality of life at Israel's settlements. Armed with this knowledge, I have the power to help bring people together instead of separating them. Now I understand how my success in this course will help others. Everything that we're learning matters.

After having this realization, class is never boring again, and by the end of the three weeks, I am ready to share my knowledge with my garin members. I'm excited about all the ways in which—I hope—this will bring me closer to them.

Shai and I exchange numbers on the day we graduate from the course, and I proudly hold up my certificate of completion.

"I did it, Shai. I did it!"

We have our photo taken together and share a hug.

"I would love to meet your garin one day," I tell him.

The power of having a positive outlook isn't lost on me at this moment. Shai helped me with that, never coming down to my level when I complained, and supporting me when I was excited about what we were learning. I think of Tania Aebi. She didn't have time or energy to waste. She was on her own as she sailed around the world, without the luxury to complain or feel sorry for herself. If she got stuck or afraid, she forged on. When I got stuck and afraid, I made friends with Shai. I couldn't have successfully completed this course without his help.

I know I have a long road ahead of me once I return to Shitim, but I also know now that I'm not alone. I think of the other garin members at the settlement—the native Israelis—and how sociable, funny, and friendly they are. Maybe it's time I stop putting all my eggs in one basket in terms of just working with my garin. Just like I connected with Shai, I can connect with the others and "build roots" that way. One root-building experience after another will give me the confidence I need to stand tall and act with resilience so I will truly be able to handle anything that comes my way.

I'm ready.

14

GIVING VOICE

IT'S THE LAST DAY OF THE COURSE IN ESHBAL. THE dreaded moment to say goodbye to Shai, my new friend. For the last few weeks, he and I have gazed at the stars at night and exchanged stories about our garins. Finally, I have connected with someone in the way I've longed to connect ever since I arrived here.

This is what it's all about, I think. *Not about launchers and systems.*

"Are you happy to be going back tomorrow?" Shai asks me, looking up from where he crouches on the ground. His hands are full of dirt. The blackest they've ever been.

"I've gotten so much from this course," I tell him. "But really, you've saved me by being my friend. I just wish some of my garin members would change so we'd be one big happy family." My hands are getting deeper into the dirt too. I'm digging out my past, allowing new life to grow into the person I'm now becoming. Some anger and bitterness still lingers, but I'm also finally accepting that I don't have the power to change certain things. I cannot change my garin members. I cannot change my mom.

"No garin is perfect, Dorit," Shai tells me.

"Yes, I know." Sadness threatens to overwhelm me.

"And what about the other garin on Shitim you mentioned, those whose home kibbutz base is Kibbutz Har-Hamasah?"

"I don't really know them," I say.

"Do you want to be their friends?"

"Of course. But they're so close-knit. Many of them grew up with each other since kindergarten." Now the tears are coming fast. "They have what I don't have," I blurt.

"What's that?" Shai asks gently.

"Real closeness with one another."

Shai squats closer to the ground. "Well, at least you have me. I'm your friend."

I rub at my nose with my dirty hand and get soil up my nose. "Thanks, Shai." I wipe my nose with the back of my work uniform. "You're, like, the only person in Israel who's made the time to get to know me. And now you're going to be so far away."

Shai just looks at me and listens.

"My garin is fun-loving and exciting," I say. "Very nice. But not very close-knit."

Shai pauses. He opens his mouth as if to say something, but holds back for a moment. Then he says, "Dorit, why don't you do something like Danny talked about during the last few lessons—the stuff about the things we should look out and plan for when trying to build a settlement? What about games or relaxation spots? Take your own spin on it to bring the two garins together. How about that?"

"Not a bad idea, Shai." I try to think about possible games and relaxation spots at Shitim. How exactly would that work?

Shai sees the consternation building up on my face. "What is it?" he asks.

"I'm trying to consider how I can possibly apply any of this on my settlement. I'm a New York City girl, you know."

"Take it easy. *Liat, liat*—slowly, slowly," Shai says. He gives me a hearty pat on the back that Israelis refer to as a *chapcha*, then he grabs me and gives me a big bear hug. "Come and visit me. Don't forget."

"I won't."

I want to bury my head in Shai's arms. I want to tell him about why I'm really here—that I came to Israel to escape my mom, to find a way to not turn out like her. If only I didn't have to struggle so hard. If only. But as I lean against Shai, he starts rubbing my head. The last time someone rubbed my head it was Mom, and I was sixteen studying for the SATs. The memory comes flooding back:

She stepped into my room just for a minute before heading back down to practice. Another important gig was coming up.

"Mom?"

"Yes, honey-bunny."

"It's the SATs. I'm scared. I don't think I'm ready. I think I need help. What do I do?"

"Oh, honey-bunny. Don't worry. It'll be alright. Don't be a worry bug, be a happy bug."

"Mom, I'm really scared."

"You don't have to be."

Two minutes later, she was stroking my head as per my commands. "Rub me there and here."

Then she stopped. "Dorit, honey, I've got to go." She turned and climbed back down the tiny stairs of my loft bed.

There was nothing else to say.

It was time to move on.

I cried until the pillowcase was wet. Tomorrow was a new day.

With effort, I shake myself out of my thoughts of Mom and return to the present, where Shai is still hugging me. I burrow my head deeper into his shoulder. *Tomorrow is a new day*, I think. I try to believe it.

∞

WHEN I'VE BEEN BACK AT SHITIM FOR ONE WEEK, THE Israeli garin announces a theme night called "An Evening for Love." I jump at the opportunity to sing in front an audience. I want to give voice to the past vocal major in me. Nobody from either of the garins knows I once studied voice at the prestigious Fame School, and I've preferred to keep it that way. I don't want to deal with the barrage of questions that might follow: *Why did you decide to leave America? Why the army?* I don't want to reveal anything about my family of origin to the people here. They only know I'm from New York City and speak Hebrew with a semi-American accent, and that seems like enough.

For the show I decide on two well-known songs: "What I Did for Love," from the Broadway hit musical *A Chorus Line*, and "Summertime," an aria composed by George Gershwin for the 1935 opera *Porgy and Bess*. The version I grew up with was sung by Ella Fitzgerald and Louis Armstrong. I contemplate singing the love song "More" from the film *Mondo Cane*, which I sang as my audition piece for the Fame School back in 1984 with Mom as the accompaniment, but today I decide it's not "jumpy" enough.

For the next few days, I practice singing in a lumpy, desolate field while the sun beats down on my head and flies swarm around me. My voice carries through the desert, but not in the same way it would in a concert hall. During these "practice sessions," I have no pitch pipe or piano, and all my sheet music is in boxes back home. Many thoughts race through my mind while I'm out there: *Can I actually do this? Will everyone just laugh at me? Will I be able to sing on key? What will my commanding officers think?*

At seven o'clock in the evening two days later, I appear on a bungalow stoop facing an empty desert, wearing a dusty civilian shirt, my hands tucked into the pockets of my army work pants. The sun's still high above me, and my "audience"—members of my garin and the Israeli-born garin—sit on the grass. Our commanding officers stand behind them.

Silence.

I take a deep breath and introduce each song in Hebrew briefly.

Some of the commanding officers' hats are pulled down to block out the glare of the sun, so there's no way of seeing their expressions. Will there be a cringing face, or whispers of disapproval?

I decide to go with the flow: I lift my chest and open my mouth.

I have the entire "stage" to myself. I trill on the high notes without belting. My voice travels. With each note, I feel the distance between my high school self and who I am today becoming smaller. My entire body shakes with nervous excitement and anticipatory anxiety.

As I get deeper into "Summertime," I try to avoid focusing on the garin and their expressions. This hot desert is the perfect setting for the song. I try my best to execute Ella's flawless, melismatic style, letting thoughts of her rich voice carry me like warm honey. Each time I end a cadence, I control and deepen my voice just like she does in the recording I know so well.

As I near the end of the song, my heart beats fast.

What's this? There's clapping. *They liked it!* Even as I run to sit on the grass, avoiding people's eyes, the clapping is still going. I squeeze in between two of the Israeli garin members on the ground. Someone reaches from behind and squeezes my hand.

The next day, Michal, Hiyah, and Miki from the Israeli garin, and even a second officer named Debbie, approach me at breakfast.

"Wow, Dorit, you sang great. We didn't know you could sing like that."

I smile widely. I didn't know I could sing like that, either.

It occurs to me: I'm not just a soldier anymore. I'm someone with a voice.

I'M FEELING MORE COMFORTABLE WITH EVERYONE IN our garin now with the exception of one person: Jake. He never stopped acting so unpredictably hot and cold toward me following our kiss at the date factory, and I got fed up with that behavior pretty quickly. I've been avoiding him for a while now.

Now that the IDF has started putting us through a series of *giboosh*—social cohesion trips that the army makes us do as a garin—I'm becoming concerned about Jake's behavior. He sometimes seems like more of a bully than a leader. He targeted Svetlana a lot when we were at Eshbal. He's also one of the guys who became most upset by the IDF's decision not to send us to basic training after ulpan, and in many ways, it seems, he still hasn't gotten over his anger.

One instance of Jake's bullying has stayed with me despite how much time has passed since we were at Eshbal. We were told to run around the camp twenty times because we didn't all appear at the same time in the same uniforms, and Svetlana paused a couple of times for water.

"Why the heck is she stopping every minute to drink from her canteen?" Jake shouted, dashing to the front of the line with his M16. After passing her, he muttered under his breath, "Fuckin' Russian twit." The anger and frustration in Jake's voice was palpable, and was made all the more intimidating by his physical size and strength. It wasn't really fair, either, because the punishment wasn't a result of anything Svetlana did—we were in trouble because Igal hadn't been able to find his jacket. It made me mad: Jake always seemed to vent his frustrations on the women in the garin, never on the men.

Today, we walk along the River David trail in the middle of the Arava desert, I'm filled with dread at the thought that Jake might turn his anger on me. The last thing I want is to be victimized in the way Svetlana was back at Eshbal.

As I climb up the rock strewn trail, I look up ahead and see that Jake has already reached the top of the hill. A bandana is plastered around his forehead, with leaves and branches sticking out every which way. He even has green paint smeared on each cheek, like the soldiers I once saw sitting in the back of a Jeep, heading to Lebanon.

Once we're over the hill and through a clearing, we reach a series of muddy pools. Jake runs through them, holding his M16 in shooting position with the *cane*—tip—forward, shouting the same lines he shouted on that first bus ride to Eshbal: "I'm gonna shoot those motherfuckin' Arabs. I'm gonna shoot every single one of them and blast each one of them out of this motherfuckin' country!" As he did before, he switches to Hebrew after that, though the obnoxious English words he muttered still linger in the air. Instead of reprimanding him,

Menny, one of our officers, starts laughing and even speaks English with him. I fear that Jake is now building a following. Why all the violence?

I try to find my inner strength. I'm not so desperate for a connection with Jake now that the Israeli garin has my back. I take comfort in the fact that I'm now so invisible to Jake that he probably won't take notice of me, just like he's been ignoring Dalia because she's aloof, and the Russians because they don't speak English.

Just as I'm thinking I'm free of him, however, Jake and I end up face-to-face in a shady patch of the trail, under a eucalyptus tree. I guess both of us are dying for some shade.

Just as I start inching away, Jake shouts, "Dorit!" He points to Svetlana, Eina, and Vered, who are laughing, and splashing each other in a pool while speaking Russian, their guns leaning against rocks on shore. "Look at those Russian friends of yours. They're hysterical!"

This is supposed to be refreshing break before we hike the next ten kilometers through the relentless heat of the desert. I don't really want to go in the water, but I don't want to spend my resting time with Jake, either. *Maybe I should join them just to escape him.*

I take a few more steps back just as a huge spray of water hits both of us.

"I know," I say. "Don't remind me. I have to deal with them all the time." I quickly tell him about our latest argument over whether we're supposed to clean our guns for a late-afternoon inspection. I only share this information with Jake as a way to vent about the situation in my mother tongue. There are times when I'm frustrated by their mentality and Svetlana seems to be the leader of the pack. I sometimes get the feeling they are jealous of me because I'm American. They don't understand just why an American volunteers for the Israel Defense Forces.

"Dorit, man, what are you doing telling me about the awful fucking way they are treating you? Go tell someone!"

"Yeah, like who?"

"I don't know. Just anybody. Tell the commanding officers. Your house mother from Sufa . . . what's her name, Orna? Anybody!"

"Oh, c'mon Jake. They can't do anything. Nobody can do anything. This is the army, remember? They'll call me out for tattling and I won't hear the end of it. I've got another year and a half with these girls. I'm the one who has to deal with them, not you."

Every time Svetlana, Eina, Vered, and I bicker over issues like gun inspections, I want to run away. It's isolating and lonely trying to deal with these three girls who constantly think they're right. But there is nothing I can do. If I initiate a conversation about our problems with an officer, I'll be perceived as someone who constantly needs outside help to deal with our internal issues. I can't afford to reveal any weaknesses.

"Let's face it," I say hopelessly. "I'm just stuck with them."

"Then ignore them . . . they're just pricks," he says disdainfully.

I appreciate Jake suddenly standing up to support me, but I also know these are my problems to handle.

On our next break, Jake finds a "seat"—a long, dusty rock formation—and we sit there in the shade to eat sandwiches we've carried along with us in yellow crates. He urges me to sit next to him. After some coaxing, I finally accept. Above us, hawks and vultures make lazy circles in the sky, hoping to pick over the remnants of our lunch when we're done.

I look up to see Svetlana making her way toward us. The crates are located on a narrow sliver of rock near us, so she has no choice but to walk by Jake in order to retrieve her sandwich. I hope he will be so consumed with eating that he won't pay attention to her, but I fear the worst. He's sure to say something obnoxious to her; he never could tolerate her in the first place, and now I'm regretting what I just told him earlier.

As Svetlana passes him, Jake says, "Aw, stop looking so sad, Svetlana" in English, and just as she looks up at him, he throws a piece of bread at her. I scowl. This is the part of Jake I hate. A part of me says to keep quiet, though. *They've made me suffer, so now they should suffer*, it says.

Jake throws another piece of bread.

"*Nu tafsick kfar*—Stop it already!" Svetlana shouts.

Soon pieces of bread are flying every which way. Some land on Eina, Svetlana, and Vereds' heads. "*Nu, Jake, tafsick kfar!*" they shout, which elicits laughter from the guys of the garin.

Stop trying so hard to get attention, Jake, I think. *Get with it.*

Finally, I decide to say something. "You really shouldn't have done that, Jake. As I told you, I'm the one who has to deal with them. This is the last thing I need!"

"They can take it up with me, then." Jake grins widely.

"Yeah, right."

When the excitement dies down, he pulls me over to the side, next to the few trees nearby, and squeezing me with his muscular arms. It's not so much a hug as it is a crushing embrace—done, as usual with him, for comedic effect. He's now so close to me that I can feel the heat where his gun is touching my side.

"So what's the story between us?" he asks in a low voice.

"Story? What the heck are you talking about?"

"You know. During our break at the date factory at Kibbutz Ketura."

He's still squeezing my arm. I try to pry it off, but it's fastened tight. There's no letting go.

I quickly think back. The surprise kiss at the date factory left me fantasizing that there was more to Jake's hot-cold nature than what I'd seen. I kept hoping and wishing Jake would become more predictable.

"Let's just be friends and leave it at that," I say now, still trying to pry his arm away.

He holds me a few moments longer before letting go. By the time he releases me there are red marks on my arm.

I pick up my gun and start heading back toward the group. Everyone is picking up their bags and starting to walk.

"Aw, c'mon," Jake shouts after me. "You know you want it."

"Excuse me?" I shout back.

"You know you want me," he says with an air of confidence.

"You're so wrong in that department, Jake," I say. "I can bet you on that!" I rush to catch up with the rest of the group.

He laughs.

He thinks he can prove me wrong. I'll show him.

Now I have all the confirmation I need. Jake's a jerk. At least I can pat myself on the back for having trusted my initial instincts with him.

As I join up with the group, I remember something Jake said in the date factory the day we kissed: "First, I want to be your lover; then I'll be your best friend."

I so longed for a connection at the time that both of those scenarios had appeal. Now, however, it's clear that he'd be an intolerable lover *and* a lousy friend.

THE FOLLOWING FRIDAY, WE'RE AT SUFA, AND AS I'M getting ready to head out to the disco to celebrate the end of a long and difficult week, I hear voices from a bungalow a few houses away. I listen closely in the cool night air as crickets chirp. It's Jake and Robin, whom he refers to as his "drinking buddy." They're shouting and laughing, bodies shadowed against the see-through slits of the window closest to me. I've seen them drink their way into a stupor before, and their cackling fills me up with dread now. Trouble's brewing.

I walk down the path toward the bomb shelter, past Robin's bungalow. The cackling has stopped, and now Jake's voice is dominant. I stop and listen. Between the blasting music and Jake's high-pitched voice, I can't make out the conversation. Then I hear "Owner of a Lonely Heart"—one of the many American pop songs from my youth—begin to blast from the bomb shelter, and I'm filled with nostalgia.

"Dorit, you should stay away from them," Andy warned me earlier this evening. "They are the two most unstable guys in our garin." I know he's right, but at this moment I can't take heed of his words. I am feeling almost desperate for connection, and the song is piercing my lost, lonely heart. Even though I know Jake is a bad temptation, one I should resist, I start toward Robin's door. I want to hook up with Jake tonight. It's emotional, not intellectual, and the idea that I can do it is somehow empowering.

You don't have to do this, a voice says. But then it's countered by a more powerful one that says, *Yes, you do.*

I knock on the door until footsteps approach. Music blasts in the background. The door finally opens, and it's Jake.

"Dorit!" He closes in on me with a hug, a real hug, and I

smell the alcohol on his breath. Before I know what's happening, he pulls me through the dimly lit room and over to Robin's unmade bed.

I laugh. *Ah, this feels good. Finally I'm being paid attention to!*

"Hey Jake, catch you at the disco, yeah man?" Robin shouts as he lowers the volume. Before I get a good look at Jake, I look around. Clothes are strewn everywhere. Both his and Robin's M16s stand against the opposite wall. Cigarette butts and empty beer cans are scattered in every direction. I try to numb out the other sensations and allow myself to fall into this moment of being enveloped by his strong arms. He leans over me and pulls me closer to him.

This big man is pinning me down. He's going to kiss me! This is what I came for. I keep my eyes closed, trapping in the vision of us that I want, my fantasy. When I allow myself to look up at Jake, I notice how his facial muscles are bunched around his forehead, his skin now turning beet red, face full of intention. *I'll just surrender to him. I'll leave it up to him to intuit my needs.*

But just as I start to get lost in my thoughts, Jake pulls away and says something surprising. "I am not going to make love to you," he says. "You're not ready."

Stunned, I straighten myself up and look into his twenty-eight-year-old face. "Okay," I say in a small, meek voice. Then I pick myself up and walk out the door without saying anything else.

The cool air refreshes me as I head again toward the disco. "Owner of a Lonely Heart" has long since finished and another well-known Israeli tune has now taken its place, but my thoughts are elsewhere. *What the heck just happened?* With each step, I try to figure out the answer.

You left New York City and Mom so you could volunteer for the Israel Defense Forces. You were hungry for a connection. You saw something in Jake that offered a connection. You hoped he would be the one. You counted on him being the one. But then he let you down. You didn't need to sacrifice yourself just to be accepted. But you did. The minute he said he wasn't going to sleep with you, you felt let down, but deep inside, you know he did the right thing. So now what?

I wish I hadn't let him speak to me like that. I wish I'd had the voice to answer him back assertively.

Years later, I will realize that in his way, Jake was looking out for me when he refused to sleep with me. But right now, on the path, having put so much emotional energy into this, only to have it fall apart, has left me feeling bereft. I need to refuel myself. I need to get away. I walk quickly down the sticky steps at the makeshift disco at the bomb shelter at Sufa and straight to the bar, where I take one alcoholic drink, and then another.

By the time Svetlana arrives at the disco, I'm already halfway drunk. I grab her by the hand and twirl her around and around. She giggles with delight. I'm no longer shaken up by alcohol the way I was back on Malkiyah because I've been dealing with real serious issues as part of my service. I know my limits. Somewhere in the back of the disco, Robin is already getting blasted. Soon Jake will join him and they'll both drink their way into oblivion. But I don't care. Jake has no power over me. He's not worth it.

Walking home in the coolish midnight air, I hear a voice—not outside, but in my head. It's Luis's. I try to pinpoint the time and place of the memory, and then I remember. The classroom at Eshbal during our first week of ulpan. As an ice-breaker activity, the teachers had us pass positive notes to other garin members. Luis's note was the only honest one of several. Everybody else wrote something along the lines of "Dorit, you're kooky but cute." But Luis wrote, "Dorit, you can be a lot more. Search for the path."

Even then, barely knowing me, Luis saw something I didn't. When did I compromise on something important within myself? What have I already given away? And more important, is it too late to change my course? Is that why I'm here—to find a better path?

Yes, Luis, I think, *you're right. I can definitely be more. Much more.*

15

PRESIDENT'S AWARD

HALFWAY INTO MY SERVICE ON SHITIM, ONE OF OUR army officers calls me and Daniel into her dark, dank office. There's no air conditioning, and yet in comparison to the 100-plus temperatures outside, the slightly cooler air of the office is a welcome respite.

Like Idit, the overseeing commanding officer back on Eshbal, commanding officer Ahuva has flaming red hair and a somewhat unnatural-looking perm.

"Have a seat," she says, chewing on a pencil.

We sit.

"I'm sending you to Jerusalem," she continues. "You two have been selected to receive the President's Award of Excellence."

I don't want to sound stupid, but I've never heard of the President's Award of Excellence before. "Excuse me," I ask Ahuva, "but what exactly is this award for?"

"Oh," she says laughing. "You probably want to know that. The IDF chooses a few soldiers each month from a number of different units, including the Nahal, for exemplary service," she says, still chewing on her pencil.

"Oh, I see. Exemplary service. Thank you." *Me, out of all the IDF soldiers out there!* I silently yip, but I keep my giddiness inside. I never anticipated receiving such an award, and I certainly don't want to draw attention to myself by questioning why the IDF picked me. And getting to go to Jerusalem is a dream come true! I visited during ulpan at Yagur, months ago, but going alone with Daniel to receive an award will be a wholly different kind of experience. The two of us get along well: we tease each other about our accents when we speak Hebrew, and joke about the shenanigans of the other members of our garin. He's one of the calmer and more easygoing guys here, and I need someone who can simply laugh things off the way he can. Other than Luis, there's no else I would prefer traveling with to this ceremony. Plus, I'm glad someone as nice as him got this award.

"You can both stay at the *Beit-Hayal*, the soldiers' house in Jerusalem, while you're there. I'm calling them now to let them know you're staying there tomorrow."

I try to hold in my excitement. *We're leaving tomorrow!*

Beit-Hayal is not exactly a world-class place, but it's a world away from staying at a settlement. I've heard about it from other soldiers who've stayed at various locations throughout the country. You get your own room and bathroom, and while the food isn't exactly home-cooked, it's pretty healthy.

An overnight stay in Jerusalem at the army's expense! My heart pumps with delight. *Svetlana's going to be jealous of this one!*

When we're dismissed, I turn around and shuffle out into the hot air. As a Nahal soldier, I know I'm doing hard work, but I cannot wrap my mind around the idea of being rewarded for exemplary service. In my mind, receiving a President's Award should only happen when someone does something significant for the country, like saving lives or completing extraordinary military duties. I'm not a commander or an army educator or a social worker. In my mind, pulling tomatoes out of the ground in a desolate field, learning about plants and irrigation systems at an agricultural course, and packaging dates in the middle of the desert hardly equals worthy work.

At breakfast, just as he's dishing himself an extra helping of scrambled eggs, Daniel bumps into me. "So we're going to Jerusalem together!" he says, beaming.

I can't help but stare at his protruding front teeth as I swallow my own eggs and high-five him. "*Kol Hakavod Lanu*— all the best for us!" *Thank goodness it's not just me who got this award*, I think. But I don't want to kill this moment by acknowledging to him that I'm not sure whether I'm award-worthy. Just by virtue of being a man, it seems to me that Daniel is more deserving of this award than I am; at least he, unlike me, will end up doing a fair amount of military work.

Just accept the fact that you were one of the lucky ones who got picked and move on, I tell myself, but I need more convincing. I pull Daniel from the breakfast line. "Do you know any other Nahal soldiers on the settlement other than us who received this award?"

"Nope, do you?" Daniel asks.

"Nope. I have a feeling we've been selected because we are immigrant soldiers from the Nahal units. The IDF probably doesn't care if we've been working in the desert on a settlement or learning ulpan. But I just—"

"That could very well be," concurs Daniel.

"You know what else I think? We haven't spent enough time in the army to really fulfill any soldier duties."

Daniel squints at me. "Stop thinking about this too much. *Ze lo kol-kach hashoov*—It's not so important."

I'm filled with disappointment at Daniel's response; he

didn't give me the answer I'm looking for. But I try not to dwell on it too much. I focus on the funny way he emphasizes the "oov" in *hashoov*, and let the laugh carry me over. But still, I crave to know why I was picked for this.

Nahal is still one of the more rigorous types of training and service available to women in the IDF. I haven't proven myself yet, but perhaps I will get the chance to do so in time. Our time on Eshbal doesn't really count as "soldier work" because we were mainly studying the Hebrew language there, but once we go through basic training, I think I'll feel more deserving of this award. In the meantime, when I can stop worrying about *why* I'm receiving this award for a minute, I become so giddy I can hardly think. I'm going to meet the President of Israel, Chaim Herzog! I try to imagine meeting the President of the United States and I can't even wrap my mind around it. It feels momentous. I think about how proud my dad will be when I tell him.

∽

THE NEXT MORNING, AT 6 A.M., DANIEL AND I BRISKLY walk the dusty two kilometers to the main road in our polished black and brown boots. At the intersection of the two roads, a rusty signpost points south to Eilat and north to Jerusalem and Tel Aviv.

As we expected, the road is empty, a long white snake disappearing into the haze, the asphalt shimmering almost wetly in the distance. The sun is already washing out the landscape. I have convinced Daniel to take a bus rather than hitchhiking, even though he insists it will be faster and "more fun" to hitchhike for the five-hour drive.

"The bus should be coming any minute, Daniel," I say

now, still nervous that he'll try to talk me into hitchhiking. "And in the end, we'll get to Jerusalem faster with the bus. If we hitchhike, we will have to wait much longer. We might even lose rides to soldiers in uniform who've been hitchhiking from Eilat."

"You've got a point there, Dorit from the USA," Daniel says. "Let's see what comes first."

Happily, the bus comes first, headlights like two monstrous, fast-approaching eyes. We clamber into two seats opposite each other on the practically empty bus. Already it's hot as an oven. I slide open the window and inhale the hot, dry desert air. I feel my heart expanding with excitement, my breath softening and muscles winding down. The sun is rising over the Judaean Hills, coloring the barren land pink. Months ago I resented the IDF for sending us out here to serve in what I then perceived to be a harsh and hostile land, but now I'm tickled by this arid landscape and how it's sprinkled with color, as if by magic.

Two hours later, the Dead Sea sparkles in the distance, and there are people already covered with mud sitting on the beach. A cluster of luxury hotels soon dot the landscape with palm trees on the far right, the salt-mining fields spread out beyond. Sweat's trickling down my face. The air conditioner's broken, an issue for which the driver apologizes over the loudspeaker. Daniel has pulled the blinds down as far as they can go and is trying to nap, using his bag as a pillow. I do the same.

Just as we pass the Dead Sea, my ears stop popping, but the early-morning heat of the day continues to penetrate. I tug off my thin, itchy cotton socks with the tops rolled over—the same style I used to wear with my Mary Janes back in the seventies—and unbuckle my black sandals so they look like flip-flops. It's my first time wearing a dressy skirt since I've been here, and both it and the blouse I plan to wear have been stuck at the bottom of my duffel bag for so long that no matter how hard I try to smooth them out, there are still creases. The skirt goes a bit past my knees showing my pale legs. I try to pull the skirt lower, but it makes it billow like a cone.

By the time we get to Jerusalem, the holiest place on earth, I've forgotten how I look—I'm too excited to be here. There is more to Jerusalem than bomb scares: it is achingly beautiful, and so rich in human history. It feels alive, like it's breathing, vibrating under my feet, and I am suddenly a tourist again, with an urge to snap photos and look at everything with awe. Jerusalem teems with unprecedented Israeli-style diversity, ranging from ultra-Orthodox and conservative Jews to police, border patrolmen, and soldiers from all units, not to mention tourists from all over the world, who are easy to identify by their monstrous-sized backpacks.

During my first summer visit to Jerusalem in 1989, the chaos and traffic made a profound impression on me, but I couldn't relate to the aggression. I didn't understand how Israelis could live in this constant state of urgency. Now, as a soldier, I see how Jerusalem is a troubled city torn between faiths, a constant target for terrorists, but I feel very much connected to it. I, along with my fellow soldiers, am the lifeline of Israel's existence and future, and this thought makes me feel special—and safe.

As we wait for the bus that will take us into the city, Daniel points out the fact that many buses heading through the Jordan Valley now have protective window shields since they go through security blockades.

"Does that mean that bus drivers have to wear bullet-proof vests and carry guns?"

"I guess," Daniel says just as our bus pulls into a semi-gated parking area.

The driver opens the doors, and Daniel and I jump down from the metal railing we were perched on.

This is it. I'm on my way to meet the President! At first this thought scares me, but then I remember: This is Israel. I'm protected. The entire country has my back. Comforted, I settle in for the short journey to the President's house.

Inner city bus 54 travels through a mélange of neighborhoods, beginning with Meah-Shearim, Jerusalem's ultra-Orthodox neighborhood. I've heard stories of how its residents used to block roads on the Sabbath and throw stones at cars if drivers came within eyesight.

The Dome of the Rock shines like a rare amber in the middle of the city, and I remember the song "Jerusalem of Gold," written by one of Israeli's celebrated songstresses, Naomi Shemer. I grew up hearing the song, which is the unofficial national anthem of Israel, as a child. It describes the Jewish people's 2,000-year longing to return to Jerusalem, and as I consider it today, I think about how this ancient city is so important for three of the world's religions: Christianity, Judaism, and Islam. Just like the Jews referenced in Shemer's iconic song, I feel called to this holy city, and now that I'm here I feel at home, despite the fact that Jerusalem will be forever contested and divided, never at peace.

I reach overhead and open the air conditioning valve. *Good. It's working.* Cool air blows every which way, and soon I'm shivering. I reach up again and close it as we turn into a narrow, quiet street, and my thoughts turn again to the question of whether I'm award-worthy. I want to let it go, but I can't. I've been throwing this question around ever since I got the notice that I was receiving the President's Award.

I turn to Daniel. "Do you really think we did something noteworthy to get this award? I mean, with all the craziness of our garin, it's hard to believe anyone should get an award."

"Our officers are watching all the time," he says non-chalantly. He doesn't seem to have any qualms about receiving this award. "They report. They know who's who and what's what."

"So you mean they know who's really a serious soldier and who's goofing around."

"Yeah, something like that."

I think back to the beginning at Eshbal. We all tried to prove ourselves from early on until Igal screwed things up a couple of times, at which point tempers started to flare and people started to lose patience.

"But Daniel, most of us in the garin are serious. We all care."

"Maybe they're looking for that extra-special soldier or two in the Nahal who cares more. I don't know, Dorit. Why are you asking?"

"I don't know. I guess there's a part of me that wants to know what I did to be recognized for this award. I've had a lot of ups and downs. It was tough at the beginning."

"*Al tidagi*—don't worry so much about everything." As expected, Daniel says, "You know, *ze lo kol-kach hashoov*—the award itself is not so important." Again he draws out the "oov" syllable so long I just have to laugh at him. I know I won't be getting a real answer from him because he's not as driven to know as I am. Maybe it's because he's a guy; either he doesn't care as much, or he isn't going to show it.

∞

A FEW STOPS BEFORE OUR FINAL DESTINATION, AS WE pass stone houses surrounded by fir and pine trees, I reach into my bag and put my itchy white socks back on, rolling over the tops with their fake lace. I can't believe how girlie-girlie they are. I haven't worn socks like these in ages.

Once we arrive at our stop, we head to the main security area. The front gate is heavily manned: some security guards sit in an air-conditioned, enclosed space behind the gate, while others stand in front of a heavy wrought iron gate. We show our invitations, and after several bag checks, we're let through.

We walk past a U-shaped courtyard filled with an illustrious array of hibiscus, jasmine, and lavender, and then through a glass door into a world of chandeliers and high-profile military men and women.

We're led to a group of soldiers—other recipients of the award—and we quickly introduce ourselves. There's a blond-haired, blue-eyed soldier named Natasha from the former Soviet Union who works for some big chief officer at the HaKiriyah in Tel Aviv, an inner-city army base that contains the Tel Aviv district government center and the major Israel Defense Forces base, Camp Rabin, which has served as the IDF headquarters since its founding in 1948.

As Natasha and I go back and forth about mindless topics, like how long we've both been in the country and what she plans to do after the army, two male soldiers come up to us. One is a paratrooper, with red boots to match his cap, whose heavyset frame and boyish face immediately catch my attention. From what I already know about the paratroopers, they are the third-best unit of the IDF, behind the air force and then the navy, so I jump at this opportunity to interact with this soldier. The other is a bony Ethiopian from the tanks division who has impeccably straight white teeth that light up his chocolate brown skin. They introduce themselves as Amal and Avi.

I quickly scan the area to see if there are any soldiers with the Nahal tag, but so far, it's just Daniel and me. Looking at the other soldiers who will be receiving the award, I mentally confirm my suspicion that the IDF has chosen us at least in part because we are immigrants from different countries—we represent the diversity of Israel.

Amal and Avi are deferential and quiet, but when I tell them I'm a Nahal soldier from New York City stationed in the Arava desert, their faces light up like menorahs. The spotlight's now on me, and they're eager to hear about my life in New York City. I tell them how almost everyone I've met in Israel has interrogated me about why I left New York City to serve in the IDF.

Avi, the Ethiopian soldier, chuckles and nods. "I can relate to you somewhat. I'm like you, a Zionist from abroad. But in my case, people know why I left. We had no choice. There was a war going on when I was a child. My family and I were just a few of many Jewish people who left Addis Abbaba and escaped via the Sudan desert."

I think back to Operation Shlomo in 1991, a covert Israeli military operation to airlift Ethiopian Jews to Israel. Nonstop flights of thirty-five Israeli aircraft transported 14,325 Ethiopian Jews to Israel in thirty-six hours—the biggest immigration mission in Israel's history. Granted, our histories and circumstances are vastly different, but we've both sacrificed to be here and I feel an immediate kinship with Avi.

I eye his silver Star of David necklace, which has just caught a brilliant ray of light from one of the chandeliers hanging above us.

"They killed members of my family in the camps," Avi continues. "We knew that as Jewish people, we had no future there. We needed to be free. The only way out was to cross the desert. There were many problems along the way: famine, disease, no water." He speaks convivially, as if he's recounting someone else's story.

In this busy hall full of soldiers who've also been selected to receive the President's Award, my mouth is frozen, and there are pins and needles running down my back. These are the kinds of stories I have read about in books and seen in movies. I want to hear more. I want to spend hours with Avi. I can feel my heart opening up. *After so much suffering, did everyone in his family make it to Israel?*

He points to his unit tag and burgundy beret and laughs. "I had just finished basic training and gotten this a few months ago before being sent to an operation in Lebanon."

Avi's so gentle. It's hard to imagine him sitting in a tank, covered with war paint, and fighting the enemy after all he's been through.

"I'm glad you're safe," I tell him. "And your family?" My heart longs to hear a happy ending.

"Yes, we've been here for ten years now. We're lucky. When we arrived, we got sent to one of those hotels the Ministry of Absorption used for us. But some of us didn't make it."

There's heavy silence in our circle. I look up at Amal. He's wearing a rigid smile.

"Anything happening yet?" Daniel asks, resurfacing after a trip to the bathroom.

"No sign of the President yet," I say breathlessly, words rushing from my throat. I can hardly contain my excitement.

I look up at Avi. His cheeks have lightened in color. *This must be a very proud moment for himself and his family after all he's been through.*

"Are these all media photographers?" I ask.

"Yes," Avi says, observing the flood of people. "It looks like it."

"They've come just for us?" I ask. "Are we talking foreign media too?"

"Nah," Avi says. "Don't get your hopes up. Look at the photographers. Don't you see the signs? *Yediot Ahronot* and *Haaretz*."

"So these guys are the real deal. They're heroes," I tell Daniel, gesturing to Avi and Amal. "You missed the entire show, but I can catch you up later."

He shrugs his shoulders. "What could I do? Mother Nature was calling."

"Ha. Funny. That's so like you."

Then I thought of something Avi said—that, like me, he was a Zionist. Funny. I haven't used the word Zionist to refer to myself for a while. It's almost as if I had forgotten. But Avi has now rekindled something for me. People who are Zionists don't just believe in the State of Israel and its right to exist. They are believers. They have sacrificed their mother country. Avi is a prime example of that.

∞

"LOOK, HE'S COMING!" SOMEONE SHOUTS, AND WE ALL turn around.

The President emerges from the rear end of the hallway, and as he gets closer, we all turn to look at him and stiffly stand, ready to salute.

Immediately I feel self-conscious. We haven't been told what to do, and I hope I'll know when the time comes, or that I'm not the first to be called to meet him.

The hallway is full of soldiers now, from units all over the country. The President looks at all of us with a generous grin and semi-closed eyes. The more he grins, the more his cheeks puff up. He goes around the semi-circle we have just formed, stopping at each of us and asking us questions.

He speaks first with Avi, and waits politely for his responses. I try to listen to their conversation, but I'm only catching bits and pieces. When the President approaches me, he shakes my sweaty hand heartily and looks straight into my eyes. My heart is pounding in my throat. He asks, "Where are you from?"

"I'm from New York City, USA," I say. "Thank you for selecting me for this award."

Suddenly, I feel stupid. Why did I add the "USA" part? Like the President of Israel doesn't know that New York is in the US?

"I see you're serving in the Nahal unit." He points at his shoulder, the opposite shoulder where my tag is raised. "*Kol hakavod*, more power to you. Where?"

"The Arava desert, for now." My throat is parched. I wish someone would hand me a bottle of water. The back of my shirt is profusely sweaty. I try to think positive thoughts, though the only thing that's surfacing in my mind right now is the IDF's "fuck" of sending us to basic training.

"We need capable soldiers to serve those areas. Serving in the Nahal is a mighty mission, especially for a woman. Your training is very rigorous."

"*Toda*, thank you, Mr. President. I appreciate it."

Wow, the president just validated my work as a Nahal soldier!

He continues along the semi-circle now, first to Natasha, and then to Daniel. I am so flustered that I can't pay attention to their conversations.

When he's done speaking to Daniel, the President steps slightly outside the circle and addresses the room. "I commend you and your people for coming here. Our country wouldn't be the country it is today without your service." He makes a quick sweep with his hand and says, "Thank you for your service and for sacrificing your home country to be here."

I notice how the energy in our semi-circle has shifted. Just moments ago, I was questioning my self-worth as a soldier; now, none of that feels important. I no longer feel a desire to prove anything. I'm no longer consumed with all the "what-ifs" that have been plaguing me. I've exposed part of my story here, and I've been accepted and validated for my courage. I'm the only American and the only English-speaking soldier here, which makes me feel special. No one's putting me through the third degree. It's as if I was meant to be here, uniting with a common people from different backgrounds, all in the name of serving Israel. Can it be that this really is my homeland, a place I'll commit to staying in after my service and for the years to come?

"Come," the President says, "now I invite you to eat a meal specially prepared for you all. You must be hungry after all this excitement."

The President reminds me a bit of my late Uncle Isaac—a little pudgier around the face and edges, but the same smile. I wish he would linger a bit longer.

"Is that it?" I ask glumly once we gather again as our small group. "No pictures?" I want to remember this moment. I want to take this moment with me.

"Take a chill pill, Dorit," Daniel says in his usual half-joking, half-serious way. "Let's go eat. I'm starving."

∞

OUR BELLIES ARE FULL AFTER A THREE-COURSE CATERED meal consisting of fresh fruits, bagels and lox, egg salad spread, fried eggplant slices, and various salads and spreads including tabouli, spicy hummus, and a zesty tahini that I cannot stop spreading on my poppyseed bagel, which reminds me of one Dad once bought for me at a Syrian market on Atlantic Avenue in Brooklyn. The spices and smells curling into my nose remind me of home.

When the photographer arrives, all five of us—Daniel and me and our three new friends—stand in a semi-circle again, and this time the President stands in the middle. There's a huge engraved menorah on the wall behind us, and light spills through the stained glass windows above.

"You'll get your photos in the mail," the photographer tells us.

Just as we step out of the semi-circle again, it occurs to me that we haven't given him our address. We're stationed in the middle of the desert. How will the photographer know where to send it? But I think of Daniel's words—"take a chill pill"—and let it go. It'll work itself out.

Daniel and I share smiles as we exit past security.

"So, Mr. Daniel. Life *is* good at the President's house," I say. "Man, that tabouli was out of this world!"

He laughs. "It sure was!"

Before we part ways, Natasha writes down her number on a piece of napkin and hands it to me.

"Call me when you're in Tel Aviv again. I'd love to meet up. You're a lot of fun."

"So are you," I giggle. "Let's do it again!"

We chat a bit more while Avi and Daniel say their good-byes, then Natasha heads off to catch her bus.

Before Daniel and I leave, Avi grabs my hand and presses a piece of paper into my hand. "It's my number in Afula. Give me a call. I hope we can see each other one day soon."

"This country is small, so why not?" I smile at him, grateful for the connection we've had today.

There's definitely no way, after this experience, that I can go back to life the way it has been on Shitim. My entire perspective has shifted. My purpose is much greater than what I originally imagined. If I'd stayed in the States, who knows what direction my life might have gone in. But here, the experiences I'm having are giving me a chance to feel at home in the country I'm now defending—a place that moves my spirit like no other. Meeting the President, and a soldier like Avi, confirms for me how accessible people are, and how we are all interconnected. The President isn't just a distant, larger-than-life "hero"—he is a real person who shares my cultural history. And Avi's story has helped me to see the light in terms of really differentiating between minor troubles and major ones.

I'm closer to learning what "real life" is all about, and it's definitely *not* about earning good grades, trying to get a good job, and making a lot of money. It's about overcoming hurdles and obstacles and believing enough in something to make sacrifices for it. Like I'm doing here.

After all this time, I finally feel I'm home.

16

BASIC TRAINING

A MONTH AFTER RECEIVING THE PRESIDENT'S AWARD, I
find myself at Machaney Shmonim (which literally means
"Base Camp 80"), one of the largest training camps in
Northern Israel. It's August 18, 1991, and we've finally made
it to basic training. Up until now, our work in the Israel
Defense Forces has been child's play. Now the real work begins.

Base Camp 80 is filled with platoons of fifty or so new
male and female inductees. Many of them are fresh out of
high school. Some platoons, also referred to as military units,
include garins like ours, groups of soldiers who do a
combination of settlement, kibbutz, and army work. Platoons
that consist of Nahal soldiers, like ours, will have to go
through the army with their garins. Our platoon consists of
several garins, including our six-girl garin, and another
consisting of three girls: Jessica from the United States,
Michelle from London, and Karina from Argentina. Since
we've arrived, I've often heard Jessica and Michelle speaking
in English. I want more than anything to interject and introduce myself, but my awkwardness holds me back. Instead I

stew, feel jealous, and ruminate on my own situation with my garin, which has been strained from the beginning. There's still a long way to go until the march, and I know I would benefit from a real friendship with the girls in my garin, but I also know that's not going to happen.

There are several other garins here consisting entirely of French immigrants, but they act standoffish, and I don't see any potential friendships arising there either. Looking around, I can only surmise that we're all together because we're immigrants.

There are a handful of platoons here whose soldiers are not affiliated with the Nahal unit on this base. They will only have to do two weeks of basic training before the IDF sends them off to various army bases, officer courses, or other training camps.

We are stationed near the small cities of Pardes Hana and Hadera, and about an hour from Tel Aviv. There's a bit of green to compensate for the mostly flat, monotonous, tan landscape of twelve tents, endless scatterings of bunks, and dust and sand. We've had a long, exhausting first day of running around the camp, cleaning our guns, and preparing for inspections. We've already stripped our beds. Our sheets and thick woolen blankets now lie in one heap on the floor.

It turned out that my basic training being delayed was a blessing in disguise for me. I've started to feel at home in this country; I've come such a long way. I'm no longer riddled with the anxiety that shadowed my childhood and early adolescence. I don't have the luxury of getting worked up about things that used to scare me. I've formed meaningful friendships, and I've come into my own in ways I could never have expected.

Still, all the hard work I've done on myself over the last

few months seems to be erased in an instant when I land at Base Camp 80. The sheer number of platoons overwhelms me, and once again, I'm riddled with self-doubt. Being surrounded by all these soldiers reminds me again of high school, and what it felt like to be surrounded by so many brainy and talented students. While there's nothing to prove scholastically on this base, I'm easily triggered by the memory of how I tried so hard to thrive in that competitive environment, never able to relax or fit in. Now, almost two years later, I'm still concerned about fitting in. With each inspection or exercise, I start getting worked up about how well I'll perform. Before I even have a chance to consider what I'm supposed to do, I start panicking. One day here, and I've taken a giant step backward.

Two female officers shout to a nearby passing platoon, "*Smol, smol, smol, yamin, smol*—left, left, left, right, left!" Observing this scene is making the whole thing real. I am relieved to actually be here, and I try to focus on that. I'm taking the next important step toward becoming a soldier.

One afternoon, just a few days into basic training, the road is empty of soldiers and officers except for a familiar soldier with short black hair who's fast approaching our tent. As she approaches I recognize her: it's Galit, my favorite Hebrew teacher from Eshbal. A braided green rope is attached to her army tag unit, identifying her as an education officer.

"Galit, Galit!" I cry, rushing out of the tent I'm sharing with Svetlana, Eina, and Vered. The other girls join me and we practically topple her over with hugs.

"What are you doing here?" we shout.

"I came to visit you guys. I wanted to see how my garin is doing." There's a soft twinkle in her eyes, and she returns the hugs warmly. "How's everything? You guys faring okay?"

"We're doing okay," Svetlana says. "It's tough here."

"It's just so different than Eshbal," Eina confesses. "Much harder. Too many inspections. Too many things to do. Too many exercises. Too much of everything."

As they clamor and talk, I wait my turn for what I hope can be a private moment to confide in Galit. She was a good listener at Eshbal, and I felt she was both a teacher and a confidant for me. In this situation, with some of my old anxieties flaring up, seeing Galit is almost like seeing a friend from home.

"*Hevreh*, friends. It's so good to see you too." She winks at me. "I've been thinking of you a lot. Here, I've got a small gift for you all." She hands us each a goodie bag with a small personalized note written on colored cardboard. I take a quick peek into mine, excited like a child. I grab the mini-chocolate-covered wafer inside and pop it into my mouth right away, allowing the chocolate to ooze in my mouth.

We invite Galit into our tent, and she looks at the piled-up blankets and cots, seemingly looking for a place to sit.

"Have a seat," I say, leading her to an empty cot.

"Man, it's been a while since I did my basic training here," she tells us. "I think we were in that tent over there," she says, pointing to a nearby tent. "This place hasn't changed one bit. What's going on now?"

"We're in between exercises and inspections," I pipe up. "Where are you now? Still on Eshbal?" I ask eagerly.

"I'm now stationed a few bases away, teaching new immigrants Hebrew, and not just to Nahal soldiers like yourselves but to soldiers from all different units."

There is a little less than an hour to go before standing in *shlashot*—rows of three—for our commanding officers. I wait for the other girls' chatter with Galit to die down before I try to grab her for myself. I'm longing to confide in her how hard everything is: the girls, the army rigor, and the emotional triggers that keep coming up for me here.

One by one, Eina, Svetlana, and Vered finally get up to prepare for our upcoming inspection, and I gently nudge Galit's arm. She follows my lead as I head out of the tent and toward the dusty road. I am sure she can sense I'm about to cry. I cover my face with my army hat, trying to pretend just to be bothered by the sun, but soon enough, all the pressure I've been feeling comes out in those tears, which fall in a tired heap down my dusty face.

Army vehicles cruise up and down the road outside my tent. I wipe my snotty nose on my sleeve. "It's just really hard here with the girls and all. We just don't see things eye to eye. I feel like whatever I do just isn't important."

"You know, Dorit," she says. "There's nothing wrong with being alone. Actually, it makes one a much better and stronger person."

I understand that Galit is suggesting that it's okay to do things independently, without needing permission from others, but this thought doesn't sit so well with me. My biggest fear is being emotionally isolated.

She slips a little note in my hand. "You can handle this." She rubs my shoulder. "I have faith in you. I really do."

My body lightens, and my muscles relax. I knew she would make me feel better.

We end our short visit with a tight hug, and Galit promises to visit again before our basic training is over.

"Come before the march," I say. "So you can sort of see us off."

"That's a good idea. Will do."

We return to the tent, where she hugs all five girls goodbye before she briskly walks away. How I wish she could just linger and watch us prepare for our next inspection, so I won't feel so alone. Already I feel I'm being left to fend on my own again.

The note she handed me is moist in my sweaty palms. I open it and read: "Dear Dorit. You don't need anyone. You can find the way. I have faith in you."

∞

OUR OFFICERS SOON ARRIVE AND WE SCRAMBLE TO GET in rows. Then they give us our next order: be at the other side of the camp in ten minutes.

"*Zooz*—move!" they cry.

We run out of the tent, and ten minutes later, on the other side of Base 80, our officers appear again. Without delay, we stand in *shlashot* with our guns draped over us like shawls. This is the part of our training I anticipated would be hard to readjust to after four months of basically "partying" at Shitim, where there were few inspections, interactions with our officers and superiors were loose, and the dress code was very informal.

One of the soldiers from our platoon shouts the same silly mantra that we always used at Eshbal: "*Hamachleka titen hakshev la'mifakedim—shtayim, shalosh, hachev!*"

We crane our necks in the air and clasp our hands behind our backs.

"Platoon," shouts one of the officers, "you all now must run to the other side of the camp next to the showers and stand in rows! You've got one minute exactly. Now, go!" Immediately I notice that Jessica doesn't rush to be first the way I do. She runs *alongside* two of her garin members, almost as if she is trying to tell them, "It's okay. We're in this together. We can do it."

Maybe I should run alongside my garin members so I won't always feel I have to compete, I think. *Maybe this is one of the reasons why I'm always feeling frustrated and alone. Perhaps I'm pushing too hard to make my relationship with the girls work.*

When we make it to the showers, we again stand in *shlashot.* We're at the head of a clearing surrounded by a few tall scattered trees, and I'm just a few heads away from Jessica. I wonder what's she thinking and feeling. All around me are dozens of beautiful French immigrants who could easily pass as Israelis with their dark skin, and I'm comforted being in such a large platoon with a variety of nationalities. It reminds me of New York City but without the anonymity, which removes some of the newness of trying to navigate a new army environment. Someone behind me whispers in French, and for a minute I'm transported to New York City, but without feeling like a stranger to someone else's language.

"That was very good!" our commanding officer, Nurit, shouts while eyeing her military watch. The wide Velcro strap practically swallows her thin wrist. "You girls all got here right on time! Good for you!"

As we await our next command, Officer Nurit asks for a volunteer to replace the French girl who's been shouting out commands. I shoot my hand in the air. This is my chance to shine. A voice tells me that I don't need approval. I can do this alone and it's okay. I'm safe. I can handle this even with so many new things to contend with in this new army environment. All I need to do is stay committed. Stay focused.

You can do this, Dorit, I tell myself. *On your own.*

"Good!" she says. "Soldier, what's your name?"

"Dorit, Officer Nurit. My name's Dorit," I say loudly, my hands at my sides.

"Continue standing there. You're going to announce the officers when your platoon arrives at its next destination."

Does that mean I'm supposed to lead the platoon as well?

"Soldier, you're going to lead the platoon in our first run," Officer Nurit says, as if reading my mind, "and then, when we reach our destination, you'll announce the officers. Got it?"

"Yes, got it!" I shout.

While I feel honored she's given me this extra task of leading the soldiers of my platoon in addition to announcing the officers, I have no idea how I'll manage.

She clasps her M16 to her slim body and shouts, "So, platoon, we're doing our first run around the camp in preparation for your march, but without stretchers or army supplies. Just stay in one long, straight line and follow me. Got it?"

"Yes, Officer Nurit!" we all shout heartily, and follow her as her strong legs carry her along with ease.

Surprisingly, our first run around the camp doesn't feel very strenuous. It's almost like running around four medium-sized New York City blocks. At one point, after we pass apple orchards and the backyards of houses, Officer Nurit stops us in a dusty field. It feels like we're in the middle of nowhere, but once our breathing slows down, I hear cars from a nearby highway and I notice more fruit trees. Civilization. As the platoon gathers into *shlashot*, I run to face our platoon and shout *"Hamachleka titen hakshev la'mifakedim—shtayim, shalosh, hakshev!"* I feel the power of the words with every cell in my body.

My platoon responds by shouting, *"Achshev*—attention!"

Immediately I think, *Hey, I can do this! This is easy! Why did I possibly think I couldn't?*

"Good job, soldier!" Officer Nurit shouts.

I smile. I did it.

∞

DURING OUR SECOND WEEK OF BASIC TRAINING, WE DO another few rounds around the base in preparation for our eighteen-kilometer march, only this time we carry all sorts of equipment with us, including a canteen belt, a fully loaded magazine holder, and a metal helmet—and, of course, our guns. The gear weighs me down, and I struggle to stand tall.

We "greet" our officers outside the bathrooms, and when Officer Nurit shouts, "*Zooz!*" for "move!" my legs know what to do, but my mind struggles to comprehend why we have to carry all this unnecessary weight. *Why all this stuff? Running around the camp the first time was so much easier without all these extra supplies.*

An hour later, the French girls are leaning over and panting, but Jessica and Dalia steadily look ahead, beads of perspiration pilling on their faces. It's August, and the heat of summer is grueling. Now I can see how challenging this is going to be, and we haven't even been given stretchers to carry each other, which is expected on the day of the march.

"Excellent!" Officer Nurit shouts, running again in front of our platoon just as a svelte French soldier shouts "*Hakshev!*"

We look up and pay attention. The sky's a dramatic patchwork of clouds and sky. I quickly press the back of my hand against my forehead before dropping my arm to my side and craning my neck upward.

"You guys performed beautifully considering all the supplies you had to carry," Officer Nurit says. "Now, the next time we run around the camp, it won't be one time. We'll be doing a few practice runs with stretchers, and you'll be asked to carry one of your fellow soldiers each time."

This is the first time I've heard that we will have to carry stretchers on the day of the march. I can feel my stomach slowly sinking.

Stretchers! How the heck will we manage?

I can hear a few girls behind me groan softly, and a part of me wants to groan too. But just when my body is about to cave in on me, I look at Jessica. As I expected, she's steadily looking forward. The strength in her face gives me the power to stay focused. I won't break down.

17

GREEN BERET

THE DAY OF OUR EIGHTEEN-KILOMETER MARCH FINALLY arrives, and it's scorching hot. For the past six weeks we've been running around Base Camp 80 with equipment and stretchers. All the exercises we've undergone have boiled down to this moment. The test has arrived.

Our "special" meal the morning of the march consists of hard-boiled eggs, cottage cheese, freshly cut tomatoes and cucumbers, bread, and hot tea—similar to a kibbutz breakfast. I eat and drink an extra helping of each.

Breakfast done, we load up our gear, including canteens, guns, and belt packs. My black boots are tightly laced, and I'm wearing a freshly pressed work uniform from the kibbutz laundry. I crisscross my two guns—an M16 and an Uzi, both of formidable sizes and annoying lengths. But the good news is that it's just a matter of time before I'll pass one of them to someone else, as each soldier takes a turn carrying the two guns during the march. I plan on sticking with the M16; I can't seem to find a way to avoid having its end jab me in my back, but at least it's lighter than the Uzi.

The guys are doing a forty-kilometer march, I remind myself, and I take a moment to give thanks that ours is so much shorter. I can do eighteen kilometers, I think.

We gather at one of the side entrances of the camp around 9 a.m. More than forty-five girls and a dozen commanding officers mill about in this open space. We congregate and chat to pass the time. I've gotten used to waiting for the officers and for the next thing to happen. In the IDF, and in Israel in general, waiting is par for the course. So different from New York City. At first I found it surprising, given how strict officers are around morning inspections, but by now I've learned to take it all in stride.

I run over to where Svetlana to Eina are standing. As always, they're chirping incessantly in Russian and I'm trying to get their attention.

"*Shilish?*" I ask. It's a Russian word I've heard many times that basically translates into "Have you heard?"

Eina looks at me like I'm some sort of clown. She pulls away from me slightly, twists down the corners of her mouth, and continues to speak to Svetlana, ignoring me. I'm too used to this to be exasperated with her.

It's clear we are going to be here on this far side of the camp for a while, so eventually I sit down on a rock and listen to Jessica making small talk in Hebrew with some of the French girls as she pulls grass from the dry, lumpy ground. I pick at my nails until one of them starts to bleed. A slight breeze cools my forehead as crickets chirp a singsong melody.

Now, in the stillness, my nervousness flares up. There's always a part of me that shoots down my ability to give the best of myself, and it's rearing its head now. To succeed on this march, I'll need to carry all this gear, as well as my fellow soldiers at some points. These are tasks we've trained for, but the intensity and buildup of this day threaten to overwhelm me.

For the most part, I have nothing to fear regarding my performance on this march. I've trained well with the rest of the girls in my platoon. I have incurred no further punishments. I've been a model soldier and have relied on Galit's words of wisdom to help me get through difficult times. Each time a wave of anxiety has threatened to overcome me, I've taken deep breaths and gotten myself through it. I'm proud of myself, and I feel up to today's challenge. Even the thought of carrying another soldier on a stretcher doesn't bother me because we've been trained to work closely together as a group. But my track record with the Russian girls in my garin hasn't exactly been smooth. On this important day, I hope we'll finally find a way to get along without any bickering. Maybe we'll even be able to work closely together. Maybe we'll get each other through.

This is one case where Galit's words do not ring true. I cannot do this on my own; I need the support of my platoon to get through it. I start to panic, thinking of how Svetlana often ignores me. What if I need emotional support? What if my emotions get the better of me? What if I break down and the other girls see my vulnerabilities?

You are responsible for managing your own mindset, Dorit.

I've got to make sure I'm staying positive and focused.

∞

AFTER NEARLY AN HOUR OF WAITING, OUR OFFICERS gather us together and announce the details of the march: eighteen-kilometers circling around the camp and its surrounding areas. They tell us to stick together and take turns carrying the stretchers, no questions asked. A Jeep full of officers and one medic will be sticking close to us the whole way in case one of us needs medical attention at any point.

It's all come to this. I feel ready to tackle anything that comes my way. I've got what it takes.

Upon completion of the march, we will all be considered fully trained sergeants, and the green beret and Nahal tag I received from our officers upon finishing ulpan at Eshbal will finally have significance. Then we'll have two options: join the Nahal Brigade and serve on a number of *machleket meshek*—army bases—or work on a kibbutz for eight months. Eina and Svetlana are leaning toward being on a kibbutz; they are sick of being in uniform and want an easier life. But I'm indecisive. Part of me is deeply attracted to the challenge of serving on an Israeli base, and after so much time on kibbutzim and settlements, I'm less enchanted by the thought of returning to one. After all, we'll have plenty of time for that when it comes to the last three months of our service, which we'll finish up back at Sufa.

I'm pondering all this as our commanding officers gesture for us to join our respective groups. I join three of the girls from my garin, along with eleven others, to form one of four groups that make up our platoon.

We fill our *mimias* with water, and, when prompted, run to pick up the empty stretchers. Before the march, our officers explain how we'll take turns lying on the stretcher for the duration of one round, which lasts two kilometers. Each time we return to the starting point, the soldier who's on the stretcher will jump off, and a new one from each group will hop on.

As we've done many times before, I repeat, "Hands on the stretcher" as I hold one side, lift it with confidence, and begin carrying it at arm's lengths along with three other girls, including Svetlana. One of the French soldiers hops on. It takes some time to get into the rhythm of carrying it together, especially with all our equipment getting in the way, but eventually we figure something out that works.

After the first four kilometers, Svetlana takes her turn on the stretcher. She giggles and laughs while looking at me.

"*Oy, oy!*" she shouts as the stretcher begins to bounce slightly.

"This isn't funny, Svetlana," I tell her, annoyed.

She mumbles something in Hebrew and lies back, and for the next two kilometers, I and the three other French girls carry Svetlana while she tries to keep still and quiet. I'm surprised by how light she is, even with her gun and other stuff. At least in this situation, her thin body is an asset.

By the seventh kilometer of the march, my right side is really starting to hurt. At first I think it's just the side of my gun sticking into me, but then I realize the pain doesn't go away when I reposition my M16. It continues to hurt, and my breathing is becoming more constricted by the second. I run faster to keep up with the others. *What the fuck is going on with me? There's no way this can be happening so early on!*

Our march leads us through the backyards of houses and orchards, and on until the landscape changes to rows of pine trees. I want to stop and take the smell in, but there's no time to dilly-dally.

With the sun hammering down on my head, my body gets weaker, and the pain takes over. As the terrain gets sandier, my boots slump deeper into the sand, making things even more difficult for me.

Our commanding officers shout, "*Yalla*—go, go!" All but a few of them pass our group. A convoy of four Jeeps now separates the platoons, two on either side, with our officers leading the way. Dust, dirt, and flies are everywhere. I vow to keep up with my group, carrying Svetlana on the stretcher until we reach the starting point again, which I can now see in the near distance. When we finally get there, I catch my breath just long enough for Svetlana to hop off. Another soldier takes her place.

There's no way I'm going to mess up this opportunity, I tell myself fiercely. *Giving up is not an option.*

Just a few meters past the starting point, however, the pain is more than I can bear. Is this psychological? I'm practically sick at the thought of not finishing, but I hear myself saying the dreaded words in Hebrew, "*Ani lo yichola yoter*—I can't go on any farther!"

Svetlana hears me, and to my great surprise, instead of shooting me a dirty look, she grabs me by the arm and pulls me forward.

I dig in with everything I have and pick up the pace.

"*Boi, Dorit, boi*—c'mon, Dorit, c'mon!" she shouts. We're at nearly ten kilometers now, and my side muscles ache with an intense, jabbing pain. I don't know how I can possibly finish, no matter how badly I want it, and no matter how grateful I am for Svetlana's support.

"*Ani lo yichola yoter!*" I cry again. This time, I mean it.

Svetlana grabs my gun and any of the medical supplies she can carry as we try to keep up the pace. "*Boi, Dorit, boi!* You can do it. You have to do it!"

One of the other girls shouts, "Put her on the stretcher!"

The platoon and Jeep stop momentarily; the girl who's on the stretcher jumps off, and I'm lifted up and on.

I lie flat as I possibly can and grab onto the sides, trusting that my fellow soldiers have my back. It is not exactly the most comfortable ride, and even lying down I still feel pain. I try to regulate my breathing so more oxygen can flow through my body, but my breathing tempo still feels irregular. *Why isn't the pain going away?*

I am soon transferred to the Jeep, and I finish out the march watching the rest of the girls do what I should be doing right now: carrying stretchers filled with soldiers and running through the sand loaded down with guns. I'm feeling dejected and disappointed. I drink water until my stomach hurts.

"*At beseder*—are you okay?" asks Ayelet, a blonde-haired officer who always laughs at jokes I don't find particularly funny. But now she holds my hand and talks me through my pain and smiles.

"Where does it hurt?" she asks. "Here?" she says pointing to her left side, my right.

I nod like a child. She waits for me to speak as I rub away my dusty tears.

"Everything hurts," I cry out. "Everything!" I'm ashamed to admit that it started hurting almost as soon as we started, worrying that this might somehow disqualify me, if I'm not disqualified already. But Ayelet does not overwhelm me with questions or make me feel guilty. She hands me a few small juice bags to pump up my sugar levels, and I suck on them noisily.

With just fourteen more kilometers left to go, I'm feeling better, but a medic in the Jeep tells me that it's probably not worth the risk to start running again if I'm feeling as badly as I say.

I anxiously glance at Ayelet. Who has the final say in this situation? Her or the medic?

"Dorit, do you feel you want to rejoin the march?" the medic asks.

I watch the girls. They're giving the march every ounce of their strength. I stretch my body a bit. *Wait a minute, there's no pain. Am I better?* I try to convince myself I'm okay, but just as

I'm about to tell Ayelet I can handle the last ten kilometers or so, I feel another spasm of pain rock my right side. Its intensity collapses me.

I can't, I can't. I can't do it.

"Ayelet, I can't join them," I confess.

She nods, and the decision has been made.

"But I feel so badly about not regrouping with the rest of the girls."

"How can you?" she asks. "Look at you. Take it easy. *Tiragi*—relax."

I sit on the padded bench of the Jeep, watching the girls in the back making their way down to the last seven, then six, then five, four, three, two, and finally the final kilometer while I take two painkillers and drink more juice.

After eighteen-kilometers, the round-trip march finishes where it started. Almost everyone is shouting and celebrating. I descend cautiously from the Jeep, one step at a time. Dizziness overtakes me at first, but I recover quickly and look around for my garin, eager to regroup with them. Finally, I find them clamoring with the rest of the French girls.

Instantly I feel left out. Eina is the only one who seems concerned about me. "*Elohim*—oh my god, Dorit. Are you okay?" she asks.

I nod. "I think so. But it still hurts," I exclaim, pointing to my right side.

"You should see the doctor." Her tone is surprisingly warm and comforting.

"I guess I better. I hope I'm going to be all right," I say nervously. "This kind of thing has never happened to me before. I don't understand what happened."

Some of the French girls ask how I'm doing now, and then finally Svetlana looks at me.

When she doesn't say anything, I look back at her with an expression of, *Well, I gave it the best shot I could, right?*

She shoots me a look of sympathy, but it doesn't sit so well with me. I don't want her pity.

An hour after the march, my side continues to throb in pain, and now it has extended into my stomach. I'm led to the infirmary by a medic who examines me and then writes a prescription for a higher dose of painkillers. I'm given *gimmelim*—medical leave—and they say they want to do further testing and x-rays. This is not how I imagined ending the march.

After a battery of tests the next day, it turns out I have mild appendicitis, which warrants a few days of bed rest.

"What about attending the ceremony?" I ask the doctor.

"That'll be up to your commanding officers to decide. But consider yourself lucky. I've seen worse cases where people can't even walk for weeks," replies the doctor.

Oh shit. Not walking? That's scary.

I thank him, take the prescription, and don't even bother to entertain my usual "what-ifs." Instead, I simply go back to my tent and tuck myself in.

Please let me be well enough to attend the ceremony, I think before I doze off.

∞

THE NEXT MORNING, AFTER CONSULTING WITH MY officers, the doctors agree that I should be allowed to attend the ceremony and given credit for completing the march. I remove the Nahal tag that has been affixed to my shoulder for the last seven months.

I feel terribly undeserving because I didn't actually complete the march. I try and accept the fact that I'm being let off the hook because of an unpredictable medical issue. *It's as if I'm starting with a clean slate*, I tell myself. *A new beginning.*

At nine o'clock in the morning, we gather in a big clearing at one end of the camp, bunched in platoons, and our officers affix the Nahal tag to our shoulders once again. Officer Ayelet shakes my hand with a smile. A big cheer goes up, and then another and another. Svetlana is beaming. It is a heartfelt moment, and I know I will *always* be grateful to her for helping me when I needed it during the march.

All at once, we throw our berets in the air—the traditional Israeli throw party—and I shout a big "yee-haw!" cowboy style, trying to distract myself from the shame of not having completed the march, as well as some of the pain that still lingers. Someone grabs me and we start jumping up and down, but I soon slow down and stop for fear I might make the pain worse. I hug some of my fellow soldiers, and our officers stand outside our circle and watch and clap along with us. Despite my disappointment about the march, I feel lighthearted and hopeful. Basic training is finally over, and in this circle, I feel safe and strong. For that moment, that's all that matters.

The ceremony officially ends when our officers hand each of us a note made of different shapes and colors. Mine consists of baby blue, red, grey, and yellow triangular pieces. The first thing I notice is my name in Hebrew in big block letters. I'm both flattered and surprised to receive a personalized note from my officer, Ayelet, who smiles as she hands it to me. I wonder what she can possibly say after spending such a day with me.

At first I'm mesmerized by the angular shapes and colors of the note. It's a special combination of colors and shapes— very much like something my father would make. As the noises from the crowd drift and dissipate and Ayelet takes off, I begin to read the note.

Dorit,

As we dig deeper,

As we go inside more,

The most important and basic of all questions do not have answers:

Who am I and when?

When am I truly myself and until when?

Sometimes we have to do the things we don't really want to do.

The most important thing is how to manage and do them in the best way possible.

Take this into your consideration.

Good luck in the future.

Ayelet

Basic Training, '91

At first, I'm shocked and stunned. I rewind the last eight weeks of basic training like a movie. When did I ever give the impression I wasn't doing any of my tasks willingly? When did I ever give the impression that I didn't want to do something difficult? Was it through my body language? Something I said? The way I interacted with my fellow soldiers or officers? I try and pinpoint a specific scene or interaction, but my mind draws a blank. Are the notes to the others as detailed and specific as mine? Is Ayelet singling me out?

To me the note reads like advice. I can either take it or disregard it. As I walk back to our tent for the last time, Daniel's words enter my mind: "Our officers are watching. They know."

I asked Daniel weeks ago what we had done to deserve the President's Award, and at the time I didn't take his words seriously. Now the truth is staring me in the face. Daniel was too right. Officer Ayelet *was* watching—and she saw right through me. Perhaps she saw a resisting soldier. Perhaps she saw my struggle as I tried to keep going. Her words now highlight an emotion that's running deep: my shame. I'm ashamed of the lack of alignment between my thoughts and actions. I say to other Israelis that I'm a Zionist, and I do feel at home here in this foreign country, but on the other hand I have consistently blamed my garin for our problems and haven't always completed my duties with alacrity and eagerness.

Officer Ayelet has seen the real me, and she's called me out. *It's up to me now,* I think, *to discover who that "real me" is, or to make her into who I want her to be.*

Our service isn't going to get any easier, especially if we join the Nahal Brigade, so I'd better start figuring this part out sooner than later.

I consider what it feels like to be called out in this way. It's both unpleasant and galvanizing at the same time. Up until this point in my life, it has always been possible for me to get away with behaving negatively—at home and at school. I came to Israel specifically to escape my mother, and to figure out what kind of adult I want to be—a different kind of adult than her. And yet Ayelet is showing me the ways in which I've been acting out, and it's so much like my mother it scares me. I do not want to go through my adult life like this. Ayelet has pointed out that I have a choice: I can choose to be a better version of myself, not to behave how my mother always did— throwing fits to get her way. And I want to be that better version. I want to be a joiner. I want to belong. I want to live a life that's more expansive and full than my mother's life. I can make my own choices. It's not too late.

18

AVIVIM

IT'S ALMOST THE END OF SEPTEMBER 1991, AND WITH
the end of basic training comes the next phase of our service:
working on a kibbutz or serving with the Nahal Brigade. More
soldiers are needed to serve on bases than on kibbutzim, so it
seems like the Nahal Brigade is the more likely option. Eina
and Svetlana, however, think they have a good chance to work
on a kibbutz because they are immigrants still navigating a
foreign culture. *Every female soldier from our platoon is being sent to
serve on an army base,* I think, annoyed. *Why do they think they
should have it any different?*

Jessica's garin is heading to an army base in the Gaza
strip. I don't expect anything different for us, and that's fine
with me—I want to serve with the Brigade. I want to experience "real" service. Eina and Svetlana, though, are horrified
by the thought of serving on another base. They immediately
try to secure an appointment with one of the higher ups so we
can be sent to *machleket meshek*—to work on a different kibbutz
for the next eight months.

Technically, we are supposed to serve together, since we

are a garin, but if I have to, I'm prepared to make a request to split from them. Our goals seem to be at odds with one another, and I feel like Eina and Svetlana just want to take the easy way out. Dalia has already announced that she will split from the garin if the rest of us serve on the kibbutz. I haven't said anything out loud yet, but I feel bolstered now by the knowledge that Dalia and I want the same outcome. This could be a turning point for me in terms of the dynamic of the group. I'm not going just to side with Svetlana and Eina to make things easier; I'm listening to what I want and what's best for me, regardless of the pressure I feel to do otherwise.

Our situation is complicated, however, by the fact that we are just four girls now: Svetlana, Eina, Dalia, and myself. Shortly after basic training, Vered left our garin to become a driver on some base in the far south, and Geraldine married Raul, granting her full exemption from the IDF. I'm not sure the IDF will let us splinter even further.

As we stuff the last of our belongings into duffel bags in our tent at Base Camp 80, to which we will soon say goodbye forever, Eina and Dalia go back and forth about their conflicting wishes regarding where we'll go next. I have let Svetlana and Eina know how important it is to me to serve on a base rather than going straight to a kibbutz, but I'm tired of their bickering, and no longer threatened by a potential split, if it comes down to that, so I let take Dalia take over this argument. I don't want to fight about it anymore.

"Eina, there's plenty of time to be on a kibbutz," Dalia tells her. "You've got three months left of your service to work on Sufa. Plus you'll be going to Sufa for many weekends, right?"

"Three months working on Sufa is not enough," Eina whines.

I listen but don't intervene. I'm saving my reserves and building my own case in my head. The concept of serving in a uniform is still very important to me. And while I appreciate the "good life" of serving on a kibbutz, opting out of the Nahal Brigade for me at this point is not an option. I've come too far. I want to serve on a base. I'm determined to not let Svetlana and Eina stand in my way.

An officer summons us for our appointment, and we follow her down a narrow path until we reach a small office. She opens the doors and we file in.

Inside the air-conditioned office, a higher up with an insignia of two leaves on her shoulder indicating the rank of a *Sgan aluf*—lieutenant colonel—welcomes us in and gestures for us to sit. She quickly pulls out a pile of papers and folds her hands. She's got a cherubic face, but I don't expect anything positive to happen.

I grab a seat impatiently and start picking at my nails. *I would do anything to not be here.*

Eina and Svetlana start whispering in Russian.

Oh boy, here we go again. There's no way these girls are getting what they want.

"So what's this I hear about the two of you wanting to serve with Nahal Brigade 931 while the other two of you want to do *machleket meshek*? I've never heard of a garin not agreeing to a military assignment. Explain the problem. What's happening here?" She speaks affably, but the tone in her voice is assertive.

Eina and Svetlana lay out the reasons why we should work on a kibbutz as opposed to serving with the brigade, the main reason being the tension in the military and how it has impacted our garin so far. But this rationale feels weak to me. If the girls couldn't handle the pressures of serving in the military, then they should have requested an exemption from the army by declaring a low medical profile. Eina could have brought a note stating she was engaged to Carlos, her boyfriend. They're smart. They know the system. But instead of doing things right, they're making me and Dalia suffer. And something tells me I'd suffer even more with these girls on a kibbutz than on an army base, too.

Now I finally muster up the courage to speak up. I think back to Galit's visit during the first week of basic training. *You know, Dorit, there's nothing wrong with being alone. Actually, it makes one a much better and stronger person.*

"What if we just split?" I ask the officer. "Dalia and I go to the Nahal Brigade and Eina and Svetlana go to a kibbutz. It's clear we don't agree."

Eina and Svetlana both shoot me a look like, "How dare you?" but Dalia's slight nod encourages me.

The officer looks at me squarely in the face. "You know, I don't think splitting your garin is a good idea. After all, you've been through a lot together, and you're a small garin of immigrants. You need each other. What would be the point of separating you now?"

She sees our unsettled expressions and runs down a list in front of her. "Look *banot*, girls, as much as some of you may want to, the truth is, you *can't* work on a kibbutz. We don't have room on any of the kibbutzim. So it's settled. You'll be sent to Avivim, the first base of Nahal Brigade 931. You leave tomorrow. Good luck."

With that she gets up, shakes our hands, and leads us toward the open door.

There's heaviness in the air, but I feel overjoyed. Nahal Brigade 931, here we come.

∽

THE NEXT DAY, OUR BUS TAKES US UP THE MOUNTAIN TO our first Nahal Brigade assignment, a remote base in the upper Galilee not too far away from my aunt and uncle's kibbutz, Malkiyah. We're now cruising along the same road I once hitchhiked on as a volunteer two years ago.

I try to pick out familiar sights, but I don't recognize anything. I finally spot a base, but it's as if it's been intentionally camouflaged, it's so much a part of the landscape. Then I see one base, and then another—they're almost like little villages lying on top of each other.

An officer on the bus starts speaking about the strategic location of Avivim: Our base is less than one kilometer from the Shiite village Saliha and from the Blue Line, a border between Lebanon and Israel established in 2000 for purposes of identifying the withdrawal between Lebanon and the Israeli-controlled Golan Heights. I have no idea what to expect in terms of what kind of job I might have once we get to Avivim, but it's clear that it won't be a nine to five secretarial job. I intuitively feel that my new job will entail something that keeps the base running, but I don't quite exactly know yet what this will mean as far as my day to day life.

Knowing we are so close now to Lebanon awakens a far-distant memory: It is 1982, and I'm eleven years old, visiting my aunt and uncle at Malkiyah. I'm with my parents and it's the height of the Lebanese–Israeli war. All along the road on either side of the border are burnt cars with dark hollow spaces like cavernous eyes. Mom is startled by the number of destroyed cars, and though she stays silent, she pulls me closer. I'm too young to understand the specifics of this ongoing war, but I sense her fear.

Although there's no threat of a war now, as we close in on the last ten minutes of our journey, I realize I'm up against Mom's deep-rooted—and unrealistic—fears about Israel. Fear knocks on my door like an old childhood friend. The difference, though, is that now I can see, clear as day, that I don't want it anymore. It's not serving me. And I know that my fear of what might happen in Israel is based on the media images of terrorism and bombings that I've seen over the years. Yes, those things are real, but I now know that the picture the media paints is exaggerated. Mom would fret over a bomb exploding on this base, or alongside the border, but the chances of that happening are *low*, and furthermore, thinking and fretting about it all the time is pointless. People who've grown up here simply don't worry about what might happen. You are cautious, but you live your life. I choose to look to these people as examples, and to separate myself from Mom's warped picture of what life is like here. The fact that I'm here, right now, submerging myself in a piece of Israeli history that I was taught to fear, is symbolic of just how much I've already separated from Mom in this one short year abroad, and I relish that thought.

Each time I begin to think negative thoughts, I catch myself. *She controlled me back in the States, but I can't let her control me now.*

This is it. The moment of truth and change. We're almost at the base. This is where I need to get a handle on my fear. Somewhere in my youth, Mom planted the seed that Israel, as a country targeted by terrorists, is a place to be feared. But instead of thinking about that, I try focusing on my mission and why I'm here. *This service is real. You're safe. You're not going to be blown up.*

In the spring of 1990, when Dad told me I needed to get

out of the States to avoid becoming like Mom, I didn't feel I had a choice but to listen. It felt like he was threatening me; I panicked. Everyone has a fear of becoming like their mother, but my case was worse than most. It's only now, months into my service, that I'm finally understanding what my dad meant. What I took as a threat was actually him urging me to give myself a chance at a better life. He saw in me a young life force that was going to be smothered if I stayed in America under my mother's influence. He wanted me to live a freer life —and now I'm here, figuring out how to do just that, peeling away Mom's fears one layer at a time.

Just the slightest trigger, however, still opens a flood of worries. For example, whenever Officer Yaron so much as mentions "the border" or "the enemy," I want to launch straight into Mom's faulty and irrational messaging: "They'll blow you up!"

These are the voices I hear in my head, whether my mom has ever said these words explicitly to me or not. These are her fears. In her eyes, the world is a destructive and terrible place. My challenge now is to rebirth myself so that her fear is no longer a part of my DNA.

∞

A LONG, STRAIGHT ROAD BRINGS US UP TO ANOTHER, narrower road, and we take a sharp left into Avivim. It's a "closed" base, which means that we live onsite. But my parents have now arrived in Israel from the States—they've been here for three weeks now—which means I'll be leaving almost every Thursday for their home on Korazim, a small settlement that overlooks the Sea of Galilee.

Knowing that my dad and stepmom are close by is

comforting, but not as much as I thought it would be. I think it's because I've become emotionally independent after putting in almost eight months of service in the IDF. I'm no longer the person I was a year ago—and that realization both startles and delights me.

When we arrive, we're told that our base was previously inhabited by one of the paratrooper units, but it has now been taken over by the Nahal Brigade. The fact that the paratroopers, one of the most elite units in the IDF, were here before us fills me with pride. For the next three months, we will help make this place run smoothly. I allow these thoughts to buoy me.

On the first night at our new base, after we've had a chance to settle into our rooms, our officers gather us in the dining room and outline some of the history of the region, starting with the well-known Avivim school bus massacre. As I soak in the history, I check my knee-jerk reaction—*Our proximity to the Lebanese border makes us easy prey for any terrorist attack*—trying not to let these thoughts override me. Each time a worry or fearful thought creeps into my mind, I back up for a minute and initiate self-talk, beginning first with the place and then the people: *You know this part of the country. It's not foreign to you. If something threatening were to happen, however, you've got your family thirty minutes away and a bunch of soldiers right here who really seem to know what they're doing. You can always call on them for support.*

Then comes the harder part: reassuring myself that it's okay to ask for help and support from all these military professionals who look and behave so much more confidently than I do.

Our base borders the narrow road now called the Malkiyah-Avivim Security Road, a bypass route that passes Kibbutz Malkiyah and enables 1,500 children to go to and from school safely. I will myself not to get worked up by our proximity to the Lebanese border—to focus on the significance of serving in this region instead. We help provide security and peace of mind to hundreds of Israeli families. Important work.

If Mom were here, she'd probably hole up in the nearest bomb shelter, where she would worry herself sick that a bomb might explode right in front of her at any minute. And as her daughter, the closest person to her, I have always been a victim to the panic that kind of behavior stirs up in me. She could never understand the extent to which she has emotionally paralyzed me. But now that I'm here, and up against these fears every day, I'm full of intention. I choose freedom over fear each day, and I can actually see that I've become a different person since arriving. Sometimes I wonder if my mother would even recognize me if she saw me now.

⚮

ON OUR SECOND DAY AT AVIVIM, SVETLANA AND I TAKE a short hike up the hill to scout out the adjoining Moshav Avivim. It tickles me that there is an army base and a moshav by the same name since they are technically two different places. (A *moshav* is a cooperative agricultural community of farms, which tend to be individually owned.) At the *kolbo*— supermarket—we squeal at the sight of a discounted Pnina Rosenbloom spray deodorant bottle. Our little tradition continues as we spray each other's uniforms with the scented fragrance, hoping no one will notice. I have fun with Svetlana, and it gives me hope that maybe our relationship isn't so soured after all.

From this vantage point, overlooking Avivim the moshav and Avivim the base, I can see the border, or Blue Line. It's the same hilly and rocky terrain that we stand on, speckled with traditional Christmas colors, red kalaniyot and green grass. Even though peace and quiet reigns for now, from up on this hill it's clear what challenges Israel faces as a small country surrounded by many enemies. I feel small and insignificant in comparison to this large expanse—but I can handle it. Being an IDF soldier has helped me grow in ways I didn't quite anticipate when I began my service.

Unlike the girls, whose garin members have to stay together, the guys are given their assignments based on their medical profile. Most are placed on a variety of Nahal bases throughout Israel, and a few select individuals—those with the highest medical profiles—are sent to Lebanon to carry out particular missions. As of now, the ones with the highest medical profiles include Larry, Luis, and Igal, along with a few others I don't know from other garins. I wonder where they might be and how they might be faring. It might be weeks or even months before we see any of them again. It's possible we won't see some of them until we get back to Sufa, our home base.

We are allowed four days to acclimate to Avivim before we learn what our work options are. I'm given the choice of being in charge of the gun supply unit over at the far end of the base, or taking over the job as the records clerk. The records clerk job has many and varied tasks, and my main priority is to be as busy as possible, so I opt for that one.

Aviv, my twenty-one-year-old supervisor, is originally from Yemen and has a boyish-looking face and crew cut. When I report for my first day, he takes me to one end of an office that has been partitioned at the far end of a long trailer, an area with just two small windows through which light barely comes, and Aviv introduces me to the ropes of record keeping.

Everything seems easy at first, until we get to talking

about the numbers. Aviv tells me that our base is usually at capacity, with about two hundred soldiers here at any given time. But when I look at the numbers from the past six months, I can see that they're quite a bit lower than this.

"Why have there been so many fewer soldiers on the base over the past months?" I ask Aviv. I want to understand what lies behind the numbers.

"Some soldiers left the base for another unit. And a few soldiers were . . ." He looks into the far distance.

I don't press Aviv to finish. I wait.

"This base consists of a large battalion of soldiers for whom Avivim is a transition base once they return from Lebanon," he finally says. "Each time a large group of soldiers returns from enemy territory, the total number of soldiers on this base is then recounted. At any given time the base can hold two hundred soldiers. Maybe more."

"But surely one finds out if a soldier is hurt or wounded over army radio, right?"

"Right. The paperwork is just the final count. The low number that you saw—back in February 1991—that's when our brigade took the greatest hit."

"You mean . . . ?"

"Yes."

As he says this, I start to shiver. All I can think is, *What will happen if I find myself in a situation where we're losing soldiers? Will I be able to cope?* I've never witnessed death firsthand before, and Aviv's words have triggered the fear that lies just beneath the surface for me, the fear I strive to manage every day.

It has been six months since the end of the Persian Gulf War, but constant threats bombard this base. There have been terrorist attacks, army accidents, kidnappings, and of course there's the ongoing worry that another war will begin.

As if reading my mind, Aviv says, "There's something you come to realize as you do the work as a records clerk. The numbers. That's the sad part of our business."

Serving here as an IDF soldier is real. I realize I've always seen myself as separate from the soldiers who put their lives on the line in service of Israel, but I won't be able to do that here, performing this job. Ever since I've arrived to Avivim, I've been asking, "What if I did some kind of work that would require me to put my life on the line?" I don't feel the need to get special attention or be heroic, but part of me does feel let down by the fact that my work doesn't amount to something life-saving. I don't put myself on the line every day like many other IDF soldiers do. Here, a soldier can die at any moment—a far different reality than I ever faced in New York City—and it's all in the name of service. Is what I'm doing enough?

∞

I'VE HARDLY SEEN DALIA SINCE WE ARRIVED AT AVIVIM, so I'm excited to finally get a chance to connect with her when we see each other at dinner the next day.

"Everything okay? How's it going with you?" I ask, dishing out a spoonful of zesty Israeli salad. "What does the famous and popular Dalia do as the clerk of the battalion?" I'm hoping she'll share some intimate details about her job, which seems really interesting.

She plays with her salad, eyeing the doorway cautiously, as if one of her soldiers might walk through any minute. "I bring the guys meals, care packages, and mail, and generally hang out with them from dawn to dusk."

"Where do you bring them the stuff?"

She points to the hill in the distance. "There's a long bunker down there. On the opposite side of the base."

"Dawn to dusk. That's a pretty long time to hang out with the guys." I smile playfully, and she seems to warm up to me.

"Well, it's not every day. It's only for a few days at a time, before they go to Lebanon and after they come back."

"What do you do when the guys are in Lebanon?"

"We chat on army radio to make sure they're all okay. If there's a problem, I let either Yaron or Ronen know."

"Are they back from Lebanon right now?"

"Yes, but only for a few days, and then they're going back."

The chances of seeing the guys who return from Lebanon are pretty low. They only come into the dining room for meals, and then they go down the hill to their bunker. I'm impressed by Dalia's insider knowledge, and a little jealous that she gets to hang out with the guys every day.

"What's life like for them when they're there?" I ask.

"They have a very hard life over there. Their lives are constantly on the line. One soldier almost collapsed from dehydration this week. Another soldier had trauma spells and tried to commit suicide."

The word "suicide" sends a jolt up my spine. I feel as if I'm having a real awakening here. We are in the IDF. This is real. But because Israel is wired to be so social, and group dynamics are so strongly emphasized in the army, I know that no one has to suffer in silence. In contrast, we are encouraged to share our burdens with others; there's no excuse for closing yourself away. Accepting this shift in mentality was a shock for me at first, but I have grown to appreciate it, though I haven't fully embraced the way I should. What if I allowed myself to be a part of this group mentality? Part of me feels this is the link that has been missing for much of my youth. This could be the beginning of everything.

∾

EVER SINCE LEARNING OF THE ATTACK IN LEBANON THAT left some of our soldiers wounded, I have felt a heightened desire for security, one that makes me strap my gun to myself everywhere I go. Is this feeling going to go away once we reach our Hoshniya, our next base? The only time I relax is when Svetlana and I leave Avivim and hike up to the supermarket to spray Pnina Rosenblum deodorant on each other. There, laughing in the aisles, is the only place I feel entirely relaxed.

Two weeks after our soldiers come home from Lebanon, Lieutenant Colonel Yaron calls all of us into his one-room office, an attachment to one of the trailers, for hands-on instruction on how to react in case of enemy fire. From what I understand, tension has been heating up in enemy territory. Sometime within the last twenty-four hours, the Hezbollah, a Shi'a Islamic militant group and political party based in Lebanon, activated an IED (improvised explosive device) at the security fence near the northern border, and an anti-tank missile was launched at IDF soldiers.

This news, of course, threatens my sense of inner peace and security. At first I refuse to give into Mom's fears, but when I fully comprehend what we're up against, fear and panic creep in on me. This time I don't fight the feelings— and, surprisingly, they fade away as quickly as they surfaced. It's not about me anymore, I realize. It's about having faith that we are all strong enough to survive this moment, and to move forward together. The group mentality of the IDF now really sinks into me. In the short period of time I've been here at Avivim, I have developed faith in it that I never had before.

"We'll continue to act to protect the civilians of Israel!" Yaron shouts over the sea of soldiers that I am a part of. "The civilians all along the border woke up this morning to the sound of Code-Red alarms and rockets. It's our job to seek out and target those who wish to attack our civilians and soldiers and to eliminate their capabilities. Hezbollah rocket terrorism is intolerable. Israelis should not have to accept this."

I wonder why *we* haven't heard any alarms and rockets. I look around the room. Male soldiers sit on the floor, lean against the doors, and sit on tables, listening attentively to Lieutenant Colonel Yaron's words.

"There's a commander of the Northern Tracking Unit that operates near the Lebanese border and consists only of Nahal soldiers of our brigade," Yaron continues.

I wonder if the guys in our garin are in a platoon of that same tracking unit, or if they are part of a different brigade. I'm confused.

Svetlana, Eina, and I sit on the few chairs in the room. Perhaps we can allow ourselves to be comfortable while Yaron talks about a fairly uncomfortable subject—war and enemy fire—because the truth of the matter is, we will not be going to war. Should war come to us, we female Nahal soldiers will be instructed to take cover. I make a mental note to ask Yaron logistical questions about bomb shelters and gas masks.

Yaron displays a surveillance-type topography map that has been created using pictures from an infrared camera. It shows our area and the surrounding army bases, and finally the enemy territory: Lebanon. There's a lot of technical vocabulary about the area I'm clueless about. Nobody bothers to check everyone's understanding; it's assumed we have the relevant background knowledge to follow along. Even though I'm struggling to take in all the information, it's nice to know that everything about our terrain and position is shared with all of us, regardless of our position here at the base. I'm proud to know I've been trusted with the power to keep our country safe. Since I'm "behind the scenes" and don't have a high combat role to deal with, this information isn't as crucial for me to know as it is for the guys who will be going into Lebanon, but I am still on this base with everyone else, and so I am included.

As Yaron begins to go over the three rules for taking cover during an enemy attack, I glance at Dalia, Eina, and Svetlana. They are listening intently, just like I am. We all take our responsibilities here seriously, but in comparison to native-born soldiers, we have to work extra hard to make sure we understand what's being said. Eina twitches her mouth every time she hears something important.

Out of the three girls, Eina's the one I trust the most in terms of her understanding of Hebrew, but I'm afraid to ask her any questions, and I don't want to ask any of the male soldiers for fear they might perceive me as a weakling, so I decide to just tough it out. Yaron continues talking. A few soldiers laugh. Eina pulls Svetlana aside and whispers something in her ear, then both of them look at me and laugh. I make a mental note: *Don't ask Eina anything. Either stay silent or ask Dalia.*

Two days later, Eina and Svetlana make an appointment to speak with Yaron to request once again that they be sent to work on a kibbutz. He does not give in to their request.

I don't know why they're so eager to leave; I enjoy life in the platoon. I have no complaints about my job. When Aviv recommends me for a human resources course, I politely decline because I don't want to leave even for a short time.

I've learned something invaluable during my time here at Avivim: I am in control of my thoughts. I don't have to be sucked in by fear. I don't have to remain emotionally paralyzed. I can choose to be the victim or not.

We have two more bases to go: Hoshniya and then Gaza.

I'm stronger than I realized. And I'm ready.

19

STUCK ON HOSHNIYA

JANUARY 1992. WE ASCEND THE BUS, OUR DUFFEL BAGS
weighing us down. There's a light carpet of snow, but patches
of green invariably peek through, indicating that spring is
almost in sight. We're on our way to our second closed base:
Hoshniya. To get there, we go back down that familiar side of
the mountain in the Upper Galilee of Israel and snake up
another, unfamiliar one to the Golan Heights, twenty kilometers southeast of the Syrian-Israeli border. I'll still be a
thirty-minute drive from my parents. Life couldn't be better.

By early afternoon, all two hundred of us, who have for
the most part been together since Avivim, gather in the drab,
grey-green, U-shaped base formerly occupied by the tank
division. Unlike Avivim, the terrain here is entirely flat, with
just a glimpse of an unknown mountain in the distance, and a
few trees scattered around. In the middle of the base, there's a
sign bearing the Nahal Brigade insignia, which consists of
yellow, blue, and red half-arrows circling through a torch and
scythe on a green background.

Our six-by-eight room is at the far left side of the U, and

has just enough room for two metal bunks for Dalia, Eina, Svetlana, and myself. We're next to the *mercazia*—communications rooms—the only place with an outside phone line.

Here, as at Avivim, my job is to cross out and enter names in the same large green ledger, sort files, and put stuff in envelopes. For the most part, we as department units and heads have traveled together from Avivim. The only noticeable difference between life at Avivim and life here at Hoshniya, really, is that the other garin of girls has been released from the IDF and a new garin known as *Garin V'zehu!*—"Garin and that's it!"—has taken their place. There are eleven of them in all.

Two weekends in, Yael from the new garin asks if I will switch weekends with her, which means I'll be slated to stay that weekend with just Svetlana. It's a logic I don't quite understand: why would the IDF order only two out of a total of fifteen girls to stay at the base on a cold, snowy weekend? There will also be a handful of male soldiers and a few supervisors, of course—a total of twenty soldiers, all told—but it's puzzling that they feel compelled to keep any girls here if there will only be two of us.

It's been a long time since Svetlana and I have spent a weekend alone together, and I'm not so thrilled about the idea. We sometimes have fun together, but we've never been kindred spirits. Plus, I'm anxious to go home to Korazim to see my parents. But no other girl agrees to the switch, and after Yael asks me several times, I finally give in at the last minute. She gives me the hearty version of "chapcha," or a hearty pat on the back in exchange for granting the favor. I'm not sure if I did the right thing, but there's no changing my mind now.

Israel is experiencing record-breaking, below-freezing temperatures, and everyone on the base walks around in snowsuits from morning to night. On the weekend I am staying at the base in Yael's stead, I wake up with a terrible urge to go to the bathroom. I slip on my snowsuit and open the door. It's stuck at first, but I push it firmly until it opens—only to reveal heaps of snow on the other side of the door.

I slog outside and swish-swash my way to the bathroom. The pipes are completely frozen, and the bathrooms are too disgusting to use. I go outside, in the snow.

All throughout the day, there are power failures, so we can't heat any food. During the day, long windy stretches mimic the sound of hyenas. Snow completely covers the *Shekemit*—the painted "goodie truck" that sells Crembos, which are dome-shaped vanilla- and mocha-flavored marshmallows covered with chocolate. Just its candy pink-and-blue face is slightly visible. The snowflakes resemble soap suds.

The IDF manages to procure a small water tank for us, just enough for face washing, drinking, and teeth brushing. By Saturday mid-afternoon, the storms have become so violent, with below-freezing wind chill, that there's now talk that all the soldiers who left the base won't be able to return on Sunday due to impassable roads. Why the heck did I make that last minute switch? Sunday's the day when the food supply trunk is supposed to arrive, and our food supply is dwindling.

"What are we going to do?" I ask Svetlana. I feel desperate, and I can't let go of the fact that this is not my weekend to be at the base.

"I don't know. This is crazy." She shakes her head.

It's an hour before my afternoon shift at the communications room and I'm starving. I passed on breakfast because the food was practically frozen. Now I'm regretting that decision.

"How could there be so little food to begin with?" I wail. "This doesn't make sense."

"Don't fret," Svetlana says calmly. "We'll figure out something. Let's go to the dining room and see what we can find."

We slowly trudge our way to the kitchen. The snow has now come up almost to our waists. We find remnants of whatever is left in drawers and the pantry—*halva*, a sesame and honey roll, grape juice, and dried cinnamon rolls.

Just as I stuff the last bit of a cinnamon roll in my mouth, Svetlana cries out, "Come! Look what I found!" She holds open the refrigerator door and we both peer inside.

At the far end of the refrigerator is a brown box stuffed with small cottage cheese containers, a huge block of yellow cheese, crates of cucumbers and tomatoes, jars of jellies, a few cartons of eggs, and a bag of olives and pickles—enough food to last for a few days. How did we not notice this before?

"This is a miracle!" I shout. I reach for the eggs. "Should we hard-boil these?"

"Yes! Let's make egg salad. We've got the mayonnaise," Svetlana says.

We fumble, trying to find matches in the cold to light the gas-operated stove so we can boil the eggs for our egg salad, and come up empty.

"Oh, now what are we going to do!" I cry.

"Wait a minute, I've got an idea!" Svetlana quietly steps into the cooks' sleeping quarters, adjacent to the kitchen. The door's ajar.

"Why are you trying to be so quiet?" I call after her. "They're gone, you know."

She returns with a Zippo lighter.

"Svetlana, you're a genius!" I cry, beaming. "Amazing!"

We both chuckle.

Our water supplies have now become so limited that there isn't enough to waste on cooking. "Why don't we heat snow for the eggs?" I suggest.

"Great idea!"

With my mittened hands, I scoop snow and dump it into the pot. We light the burner, and bubbles soon begin to emerge from the lid.

I breathe a sigh of relief, pull off my mittens, and put my hands closer to the flame so I can warm my body at the same time. "Ah. This feels so good."

Svetlana rummages in the pantry. "Ooh, forget the mayonnaise. I've got something better—this!" She holds up a can.

I lift my fogged glasses and peer closely at the plain white wrapping under the words "IDF." I make out the word "beets."

"Ugh," I say, making a face. "I can't stand beets."

Mom loves borscht, beet soup. When I was a kid, she'd often buy the Manischewitz brand in the kosher section of our local supermarket, or she'd eat Grandma's homemade version when we visited her for the Jewish holidays in Far Rockaway. She would breathe deeply between each slurp. "Have some, Dorit. It's delicious. It'll build up your immunity." She'd push a bowl toward me. "A *bissele*?" she'd ask—Yiddish for "a bite?"—and she'd push it toward me. "This is what we ate in the old country with your Grandma."

I always shook my head. I got nauseous just smelling it. Just like with everything else, Mom was completely out of touch with my tastes. Whether it was food, music, or fashion, I had to advocate for myself if I wanted to get what I actually wanted.

Then again, being here has been a constant practice in being more open. So rather than continuing to resist, I figure I can give the beets a try—make giving them a chance a small way in which I'm accepting into my life the things I think I dislike due to associations I have with my mother.

C'mon, Dorit, a voice says. *That was a long time ago. Give it a try.*

"Actually," I say. "I haven't had them in a long time. Maybe I will like them."

Svetlana flashes me a smile, and she slices the beets while I slice the eggs. She rummages again in the pantry and procures a number of spices I don't recognize, but I don't question her. *Trust that everything is going to work out for the best.*

Together, we whip up an egg-beet salad concoction. It looks quite tantalizing, but still I hesitate. *Am I really going to like this?* At this point, I don't have much of a choice—I'm starving —but I'm nervous.

"Here, Svetlana. You try it first. It looks mushy."

She eagerly scoops a bit. "It's really good. Creamy. You'll like it. It has the same texture as a Crembo. We ate this practically boiled in Russia—like a soup."

"Okay, let me try!"

Svetlana laughs as I gingerly scoop a little and taste it.

"Wow! Not bad. Not bad at all." With each bite, I slowly move away from the past. I take the smells, the creamy taste, everything, all in. It's another way of connecting to the here and now of this moment. Just like I connect to the "real" Israel as I'm experiencing it, I connect to tastes that enliven my senses instead of filling me up with anxiety.

Still, I can't help but say, "You really ate this stuff boiled? Are you kidding me? Like double yuck-yuck!" Although it tastes perfectly fine now, the idea of eating it boiled just conjures up images of Mom's borscht.

Svetlana laughs and shrugs. "It's better than you think!"

Between mouthfuls, we talk about our plans for our next *regila*—week off—which is coming up in a few weeks. My last one was right before basic training.

"Don't you ever wish you could just go back to your home

country?" Svetlana asks between mouthfuls while I pick a bit of beet from the back of my mouth with my tongue.

"Hmmm. No. I don't think I want to go back to New York City."

"I'll never understand people like you, Dorit. Why are you even here? If you ask me, you should be in America right now."

Since we met, the way we've perceived each other has only been based on judgment and observation. I'm the American who left the good life. She thinks I have it easy, and so she projects her issues onto me. I can go back and she can't—that has been the source of our tension since the first day. She fled Communist Russia, the hard life, for an even harder one in the IDF. I empathize with her plight, but it's never been easy to sympathize, since she's been nothing but a thorn in my side for all these months. Plus, there's nothing I can do about the fact that I come from where I come from. But now that Svetlana and I are on neutral territory, and things have gotten better between us, I am feeling a new openness with her that compels me to want to share the real reason I'm here.

The one thing keeping me back is the fact that, based on what I've seen, Svetlana couldn't care less about building an emotional connection with other soldiers—the very thing I've been longing for since I got here. If I open up about Mom, will she understand, or will it make me feel more isolated than I already do? I'm not sure, but Svetlana restored my faith in her humanity when she tried to help me during the march at Base Camp 80.

It's time to share, Dorit, I decide.

"Svetlana," I blurt. "There's something you gotta know. I left America because of my mom. She put me through some difficult situations. We didn't agree on a lot of things. We had some serious problems. So that's why I'm here."

"Your mom in New York City, or your stepmom who lives here?"

"No, my real Mom. *Ima amitit.*"

Svetlana nods her head as if to say, "I see." I know she's especially close to her mom, whom I've met a few times at their small apartment. I don't know if I'm looking for reassurance, or just a bit of sympathy, but it feels good to open up in this way.

The winds drum up again and pelt the front door, sending it swinging shut. Then another gust comes, and it bangs open. Back and forth it flies.

I find a large rock and wedge it against the door to keep it in its place, then return to the kitchen counter and pile the dirty dishes in the sink. The dishwashing liquid is frozen as solid as the pipes.

Svetlana zips up her snowsuit. "Let's take some of these," she says, stuffing some cottage cheese containers and a few crusty rolls in her pockets. I do the same. "I don't know about you, but I don't want to keep leaving my room for food each time."

Despite the cold, I feel better than I have in days as we trudge back to our rooms.

∽

BY ONE O'CLOCK IN THE MORNING ON SUNDAY, WE'RE completely snowed in. Winds strike up an eerie sonata against the window of the far communications room, where I'm about to work my shift. It seems to be a message that I'm going to be staying here for a while. I'm alone.

I gently nudge Svetlana, who has been in the communications room for the last twelve hours and has fallen asleep. I wistfully eye the cot that's set up for us in case we need to rest, knowing that I've got to stay awake, then thumb to the page I'd left off on in the well-worn edition of *David Copperfield* I've been making my way through. The army radio—thankfully, the generator the IDF brought us is still working—plays a slew of classics: The Moody Blue's "Nights in White Satin," Duran Duran's "Hungry like the Wolf," and Cyndi Lauper's "Time after Time." For a moment, I allow myself to get lost between space and time—neither here nor there. These songs connect to the raw emotions of my heart. I try staying awake for Elton John's "Sacrifice," but I'm too zonked, and I fall asleep.

I awake to a nudge, and sit straight up. A glance at the clock tells me it's six in the morning; it's been five hours since I fell asleep.

"C'mon, get up Dorit," Svetlana says. "The Deputy Battalion just called. We need to phone all the soldiers who went away for the weekend to tell them not to return today. The phone lines are working. We've got more than a hundred soldiers to call."

My eyes are wide open now. "A hundred soldiers? You got to be kidding. This is totally unfair!"

"I know, I know. But what can we do?"

"But there's just one phone. It'll take hours," I wail like a child.

"C'mon, c'mon," Svetlana says. "You can do it."

I get a grip and think about Ayelet. *Sometimes we have to do the things we don't want to do.* I know it's true, but I'm still pissed. *Fuck, fuck, fuckity-fuck. Can someone remind me why I'm here? Why the heck am I doing this?*

I trudge to the *mercazia* in my snowsuit. Snow isn't falling, but the wind is moaning, and some snow manages to get past my snowsuit and into my boots.

Once I make it back safely to the communications rooms, I peel off my wet woolen socks and plug in the spiral foot heater. *At least the stupid foot heaters are working.* I raise my feet to the heater to defrost them, then look up at Svetlana, who's eyeing me with concern. She senses my tension.

"I'll do the first fifty and you do the second fifty," I say. "Fair?"

"Fair."

The first ten parents are pleasantly surprised to know their loved one can stay an extra day.

"Really? Wow. Thank you so much."

"We'll call you again tomorrow to let you know if the roads are cleared and if they need to come back to the base." Our officers have told us that this will be the protocol for the next few days. But I am full of dread. How am I going to muster the strength to call fifty soldiers each day when I'm stuck here in the freezing cold?

By the time I inform the eleventh parent, I'm fighting to keep my voice level—fighting to keep myself from breaking down. *Why the heck did I agree to switch with Yael? Why?*

"Where are you calling from?" one of the parents asks.

"I'm calling from the base in the Golan Heights. Hoshniya."

"Oh, wow. Be careful, and stay warm and dry. I heard it's really rough up there."

"It is. We've been stuck here for the last four days due to a snowstorm. Power outages, Frozen pipes. A dwindling supply of food." Tears threaten to choke me. Almost all of the soldiers on this base have families in the center of the country—about a four-and-a-half-hour bus ride away. Svetlana, Eina, Dalia, and I are the only immigrants. Having our families in the country makes coping with army life easier, but right now my family seems so very far away.

"Oh my god. If I had a way to get it up to you, I'd deliver a care package to you. You soldiers are the lifeline of this nation. I treat all the soldiers in Israel like they're my own sons and daughters. You're one of them."

"Thank you so much. I appreciate it," I say, hanging up the phone. The woman's words help to sweeten this sour moment. I'm still upset, but I also feel I've just completed an exercise in reinforcing my sense of national duty.

I approach the next batch of calls with a renewed sense of positivity. Connecting with the parents of fifty soldiers from this corner of the communications room is my lifeline to the outside world. It's as if all their parents are all a part of my family. We chat and laugh as the winds howl outside, And I can sense their excitement with each call. By the time I'm halfway in, I'm feeling pretty good about this rigmarole. This isn't just a duty—it's a goodwill exercise. I've just called fifty soldiers to tell them they have an extra day to stay at home. It's actually pretty nice to be the bearer of good news.

∞

EACH DAY FOR THE NEXT FOUR DAYS, WE BOTH CALL OUR share of fifty soldiers with updates. By the end of the fourth day, I've gotten to know the parents' voices.

"Hello again. It's me again, Dorit from Hoshniya. Your son has another day to stay home. Roads are still impassable."

"Oh, wow. Thank you. This couldn't have happened at a better time. I just feel bad for you guys. I hope you guys get off the base soon. This seems to be going on for a long time already."

"Thanks. I hope so too."

I end up having a thirty-minute conversation with one of

the parents. Turns out that her son is one of many who has just returned from Lebanon.

"You know, before this surprise visit, I hadn't seen my son in over three months."

"Wow. That must be hard."

"It's okay. I've gotten used to it," she says.

Until now, I haven't given much thought to how Mom might be feeling, not having seen me for almost eighteen months.

"Do you want to come for a meal the first weekend you're off the base?" she asks.

"I'd love that," I say. "We've been talking for three days straight already—I feel as if I already know you. I'll let you know, okay? Hopefully it will be sooner than later." I chuckle. *Making these calls really isn't that bad. Look at the good things that are emerging as a result of them.*

"And don't forget to bring your Russian friend with you," she says. "The more the merrier."

"Wow, thank you. These last few days have been rough. Our conversation is really lifting my spirits."

"*Al tidagi,* don't worry. The snowstorm should stop soon, the reports say."

"I hope so. It certainly doesn't feel like it."

I hang up the phone, cross another family name off the list, and turn around to face Svetlana.

"Wow!" I exclaim. "Just wow."

"What? What is it?" asks Svetlana looking up from her Russian magazine. It's clear she's desperate for some good news.

"You wouldn't believe what one of the parents of the soldiers just did—she invited me for a Shabbat meal the first weekend we get off the base! So cool. Just what I needed to hear. And she told me I could bring you too! Wanna come?"

"Sure. Where do they live?"

"Ashqelon. Your neck of the woods." I smile.

"Awesome!"

Where in the States can one feel a sense of community and safety like this? I've experienced it only in Israel. My situation may be tough, but the people in this country are making it more bearable.

∽

HOMECOMING. TODAY'S THE DAY THE REMAINING soldiers are supposed to return from their extra four days at home. All twenty of us soldiers who have been stuck here, including the supervisors, are waiting with fierce anticipation. After four exhausting days, signs of life are finally emerging. The winds are dying down. Melting snow reveals faded patches of green. A food truck finally makes its way to the base. I wake up to the sound of an engine.

I must be dreaming. An engine!

I pull the curtain and dash out. Other soldiers are already waiting.

"Svetlana, the bus!" I call over my shoulder as I burst through the door. "A bus full of soldiers! They're here!"

She moves lethargically, having spent practically an entire night at the communications room. Between the two of us, we managed to cover four eight-hour shifts for almost the whole past week, twelve hours for each of us every day.

A barrage of soldiers, all dressed in freshly pressed travel uniforms, piles out of the first bus. First to emerge is Tzili, the one in charge of operating the "goodie truck."

"*Oh Elohim, eize balagan poh*—oh my god, what a mess here!" he shouts.

He eyes me. I can see how almost six days at home has

lifted his skin, softened his face, and made his brown eyes glow. I'm sure I look haggard and pale by comparison.

Svetlana rushes out. Her eyes are puffy, her hair is unbrushed, and her snowsuit is unbuttoned, but she's a barrel of smiles.

"*Oh, eize yoffi*—how great!" she shouts. "Now we'll get Crembos!" She claps wildly with delight.

I share her excitement, but I'm less concerned with sweets and more concerned with getting off this base. "Forget the Crembos, silly! Let's speak with Ronen about taking that *regila* early—as in, *now*. We've earned it!" I point to a Jeep that has just turned a bend and is now slowly pulling up to a curb closest to the U part of our base.

Yaron and Ronen quickly make their way toward us, their guns banging behind them. I feel tingly all over.

Yaron's the first to speak. "You girls deserve a medal. What you did was incredible—holding down the base like that. You guys are heroes. That wasn't easy."

We smile—weakly, but with pride.

"Tell me about it!" I shout. "Now about that *regila* you mentioned on the phone . . . can we get it now instead of waiting a few more weeks?"

"Sure, why not?" Ronen beams. "As Yaron said, you guys deserve it."

∞

TWO HOURS LATER, SVETLANA AND I HITCHHIKE DOWN the mountain. Although I should feel nervous about hitchhiking, I'm actually quite at peace about it. There's aren't that many soldiers hitchhiking at this time of day in the Golan Heights and second, I feel safe with Svetlana.

"We need more than just a week off from the army—we

need to get released, like right about now!" I say, and we laugh like crazy.

Once we reach the main road, we head in different directions. I'm heading straight to the soldier's hitchhike stop hopefully to get a ride to see my parents. Svetlana, meanwhile, will wait at the bus stop for the 845 express bus bound for Tel Aviv, where she'll then catch another bus to Ashqelon, some two hours away, where her family is.

Although we need time away from each other after such an ordeal, I'm taking a very important lesson with me: snap judgments can come back to bite you. Both Svetlana and I have suffered from having projected our own issues onto each other, and this weekend has given us an opportunity to see each other for the truth of who we really are. We have always ended up pulling away from each other when things have gotten tough, but our relationship is finally showing signs of promise. Last week's ordeal has taught us a lot, and brought us closer. Without patience, tolerance, compassion, and under-standing, we could have spent the week fighting, screaming, and blaming each other for the difficult situation we found ourselves in—but instead we both chose to work it out without holding grudges, and to see the good in each other instead of getting on each other's nerves. Finding compassion hasn't always been easy with Svetlana, but I managed to locate it this week, and I'm so glad I did.

No sooner do I stick out my index finger than a ride arrives. Just before jumping in, I rush over to Svetlana and give her a hug.

"Thanks for surviving with me. Maybe I'll see you on Sufa, at the disco?" I'm not sure I want to make the six-and-a-half-hour trip south to the Negev desert, where Svetlana and I still share a room, but I'm thinking about it.

She gives me a thumbs-up and smiles. "I'll give you a call."

"Sounds good!"

We give each other another tight squeeze.

"Safe trip. Don't fall asleep anymore!"

"Don't worry!" she cries.

For the first time, I feel I've made a real connection with Svetlana.

It looks like we've finally come full circle.

ONCE I REACH THE KORAZIM JUNCTION, I CROSS THE BUSY highway and take the back entrance to my parents' settlement by climbing over metal barriers and walking down a paved road with parked cars on either side. Beautifully designed villas line both sides of this relatively young settlement. It's early Friday afternoon—just a few hours before sundown and Shabbat, the celebration of the Sabbath.

At one point, I bend down and notice a cluster of yellow flowers trying to peek their way through the light white carpet of snow. Having just left a snowy base, I feel transplanted to a completely different place and time. It's utterly surreal.

I continue walking down the road. The transition from a military base to a beautiful settlement filled with families I hardly know is beyond weird, but I'm happy to know that what I've been missing for the last five stays by staying on a base is still here waiting for me.

At the first junction, I turn left and continue walking until I reach the first villa overlooking the Sea of Galilee—my parents' house.

I turn the doorknob of the back entrance of the house and walk up the marble stairs.

"Hello! I'm here!" I cry.

I'm greeted by the smell of onions frying; the house is warm and toasty.

Now I know I'm not on a base.

My stepmother emerges just as I reach the stop of the stairs. "Hey, it's Dorit! You made it!" she cries.

"Phew. What a week!" I exclaim, giving her a big hug. "I don't ever want to go through *that* again."

The aromas of tonight's dinner—a tantalizing concoction of meat and potatoes—emanate from the kitchen. I sniff the air, feeling more excited to eat than I have in weeks.

I walk into the kitchen to find Dad chopping fennel and other vegetables for our special Friday meal.

"*Ahalan*—hello!" I exclaim heartily. "It's feels so good to be home."

As weird as it may sound, I feel a vague sense of disappointment now that I'm here. After enduring the larger-than-life obstacles of the past week at Hoshniya—things I've never experienced back in New York City or even here in Israel—I'm not so sure what to make of a tasty meal, family, and a warm shower. In the past few days, I did the impossible: I weathered the cold in a remote base; endured the hardship of little water and food; and forged a friendship with Svetlana, someone I'd given up on ever connecting with. Now that I've intimately experienced what it means to survive, I understand how fear and uncertainty prevent us from working hard to overcome something difficult. Knowing we were stuck in the snow with limited food put me into fear mode, but with each passing day, I reprogrammed myself to work with the conditions, see the positive, and keep the faith. Here in this cozy and homey environment, there are no obstacles—there is no need to endure—and somehow this in itself is a bit of a letdown. I'm nowhere near being tested and put to the edge.

"What's up?" Dad asks, noticing my glum expression. "Is everything okay?"

"Yeah, everything's okay. Just point me to the nearest shower—I've got to get these clothes off!" I joke. "I've been sleeping, walking, living, and breathing in my uniform day *and* night for a week!"

Within minutes, I'm soaping my grimy body under scalding hot water. The steam practically burns me, but I don't care. It's heaven. When I finally open the window, the steam rushes out and I allow myself to ponder this past week's ordeal. The fact that I didn't crack under the pressure makes me feel like a hero. I didn't save anyone's life, but I did keep the base running, *and* I kept my relationship with Svetlana alive. My sense of achievement goes much deeper than just knowing I manned a communications room or received accolades from my commanding officers. It's knowing that I've finally found a way into Svetlana's somewhat cold and unpredictable heart, and that we made it through together.

20

FINDING LOVE IN GAZA

IT'S NOW APRIL 1992, AND EVER SINCE WE ARRIVED AT our new base in the Gaza Strip two days ago, I have been wandering from one side of the tent netting to the other. I want to know if there is life beyond this base beyond what the media has taught me. But taking a walk outside is not an option right now: there is a dust cloud so ominous outside the netting that any kind of exploration outside is out of the question.

I'm exiting my office—a room partitioned by fabric and netting—when Maoen, an Arabic-speaking soldier in charge of the weapons and supplies from one of the Druze villages up north, jumps down from a Zim shipping container and comes my way.

Maoen is the newest addition to this base, most recently assigned to the weaponry unit. Speaking to an Arabic-speaking soldier is intimidating for me—in my mind and my limited experience, Arabs are Arabs. They are the enemy. But this is not true of Druze, who are on our side. Druzim do not live in the Israeli-occupied territories—they typically live on remote villages scattered throughout the country, primarily in the North of Israel—and therefore are required by law to serve in the Israeli army.

"*Ma Yanim*—what's up?" he says loudly, reaching for my hand and squeezing it. "I'm so glad you're here! Last night was rough, with all the soldiers leaving. But today we'll have an easy day—just you and me."

I'm not sure what to make of his enthusiasm over us spending an easy day together. I've only been on this base for a little over a week, and we've only casually run into each other, mainly in the dining room. We've gotten some stares and raised looks from other soldiers when we've talked at dinner— I guess because Druze men are typically not supposed to have relationships with other women outside their village and their marriages are arranged. But Maoen is gentle and unobtrusive. He seems sweet, and I'd like to get to know him better.

Today's lighter paperwork load is conducive for doing just that. We're working in the Zim container—a makeshift office on a raised platform situated a bit away from the tent, which offers just enough privacy to have a conversation. I sit cross-legged on the floor next to Maoen's desk while he fills out slips tracking last night's checked out uniforms, supplies, and guns. He has beautiful penmanship—his Hebrew is clear and easy to read.

I notice a black beanbag in the corner, and instantly flop over onto it. "I miss these kinds of hollow spaces; they're like play spaces."

"Play spaces?" he asks. He knows some English, but Hebrew is our common language and the language we always speak together.

"Yeah—didn't you ever have a secret play place as a kid that you could get lost in forever?" I ask. "This container reminds me of my father's studio in the building I grew up in in New York City. That was one of my favorite play spaces."

"Tell me about New York," he prompts.

I tell Maoen about some of the highlights: weekend trips to Central Park and bike rides along the Hudson River; growing up in Greenwich Village and living in Westbeth. I share with him, too, what it was like to go shopping on Atlantic Avenue in Brooklyn on Sundays—taking the subway and buying warm, fresh pita bread and hummus from Arabic-speaking Syrians.

As Maoen listens to me, I can feel a special kind of openness from him, and his face lights up in response to the memories I'm sharing. Perhaps getting lost in someone else's memories, from a country he's never been to, offers him a momentary reprieve from the stress of his life here.

Up until now, any conversation I've had about America has ended in an interrogation about why I chose to come to Israel, but Maoen is genuinely fascinated with my world, which in turn fuels my desire to get to know his. Where does this twenty-one-year-old soldier come from? What is life like for a Druze like Maoen? How are his social customs different than the non-Druze community's?

"If you come to my village, you'll see exactly how pita is made," he says. He tells me about the huge brick ovens people make pita in, and how the dough is laid on top of the ovens.

"Bubbles start forming at the top, until it becomes hard, and then we take a big wooden server and dish it out," he tells me. "The doughy balls are usually made the night before—but also sometimes right before they go in."

"I'm getting hungry just listening to you," I say. On our last base, we took a bus trip from the Upper Galilee to the Golan Heights and passed through Majdal Shams, a Druze town in the southern foothills of Mount Hermon, north of the Golan Heights. We stopped at a restaurant there, and I saw one of these brick ovens full of pita. I had just enough time to spread *Labane*—a soft, tart cheese—and za'atar, a Middle Eastern spice mixture on mine before we had to go. It was heavenly, and I'm happy that I had this experience so I can envision exactly what Maoen is sharing with me.

"Usually every household has one or a group of families that share an oven. Hmm . . . let me see if I can make a pita for us," he says, his face lighting up. "This will be fun! Wait right here!"

I love that Maoen is so hands-on and eager. How the heck does he know where to get flour on this base in the middle of nowhere? Minutes later, though, he's set up a pita-making station complete with a rolling pin, lots of flour, water, olive oil, salt, and sugar, and we're mixing and rolling together. I'm conscious of the space between us. Between grabs of dough, our hands touch.

He grabs my hand under the gooey dough. "Gotcha!" he cries.

I let his hand rest on mine, our fingers intertwined in the cool, moist dough. "Maoen," I tell him, knowing full well I'm changing the subject, "I've never made dough before."

"Never made dough?" He looks at me like I've just said the most shocking thing in the world. "Dough is a big part of our lives." he says.

"There's a first time for everything," I say, smiling.

Maoen returns my smile. "I like you. You're very unique. An American Israeli."

I'm touched by his sincerity, and yet at the same time I'm wondering if he is crossing a line he's not supposed to cross, given what I know about his culture. Druze are deferential and respectful, and they're not supposed to have relationships with women outside of their community. And yet he does seem to be adhering to those rules—he's polite, and he gives me ample space. I like that he's not a typical Israeli. He feels more accessible to me, more sensitive and expressive, and I'm intrigued by everything about him.

∽

AFTER WE'RE DONE WITH OUR DOUGH, MAOEN QUICKLY tidies up the floor, sweeping the remaining flour into a small dustpan. He has a stash of cleaning supplies way in the back. I wonder if there are other goodies tucked away in this container that only he knows about.

"Now, the question is . . . where are we going to bake this beauty?" Maoen asks, careful to keep the dough level.

"That's what I was wondering," I say. "Everything here is generator powered, and I want to taste our creation."

In a flash, he jumps down from the raised platform of the container, off in search of something, apparently, to bake the pitas on. Minutes later, he returns with a small foot heater. *Where did he manage to procure a foot heater in a base with blasting hot temperatures?*

"You're going to bake pita on a foot heater?"

"Not one foot heater—three foot heaters!" He looks up with a twinkle in his eye. "Wait a minute!"

He disappears again, and returns with two more foot heaters. "Ta-da!"

He notices the consternation in my face.

"Oh, don't worry, Dorit. The metal bars will act like a baking tray. We're not going to blow up the base."

"Oh my god. This is ridiculous."

I watch as he lays the pita dough across the three heaters,

deftly flipping it to its other side after a few minutes. I'm afraid even to watch, convinced that the dough will catch on fire. But minutes later, Maoen is holding a soft, warm pita up for me to try—and it's not just edible, it's delicious. He watches me as I pop a piece in my mouth and then laughs with delight when he sees me smiling.

"I told you so. It's not that bad."

We break it into two. On one side, Maoen spreads olive oil, za'atar, and feta cheese. On my side, I spread *Shachar*, a creamy chocolate spread.

This is one of those moments where time seems to slow down. Together we are transcending culture, race, and religion, and this moment is, for me, one of utter peace and harmony. My unfolding relationship with Maoen is showing me my limited understanding of the nuances of race and culture. Each conversation spells an intimate world I know nothing about. In New York City, diversity swarmed around me, but I never really had the opportunity to experience what it was like to live and learn alongside another culture. The media and Mom influenced how I felt about other people and set the tone for my fears, especially where Arabs were concerned. But here I am, actively forging a friendship with someone whose Arab heritage is exactly what draws me to him. I'm formulating my own opinions. From here on out, I promise myself, I'll continue to stay open and interactive. Mom once said, "Be open with people you meet." Now I'm taking her advice to heart.

∞

DURING THAT FIRST WEEK AT THE BASE ON THE GAZA Strip, I explore the tent itself, which is like a labyrinth created by twists and turns of the netting and fabric, hoisted by fifteen-foot wooden poles dug deep into the ground. One part of the tent opens to a rather large, airy "room" consisting of a dirt floor and the fifteen cots we female soldiers sleep on.

The other side of our tent has nooks of varying sizes, including small offices and a dining room. My records office consists of a small, closed off space just big enough for a filing cabinet, chair, and desk. Overhead is netting. Miraculously, this netting never falls, not even in the strong winds. This is the one place where I am protected from swarms of flies and sandstorms.

The day after making pita, when my work at the office is done, I open my journal. It seems another sandstorm is starting up; I can't hear what's coming through on the walkie-talkie system. I turn up the volume, but all I get is static.

I've just started writing when Maoen peers into my office and sees me working. Before I even know what's happening, he slings his arm around me. I stiffen slightly. I'm not so sure I should let his arm stay there. I want to relax and enjoy Maoen's company, but I'm deeply worried about being found out, and about what others might think if they saw us like this.

"What are you writing?" he asks, peering over my shoulder. "Oh, you're writing in English. Nice."

"I'm writing about my life here on this base. My thoughts. How tired I've been. How much I miss America. My mom. That kind of stuff."

"Hmm. America. Do you want to go back?"

"I miss parts of it, but not enough to want to return just yet."

Afraid to expose myself too much, I open to a blank page, write my name in Hebrew, and gesture for him to write something. I know Maoen is fluent in English because he's been learning it since primary school, but I don't know how well he can read my writing.

He takes my journal from me and starts writing in English, in beautiful penmanship. When he's finished, he hands the pen back to me.

"Read it when I'm gone," he says, and with that, he closes the journal and cups my hands in his. He lingers for a moment longer, looking deeply into my eyes, before he disappears behind the netting. I can see his shadow getting smaller beyond the thick netting until it becomes just a small dot and in its place are intense rays of sun.

I open the journal and read:

Let the good luck be with you everywhere you go. And let love attack your little heart to live sweetly with it all the days of your life.
Someone loves one, someone two. I love just one. That is you.

∞

A FEW DAYS LATER, I'M IN FRONT OF THE ZIM CONTAINER again. This time I'm leading a fairly long line of girls from both garinim. We are getting ready to be fitted for our metal helmets so we can participate in our first military exercise outside the base. Our exercise fills me with dread, mainly because it sounds so serious. All we've been told right now is that we'll be doing a series of "attack" exercises a few kilometers away from the camp and in full armor, including our helmets, guns, bullets, magazines, and other supplies. When I ask for more details on what we'll be doing, I'm told that we'll be crawling with our guns toward manmade targets. This is nothing like any exercises we've done at Base Camp 80, Avivim, or Hoshniya.

"I've been waiting for you," Maoen says, laughing. "What took you guys so long to come?" He pulls out a Noblesse cigarette, hands one to me.

"No thank you," I say, not understanding how he thinks I could have time for a cigarette in this moment. "Sorry for the delay. Our officers were talking us through the exercise." I look steadfastly into the container.

"Okay girls, *banot*. Let's get started fitting you all for your helmets!" Maeon shouts over the sea of faces.

Girls fidget behind me, chatting about random subjects. Maoen's job here is to pass along the helmets and supplies. He promised me I'd be the first one to get fitted for a helmet, so I won't have to stand in line.

He jumps down from the container and I stand still as he places a helmet on my head and fastens the straps.

I try not to teeter-totter, but I'm not used to carrying thirty pounds of metal on my head. It feels extremely bulky.

"Wow, this thing is heavy!" I exclaim. I feel like I'm balancing a concrete block on my head, and it's knocking my legs out of whack. "Are you sure I'll manage?" I ask with trepidation. I'm proud of myself for how far I've come—I'm more confident now than I've been in my entire life—but I still get tripped up by totally new experiences sometimes, and I've never experienced anything in the military quite like this. I can feel my old anxieties surfacing.

"You'll be fine," Maoen whispers in my ear, which immediately draws stares from the girls behind me. "Really," he says reassuringly.

I take in his strength, his face. At twenty-one, he's more of a man than many of the other soldiers I've been serving with over the past year.

"It's not as bad as it seems," he says. "You'll get used to it."

"It's too tight," I complain.

Maeon, as always, is gentle with me. As he adjusts my helmet, I imagine that the vibe we put out suggests that there is something between us, and I try not to blush. I'm conflicted about my feelings toward him. Sometimes when I look at him, I'm surprised to hear my mom's voice in my ear: *"They're the enemy! They're the ones who are going to blow Israel up."* It's a disconcerting message to be confronted by when facing this man I've grown to care about so much.

I look now at Maoen, who gazes at me with a twinkle in his eye. He's so close to me right now, I can smell the cigarette smoke on his breath. Part of me wishes I could share with him the mess of emotions I'm feeling right now, while another part of me is embarrassed by it.

As he readjusts my helmet straps, I ask, "Why do we need these helmets?"

"What do you mean by that?" he says, laughing. "You're in Gaza now, past Rafiach." He hands me a paper to sign. This helmet's officially mine but on a temporary basis. In a few months' time, it'll sit on some other girl's head.

Moaen is referring to Rafiach junction, a small strip of land that's several hundred meters long and consists of several wide concrete slabs—checkpoints—that are passable only via Jeep. At each checkpoint, there are several Israeli soldiers in metal helmets and heavy army gear who hold their M16s high. They look terribly fierce, but their job is to protect us.

The first time we passed through these checkpoints, on the way to our new base, I felt like I was living in some sort of news documentary. The images were familiar to me; I'd seen this area on TV back in the States, and it was almost easier to visualize myself as if on a screen than to fully connect with the real-life feeling of being there in that moment, crossing into

Gaza. I couldn't help but think about what my mom would say if she knew where I was.

∞

A FEW HOURS AFTER BEING FITTED FOR OUR HELMETS, we are all crouching on the top of a small hill. Our officers soon appear from a group of swaying trees. They've been supporting us since the days of Avivim; they're our big brothers and sisters. We're still waiting for our first orders for this military exercise, which should take a few hours. Upon finishing, we'll go back to the base.

"*Yalla, Yalla!*" our officers shout in unison. "Go, go!" Just as we've been instructed, we jut our legs out in a V position and inch slowly along the ground from the top to the bottom of the hill with our guns positioned in firing mode.

"Heads down now!" one officer shouts.

"Move forward!" another one commands.

We're told this military exercise is necessary in the event we're attacked by the enemy. We are told to cross our guns so that they cannot be taken away from us if we are ambushed. We need to camouflage ourselves. In this way, we can observe the enemy without being seen.

Under the metal of the helmet, I feel I can handle anything, even though this is just an exercise.

We continue moving forward along the ground, little by little, and I feel like I'm in a World War I movie.

We finally reach a clearing devoid of bushes, thorns, and shrubbery.

Suddenly, a flood of lights are aimed in the distance, illuminating a row of cardboard cutout soldiers in enemy uniform.

"Ready, aim, fire!" a familiar voice rings out in the distance. I recognize it immediately as Maoen's.

Maoen? What's he doing here?

I promptly load my gun with more bullets from my magazine. When the first magazine is empty, I reload my gun and fire until the second one is spent as well. I have two magazines left.

There's lots of metal and gunfire. It's hard to pick out a particular soldier's face; I can only rely on voices. Suddenly, someone's crouching and slowly inching their way up until our bodies practically touch. *Maoen.*

"You've got to balance it on your shoulder," he tells me. "You're nowhere near the firing range."

He angles the gun so it's better positioned on my shoulder. He's trying to give me advice, but amidst all the gunfire and smokes, it's hard to focus, and I'm getting overwhelmed.

"Hey, Maoen. Stop it. It's starting to feel too heavy."

He quickly pulls back and I let the gun drop from my shoulder.

"I'm sorry," he says. "I didn't mean it."

I thought I had this gun thing under control, but I'm struggling now to keep it balanced. My arm's hurting and I can longer keep up with the pace of the other girls. *But this is not a race*, I remind myself. *I'm not in a competition.* Even so, I falter.

Maoen's still here, even though I've just chastised him.

"Still need help?" he asks.

"No."

"Okay," he says without even a hint of impatience in his voice.

I relent. "Well, maybe. Yes."

Maoen holds my gun, but only for a minute. All our

officers have steadily moved forward, about a quarter of a mile down the long stretch of land before us. Thorns and shrubbery attack me from all sides. I flinch at the pain, but bear it.

Suddenly one of the officers in front of us shouts, "*Mifaked Maoen, Bo*—Officer Maoen, come! We need your help!"

Officer Maoen? I want to say something, but what would I say—that I had no idea? Did he intentionally keep this information from me, or did I just not notice?

I inch forward, and Moaen steadies my gun. *Officer* Maoen steadies my gun.

We move forward. Together.

I steal a glance at him, and it occurs to me that I've never seen him wear those three stripes that would have allowed me to detect his rank. But how can that be? The only explanation I can come up with is that I've never seen him in his travel uniform; I've only seen him in his work uniform. Maybe he did withhold the information, not wanting our relationship to be defined or dictated by our respective titles and ranks. Perhaps he thought this might ruin our relationship—or our chances for one. But regardless, now I know he doesn't thrive on authority. He's a human being first, and then an officer. My officer.

∽

ONE DUSTY AFTERNOON, WE ARE TAKEN BY JEEP ON A tour of our surroundings. After we've been driving for a bit, our base disappears behind us, and a beach materializes in front of us. To my left there's a makeshift tent and some dilapidated structures. Before me, far out in the distance, is the faint dot of a ship on the horizon. We stop right alongside the beach, and our driver turns off the engine and urges us to get out.

Maoen and I are the last to exit. I want to stay slightly longer, alone with him in that Jeep, but instead we follow the driver and a few other soldiers as they race toward the beach like children.

The water is supremely clear, and I peer down to see little fish swimming around. Seemingly from nowhere come some screaming kids, no older than five or six, with dirty faces and clothes made of multicolored rags. They utter a few words in Arabic and run over to the beach, where they throw stones, squeal with delight, and then run back and pick up a few more stones.

I've never thought of Gaza Strip as a "beachy" place—but now that I think about it, I realize it is along the Mediterranean.

Hanufa, a lanky soldier, emerges from behind the Jeep and pulls off his boots, then peels off his socks, and finally rolls up his pants and shows his hairy legs. *Can this be?* I wonder. *Aren't we in the Israel Defense Forces? Are we allowed to go wading in the water?*

But other soldiers soon follow suit, rolling their pants to their knees and draping their guns to their sides or slinging them on their backs in a crisscrossed position. Their legs disappear in the water, and I smile as they cry out with glee. Waves rush in and out. I could be on any beach in the world; I have to remind myself again that we are on a Gaza Strip beach.

Maoen and I are the only ones who remain on the beach. It's our private moment, finally. He reaches for my hand under the sand, and just as our hands meet, he pulls me closer. We wait until no one is looking and then we kiss. Our lips fasten just for a moment, and then we break apart.

"You know," he says, "you really handled yourself well during that military exercise. Just like a real, high-profile soldier."

"What?" I squeal. "Are you serious? I was freaking scared. I had no idea what I was doing. You helped me half the time. I was in pain. I barely made it to the targets. And I have to say that when you were acknowledged as an officer, I almost died. Why are you so modest?"

"Modest? I thought you knew."

"How would I know?"

He just smiles at me, his kind eyes meeting mine.

Pride now fills me up in the space where I was once filled with concern. I wanted to succeed with the military exercise, and didn't anticipate that an officer like Maoen would help me. He's made the IDF officer's world look accessible and human to me.

"You continued," he says, smiling. "You did it."

I allow those words to fill me up. No one up until now has ever given me positive feedback about my physical ability to carry myself in the IDF.

If I was back in New York City, holding hands with an army officer, I would probably pinch myself over the fact that I was dating an officer. And I do have a moment like that here, but then it quickly fades away. None of these appellations or titles matter. We're just two young people entering into something exciting, and we have no idea where it will lead.

I turn to him and say, "You are so sweet. I'm so glad you're here. But next time tell me you're a sergeant and not just someone who works at the weaponry and supply unit, okay?" I smile. "But you have the heart of an officer. Not just any officer."

"I don't believe in all that stuff—ranks and everything,"

Maoen says, shrugging. "I just do the service." He pulls me toward him for one more quick embrace while the other soldiers are still out in the ocean, distracted.

I close my eyes. Nothing in my service so far has prepared me for this moment. This is definitely not something I imagined would happen. *Am I really falling in love?*

Maoen reaches for my hand under the burning sand, and we watch the other soldiers splash each other. One is now completely drenched.

Gaza. A military base, but yet so much more.

Maoen steals kiss after kiss, then offers me a tender smile.

I want this moment to last forever.

21

MISGAV AM

Toward the end of our third month on the Gaza
Strip, Ronen, the deputy battalion commander, calls Dalia,
Eina, Svetlana, and myself into his office.

"Have you heard the news?" he asks, his muscular hand
resting on his M16. "You girls have been assigned to *machleket
meshek.*"

Serving on another kibbutz? Since when?

Eina and Svetlana smile at each other. But Dalia and I
don't exactly know how to respond. What just happened? Eina
and Svetlana have been hoping that we will all return to serve
on a kibbutz ever since we were sent to our first base, but until
now, their requests for a transfer have always been denied.
Dalia and I, meanwhile, have both continued to enjoy our
service in the Brigade. After all these months, I still prefer
serving on a base to what I know will be waiting for me on a
kibbutz—basically just busy work and keeping house. But it's
also true that these last few weeks on the base have been
tedious, and I'm burnt out on the mountainous heaps of paperwork of new soldiers entering and leaving. Part of me wants to

stay with Maoen, but there's another stronger part that wants to finish my service with the girls in my garin.

He continues. "There's an opening at a kibbutz in the north for a small garin like yours. I was told you'd all be interested in serving on another kibbutz before ending your service in Sufa. Still interested?"

Eina and Svetlana immediately exclaim, "Yes, yes!"

Ronen looks at Dalia and me. "You two in as well?"

"Where is it?" I ask.

"In the Upper Galilee. It's called Misgav Am."

I silently yip. It's been more than six months since we served in Avivim. The idea of mountains, verdant valleys and pastures, apple orchards, waterfalls, and wildflowers fills me with excited anticipation. And I would be closer to my family again. In some ways, this transfer would feel like coming home. Maybe I am ready for a change after all.

"Yes," I say meekly. "I'm in. I'll go."

"I'll go, too," Dalia chirps, which astounds me. In a strange way, we've bonded. I'll miss her when she heads to her kibbutz along the shores of the Mediterranean Sea instead of back to Sufa with the rest of us.

∞

WHEN I BREAK THE NEWS TO MAOEN, HE GETS TEARY. "So when do you leave? Where will you go?"

"Friday's our last day. *Machleket meshek* starts Monday. Officer Ronen said we're going to a kibbutz called Misgav Am in the Upper Galilee. Have you heard of it?"

"Nope. *Eize basa*—this sucks. Man, I can't believe you're going."

"I can't either. Now that I'm here, I don't want to leave.

And part of it has to do with you. I'm gonna miss you. A lot."
I wish Maoen knew how torn I feel at this moment. Making
the heartfelt decision to leave this base to serve with the girls is
logical, but they are not tender and warm like Maoen.

"At least you'll have an easier life. You'll get to see your
family more often. From here on out, you'll be close to *ezrachi*
—civilian life."

I nod and try to hold back the tears. Maoen starts rubbing
my shoulders to try to make me feel better.

My only major reservation about going to Misgav Am is
the domestic work I know I'll probably end up having to do
there. How will cleaning toilets and doing dishes equate with
the kind of "hardcore" work I'm doing now? Here in Gaza,
I'm actually doing something to help protect and serve the
country. There, I won't feel so integral to Israel's safety.

I try to find comfort in the fact that I am now a seasoned
soldier who understands the implications of serving on a
kibbutz near the border. *Machleket meshek* may not be serving on
a base, but I know I have skills to offer them. I still feel I can
make a difference there.

I slip my hand into Maoen's hot, sweaty palm. Other
soldiers still give us looks when they see us together, but I'm
past caring about what others think. Since that kiss on the
beach, the other girls think that I'm a flirt. In their eyes, I'm
some kind of free spirit who enjoys sleeping around.

We walk hand in hand to the dining room. There's a small
group of male soldiers to our right, and they all stare. Putrid-
green tables are being cleared of stacks of plastic plates with
bits of salad, hummus, and canned corn—a typical army
lunch—left on them.

In the middle of this partitioned tent dining room sits
Ronen, surrounded by a few officers. They're deep in army talk.

I turn to Maoen. "I'm so conflicted. Maybe I should ask Ronen if I can stay here instead of going with the girls. I just know I'm going to miss you."

We make our way outside the tent. Flies attack us from all directions. From behind Maoen's shoulder I notice a few Israeli soldiers who've just stopped chatting. Clearly, they're looking at us. I know what they're thinking, but I still don't care.

"What's that, *motek*—sweetheart?" He caresses my face with the gentlest of touches.

I sigh. Staying here is no longer an option, and I know it. I'll just have to figure out a way to deal with this separation. "Visit me," I say. "Please promise. I'm going to be lonely."

"Don't worry, *motek*. I will."

∞

TWO DAYS LATER, I ARRIVE AT MISGAV AM ON THE early-afternoon Friday bus from Kiriyat Shmona, a heavy duffel bag draped over my shoulder.

The first thing I notice about Misgav Am is its huge, panoramic view. The kibbutz is perched on a mountaintop overlooking the Hula Valley, an agricultural region that has abundant fresh water and is also a major stopover for the more than 500 million birds that migrate along the Syrian-African Rift Valley between Africa, Europe, and Asia. The snow-capped Mount Hermon lies in the far distance. I'm overwhelmed; we've been sent to one of the most beautiful kibbutzim in all of Israel.

Later that afternoon, I meet up with Mike, a longtime American kibbutz member who's in charge of security. He tells me about the "Good Fence" that encloses a *moshava*—an agriculture community—known as Metulla, which dates to the

19th century. The "Good Fence" dates to 1978. It serves the purpose of security checking any Lebanese who wanted to come into the country. It's a constant reminder of the tensions between our two nations.

Up until two days ago, I was convinced that our new kibbutz service would be entirely domestic, so I'm grateful to soak up this bit of information. It reinforces my soldier identity and helps me understand this area's political connection. Still, I feel very removed from the IDF in terms of duties. As far as I'm concerned, being here is still a big letdown. It takes me weeks to adjust to the fact I no longer have to report to work in a uniform. Early each morning I strain to listen for any signs of the army, only to wake up to silence, and thus disappointment. There are no commanders passing by our tents and shouting out orders. In their place, I hear a tourist bus rumbling on the narrow road below. My big room is too quiet, and the metal bed frame and foamy mattress make me feel domesticated. I push open the rickety green shutters on my window and look down at the curvy cemented path below leading to the children's house, and I feel like I have to pinch myself. How did I end up here?

∞

WORKING ON MISGAV AM REQUIRES ME TO FIND WAYS to be of service without really feeling like a soldier. I've been completely stripped of my accustomed military routine. I now wear army work pants with a flowered top for my shift at the dining room. I tell the *sadran avoda*, the person in charge of setting up the work schedule, that I want to work in the most difficult jobs possible, but I end up cleaning dining room tables and working the dishwasher. Misgav Am has a plethora of industries, including a factory that manufactures a wide range of elastic bandages for industrial purposes, but I won't be chosen for any of those jobs for now.

After a few weeks of cleaning tables and toilets, I learn that there's an immediate opening to work with the one-and-a-half-year-olds at one of the children's houses. As part of its self-sustaining and communal framework, each kibbutz houses various children's houses, ranging from infant age to kindergarten. Some kibbutzim also house schools, elementary through high school. Typically, parents will drop off their children on their way to work. Some parents may work at the kibbutz, while others may hold an outside job.

I put in my request to work with the children and am pleased when I get the job.

Dina, a matronly woman from Yemen who is also a veteran kibbutz member in charge of the children's house I'm working at, tells me she's been working with young children on Misgav Am for the past thirty years. I quickly learn that my job is usually given to an experienced childcare worker, but I was hired largely because I'm fluent in Hebrew but still young, which is important to Dina because the job requires picking children up and staying upbeat and energetic with them all day long.

On my first day, a small crowd of children gathers, eyeing me with curiosity. Dina, too, eyes me, scrutinizing my IDF work uniform. I immediately become self-conscious. *Surely she knows I'm a soldier.*

I figure she isn't quite sure what to make of me yet, most likely because I'm American, so I try to break the ice: "You know, Dina," I tell her, "I worked with children from a similar age group on Kibbutz Ketura for a week when our service brought us to Shitim in the Arava desert."

"Oh really?" she says. "Tell me about that experience."

I have the sense that this is the real interview, even though I'm technically already in. I certainly feel as if I need to prove something to Dina, the one who really calls the shots here at the children's house. Later I will understand why it's so important that she trust me. She is the protector not just of these children's emotional and physical safety and security but also to that of their parents—many of whom were once under Dina's care themselves. Kibbutz life is close-knit, and people guard their reputations fiercely. In the IDF, the biggest risk to your reputation is if you do a "fuck" that costs your garin a punishment. But that "fuck" will quickly be forgotten when you move to the next base. Here, on Misgav Am, there's no escape—you see the same people in the dining room year after year, and they talk about you behind your back. I won't be here for that long, but I am acutely aware of how important it is to get along well with everyone, and from the very beginning.

Over time, Dina and I develop a rapport. I tell her about the service I've done, and about my garin. The heavy lines on her face tell me that she's experienced a lot during her thirty years on the kibbutz. Maybe I've been quick to judge this service as "less than" in some ways. Being at a base is rigorous work, but is there anything more important than raising the next generation? I feel privileged that Dina trusts me. I want to work hard to continue to affirm that trust.

"Let's get to work," she says.

❧

FOR THE FIRST TWO WEEKS AT THE CHILDREN'S HOUSE, I feel like I'm channeling my inner child. Having held M16s for a majority of my service, I now hold eighteen-month-olds who cry, "Orit!" for "Dorit!" They try my patience by pulling my hair, and make me smile when they laugh at my goofy facial expressions. They don't care whether I am an American or if I did well during my last target practice shooting in Gaza. We speak a universal language of connection: innocence.

Connecting with my inner child helps me pass Dina's "test." She quietly observes me and the way I handle the children's behavior, and she seems to approve. The transition to having me on staff is relatively seamless. I've got a good handle on the Sabagi brother-sister twins, who tend to push each other, and chubby-faced Tom, who loves to try to get her way with the other children. Their cries make me feel needed and wanted in a way that is so different from serving on a base in Gaza. I try not to get too unnerved by Dina's watchfulness. In every trying situation, I follow my intuition. So far, it seems to be working.

∞

ONE QUIET MOMENT DURING LUNCHTIME, I ASK DINA what she knows about the history of this specific kibbutz in relation to terrorist attacks.

"Do you really want to know, Dorit? It's kind of frightening." She looks at me with consternation as the Sabagi twins munch on their chicken and noodles. Irena, the full-time paid worker from Russia, leans closer. It's obvious that she too, wants to know.

"Yes, I do. Remember, I served in Gaza," I say, trying to sound brave.

It turns out that on April 7, 1980, five terrorists from the Iraqi-backed Arab Liberation Front penetrated Misgav Am in the night and entered the nursery. During those days, children slept in nurseries and not with their parents. They killed the kibbutz secretary and an infant boy.

"What happened to the rest of the children?" Irena and I ask.

"They held the rest of the children hostage, demanding the release of fifty terrorists held in Israeli prisons."

Irena looks up and stops slurping her soup. "Oh my god, that's horrible!" she says loudly. The Sabagi twins start crying.

"But what about the IDF?" I ask. "How did they respond? They must have appeared right away!"

"Of course. The first raid was unsuccessful, but a few hours later, the army succeeded, and all the terrorists were killed."

"Phew. Thank god."

"But two kibbutz members and one soldier were killed, and four children and eleven soldiers were wounded." Dina gets up and points to another children's house not too far away from ours. "That's where it happened," she says, "and the pain of that tragedy is still there. That little boy who was killed, I took care of him for the first six months of his life. I took care of his brothers and sisters, too."

Tears well up in Dina's eyes. Irena and I look at each other solemnly.

"If I could, I would have given my own life to save those children. But I wasn't on the kibbutz that day. It's something I'll always regret."

I'm stunned by this story. If I had known while I was still in New York City that I would be stationed here on Kibbutz Misgav Am, the place of a terrorist attack, as part of my army service, I would have been terrified. I probably wouldn't have even come. But like all the other trying moments I've experienced in the IDF, I'm not intimidated by this news. I only wish this kibbutz wasn't so vulnerable. Dina fights back tears, and all I can do is hold her.

"The children. Those poor children and their families," I say, trying to console Dina, and feeling quite able, in this moment, looking around at all these precious children, to feel her pain.

∞

LATER THAT AFTERNOON, JUST AS I'M ABOUT TO FINISH UP work at my usual four o'clock hour, I hear a bicycle screech to a halt right outside the gate.

I look out the window and see a girl with wavy, dark brown hair.

"Eliz! Long time no see!" Dina shouts from the entrance to the children's house.

"I haven't seen you in ages!" the girl calls back. "How's it going?"

"Eliz used to be one of the kids here," Dina tells me as she goes to give her a hug. "That was many years ago, right?" she says.

"Right," Eliz responds.

I follow Dina to the gate and listen.

"So how's it going?" she asks Eliz.

"Pretty good. I'm back here now, working at the pub."

"Tired of Tel Aviv? City life is too much?"

"Yeah, something like that. I want to be back with *Aba and Ima*—Mom and Dad—you know?"

"I totally get that. So glad. Well, good luck with everything. It was great to see you!" Dina heads back inside, and I open the gate, on my way out.

"You work here?" Eliz asks.

"Yes, I'm here with my garin as part of our work here with *machleket meshek*."

"Oh *magniv*—cool! So, you're one of the garin members that just arrived from America?"

"Well, yes, but I've been here for a good few months already."

"And you're adjusting well to kibbutz life?"

"Yeah, it's all good. I really like it. And Dina's great."

"Yes, she is. She used to be my *mitapelet*, my child care worker. But we'd always call her Dina, *ha Ima*—Dina, the mom. She was like our second mom. Man, I haven't been inside that children's house for ages."

"So you're working now at the pub full-time?"

Eliz tosses her brunette hair. Her voluminous locks remind me of Farrah Fawcett.

She widens her smile as she continues talking. "Yeah, I'm the bartender every Tuesday, Thursday, Friday, and Saturday and sometimes Sundays—say, what time is it?" She nudges me in the elbow.

I like this girl. She's so easygoing, and acting like we're already friends.

"It's four o'clock." I can't take my eyes off her wide-eyed smile. "You're a kibbutz member?" I ask.

"Yes."

"Wait! I know who your parents are, I think. I've seen you hanging around at the accounting office. Amnon and Aliza?"

She nods.

Now I remember. My first night at the disco here, I realized how late it was and zoomed out the door, and on my way I sailed past Eliz, who was flirting with a bunch of soldiers from behind the bar. She was wearing a lacy black top and a gold necklace that sparkled under the spotlights, and every time she served a drink, she smiled that same effervescent smile she's offering me now. Putting this together is kind of fun for me, now that I'm realizing how approachable she is. Maybe I've found a friend on my new kibbutz.

I tell her about seeing her that night at the bar. "You can get really busy over there. I saw you pouring drink after drink."

"Yeah, it's always the same crowd that comes from Kiriyat Shmona. But don't worry, you can push through those guys next time you see me working. In fact, I'm working tonight. Can you come by?"

"Sure thing. See you there!"

This is a fulfilling moment for me. I have an invitation to hang out with someone who lives on this kibbutz. I feel like I've arrived somehow; I can see a future in which I'm integrated both as a soldier and a civilian. I find that I'm actually looking forward these last three months on Misgav Am building social connections before returning to serve on Sufa —though I still miss Maoen.

22

ELIZ AND GOODBYE

ELIZ'S APARTMENT DOOR BANGS CLOSED BEHIND ME. I turn and lock it, stick the keys in my back jeans pocket, and head down the dimly lit hallway and down the hill that brings me past the laundry, children's house, and dining room. There's that *thump, thump*—the mighty dance beat signifying freedom and excitement. I strain my ears to pick up the familiar tune. My heart quickens.

Ever since our first conversation three months ago, Eliz and I have been hanging out constantly, mostly at her place. A few hours before she heads off for her bartending shift at the disco, we create our own little disco. First, we move all her furniture to one side, then we blast our favorite '90s tunes, like Snap!'s "Rhythm is a Dancer" and "Power," Corona's "Rhythm of the Night," and Technotronic's "Pump Up the Jam." My feet take to the floor, feeling the rhythm. No worries. Just us and the music. At some point, I always start wondering if any of her neighbors will complain—her apartment reverberates from the convulsions of sound—but no one ever says anything. We wildly shake our freshly shampooed heads, and she copies my Herbie Hancock crisscross moves, which tickles me.

Tonight I'm wearing a lacy black top.

"See?" I shout to Eliz over the music. "I bought this black top in honor of you."

She laughs. "Now we're twins!"

So far my friendship with Eliz has defied all the expectations and rules I've long thought were typical of kibbutz life. My experience with kibbutzim so far has been that they are closed, tight-knit communities, very difficult to penetrate if you're an outsider, and especially if you're a foreigner. But it's been easy to become friends with Eliz. And she has been a blessing in that she's been a distraction from my relationship with Maoen.

I've been struggling to figure out how to accept life without Maoen since I got here. Over the last three months, we've written incessant love letters, which finally culminated in his one visit to Misgav Am a month ago, on a Thursday afternoon.

He surprised me with his visit: there he stood in the middle of the entranceway to my apartment, wearing his impeccable travel uniform and a wide grin. His duffel bag was tipped sideways, making it impossible for him to enter the apartment. I cupped my hands over my mouth.

"I got a *regila* so I can spend time with you," he said.

"Wow! A week off!"

"It took a lot of convincing to get that time off. Everyone knew that I was coming to see you. But in the end, Ronen said it was okay. "

He swept me up in a wide embrace. I was anxious to show him my room, and he delighted in the Bedouin tapestry on the main wall. When I opened the door to my dirty terrace, I giggled a little about the dirt, knowing that Maoen cannot tolerate messy spaces. But that day he seemed not to care at all; he grabbed the three-legged wooden chair that had been lying there on its side for months and cast it aside, then swooped up and pinned me against the wall.

He held my hand, kissed my lips, and nuzzled into my ear. "Man, I've missed you."

The kiss felt good but then he pushed his groin close against me and pinned me closer to the wall, and I was immediately nervous. I'd been holding off from having sex with him all this time, and the tension had been mounting. On the base, we flirted and had fun, but I'm still a virgin, and I was afraid to sleep with Maoen because I wasn't sure I was ready. In my book, having sex equals commitment, something we hadn't talked about. And now that he was here, I was second-guessing our relationship. Did I really want to be with him? I had worried a lot about the fact that he's Druze, and what his family and community would think of me. What would they do if they found out he was dating an American? These thoughts flooded my mind, and now I was anything but turned on.

I pulled back. "Maoen, I can't really go on like this." I tried to wriggle myself free from my position against the wall. In addition to everything, I didn't like being in such a compromising position.

"Why, *motek*? What's wrong?" He was dumbfounded.

In a low voice, I whispered the reason: "I can't sleep with you. I'm a virgin, you know." I didn't share that I was actually a little afraid to have sex with him, or the fact that I was saving my virginity for the right person, and I wasn't sure it was him.

When Jake told me that he couldn't sleep with me back on Sufa because I wasn't ready, I was incredulous at first. And yet now I think he was right. That day with Maoen, I realized I still wasn't ready to open myself up in this raw physical and emotional way with him. What if he didn't want to see me again after we had sex? Up until that point, we'd just been having fun. Perhaps I was overreacting, but I feared that such an intimate moment might change everything between us.

At my words, Maoen lowered his head and started crying. I'd never seen a male IDF soldier cry, and I hated to see him hurting, but in my heart I knew there was nothing for me to do but let him go. I hadn't gone into the conversation intending for it to be the end of our relationship, but I realized in this moment that that was exactly what was happening. I handed him a tissue.

"I love you so much," he said. "You know how serious I am about you. I wouldn't behave like this with anyone."

"I know, Maoen. I care about you a lot too. But I can't sleep with you. I'm not ready."

He continued to cry.

I strained to find his eyes through my own blanket of tears.

I felt guilty having led Maoen along—but the truth is, I didn't realize I was doing it. I never thought he was so sensitive; I'd taken him for granted, and had taken our whole relationship much more lightly than he had. But I couldn't buy time back now; what was done was done. I felt resolute in my decision.

Maoen was upset, but he had never been one to argue. He accepted what I said. He seemed to know there was little he could do to change my mind.

He didn't stay the night. In less than an hour, he was out the door, duffel bag in hand, and heading back down the hill, wiping the last of his tears away as he went. It would be the last time we'd ever see each other again.

That night, I lay in bed and agonized over what had

happened, blaming myself. In the morning, I woke up with a tear-stained pillow and the realization that Maoen and I probably would have been better off as friends.

∾

AS I GET CLOSER TO THE DISCO, I TAKE IN THE MAJESTIC Hula Valley, which suddenly opens in front of me like a black cloak studded with resplendent diamonds. I try to see if I can make out anything familiar in the valley below, but darkness overpowers everything. I peer over the hill and take it all in. The lit-up kibbutzim and moshavim resemble the Haden Planetarium back in New York City. Leaning over a cliff, all I see is darkness and light, and I feel as if I'm floating in space. I'm in awe of the beauty of this sight. I'm mesmerized by these "stars" that illuminate an entire world out there, all connected to me.

I saunter past the ticketer. As usual, his long black hair is pulled back into a ponytail. He's always haggard, and he barely acknowledges me when I come in. Since I work on the kibbutz, I don't have to pay an entrance fee.

I spot Eliz deep in a blanket of cigarette smoke and make my way over to her. I squeeze in between two familiar army post men wearing heavy gold chains, their black hair slicked back with mousse and gel. Sitting front and center seems to be the only way to get Eliz's attention.

"Hey, what's up?" I shout. "I'm here!" She waves to me enthusiastically, but is too busy to talk. Once in a while she rolls her eyes and gives me the look—*These guys are killing me*—but other than that, I'm on my own at the bar, forced to make small talk with the male soldiers on either side of me.

Eliz hands me a lit cigarette and pours me a cup a beer.

I'm not a beer drinker, but I drink anyway. I'm not a smoker, but I smoke anyway, waiting as patiently as I can for my friend. Eliz can join me on the disco floor during her break, which I hope is coming soon. I need to dance out the feelings that have started to gather inside me in the last thirty minutes or so. I'll hold out till Eliz can dance with me, though.

She leans across the bar. "The guy you've been talking with, Shimon . . . I think he's interested in me," she whispers excitedly in my ear.

"He looks okay. But truthfully, he seems a bit *chach-chach*— sleazy."

She laughs. "*Chach-chach?* Come on, Dorit. You're exaggerating. These guys aren't what you think they are. They're actually pretty decent. They just want to have fun like the rest of us . . ."

I take another sip of my beer and puff on my cigarette. "When are you going to get a break? Anytime soon?" I ask. Suddenly I feel a little desperate, like a third wheel.

"Soon, Dorit," she reassures me, but her tone of voice only reinforces my feelings. She seems almost put off, and I can't help but feel an edge of condescension in her answer as she turns back to her duties behind the bar.

Eliz serves one drink after another. Usually she has time to chat and dance with me, but tonight her focus is elsewhere. As she interacts with the other locals, I withdraw deeper into my thoughts about what will happen after my service is over. The insecurity I feel at not knowing what's next is threatening to overwhelm me.

Finally, I head to the dance floor alone. I take occasional breaks from the hot center of the crowded dance floor near one of the fans built into the wooden walls. As I reenter the middle of the floor after one of these breaks, I see some of

Shimon's buddies closing in on me, and I recognize some other IDF reservists I know moving in from the outer circle, too. I quickly dance my way out to the edge of the floor. I don't want to dance with any of these guys. I want to be free and unrestricted.

Finally, at three in the morning, Eliz locks up the bar. Shimon follows us outside and gives his buddies a thumbs up, indicating that they can drive off. I sense Eliz's discomfort; she's not pleased that we've suddenly become a threesome, and it's clear that she and Shimon have some sort of unspoken arrangement that he's going home with her. I say goodnight and start back up the hill to my apartment. My head is pounding. My clothes reek of alcohol and cigarettes. This is not how a typical night at the disco unfolds. Usually Eliz is off by midnight and we dance and hang out together.

"Bye, Dorit!" she cries, but that's all. We would normally hug goodbye, or she'd at least say, "I'll catch up with you later." The tension between us is thick. My eyes brim with tears. I'm frustrated by her flakiness. She hasn't done this to me before, but I've seen glimpses of her flakiness in the past when she has beckoned me to come to the bar and then become engrossed in conversation with some of the locals and ignored me.

I'm mad now that I come to the disco every night she works. This is the only context in which we hang out; we don't do stuff together unless she's working. After tonight, I feel like a hanger-on—and I don't like it. Surely she hasn't intended to use me, but tonight I feel very much like she has.

Tonight, given my pensive mood, I had hoped Eliz and I could hang out a little bit longer at her place after the pub and talk about the possibility of my staying on Misgav Am after my service. But now I'm alone in my apartment, mulling over the serious decisions I need to make over the next few months about what I'll be doing after my service. Time is closing in on me. Should I stay in Israel or go back to the United States?

∞

AFTER JUST A FEW HOURS OF SLEEP, I GROGGILY MAKE MY way to the dining room. I've purposely gotten up an hour before my work at the children's house, which begins at eight o'clock, so I can have breakfast in the dining room by myself, which is highly unusual.

From the dining room window, I look out again at the vista that was enveloped in darkness just a few hours ago. I'm really going to miss this place when I go back to Sufa. This area has become my home. When I was a lone soldier without parents in the country, it was easier to hop on a bus and travel six hours to a remote kibbutz in the middle of the Negev desert. At the time, it was the only home I knew here in Israel. But now that my family is in the Upper Galilee, going back to Sufa doesn't exactly feel worth it.

I wonder if there's any way we can do our last three months of service here at Misgav Am. The hours of traveling that would mean for Eina and Svetlana when they wanted to visit their families might be somewhat of a hardship, but we have all been having a much better time on Misgav Am than we ever did at Sufa. I can see them going for the idea.

Although Eina and Svetlana regularly show up for meals at the dining room, we usually don't sit together. Today, though, I feel compelled to grab them and share my bright idea.

"What if we requested to stay here for our final three months of kibbutz service instead of doing it at Sufa?" I suggest as I lay my tray down next to theirs.

Their eyes light up. We all know how much easier working here has been as opposed to Sufa. Svetlana and Eina finish their work by lunchtime and have the rest of the day off, and I have grown to really like my job with the children. We all know that if we move back to Sufa for our last three months of kibbutz service, we'll likely end up doing agricultural work, which none of us particularly likes.

"Okay, let's try for it," they agree.

Within a few days, we get our answer from one of our officers, who telephones us from the Nahal Commanding Unit: "No problem. You three girls can stay on Misgav Am instead of moving to Sufa."

We're thrilled! We give each other little, tentative hugs. We still aren't that close.

The only thing left for us to do now is to retrieve the rest of our belongings from Sufa and bring them to Misgav Am. Then the final countdown begins. But I still have a decision to make: Will I stay in Israel after my service? And if so, what exactly will I do?

FOR THE NEXT FOUR MONTHS, LIFE CONTINUES TO BE stable and secure on Misgav Am. I participate in a number of kibbutz activities: I take nature hikes and bus rides around the region, as far north as "The Good Fence" and up to the Golan Heights. I party at the disco four times a week and still hang out with Eliz, though on a more limited basis than before. I've gotten used to her flaky behavior, but it's still hard to deal with her at times.

With each passing day, my mind is consumed about what to do post-service. There's an option for soldiers to stay on

Misgav Am following their service, but I'm not sure for how long, or what I would do if I elected that option.

A week before our final release day, I host an army release party at my apartment. I invite Eliz, a number of kibbutz members, and some IDF soldiers, and we take tequila shots and dance to the Israeli pop I blast on the boombox I brought with me from the States. I turn the volume up as far as it will go.

One week later, I find myself at the induction center—the same place where I checked in as a new soldier almost two years ago—with Dalia, Eina, and Svetlana. I trudge to the checkout counter with all my stuff and lay out each of the articles I was issued by the IDF when I started my service: a pair of well-worn boots and a pair of sandals, socks, three pairs of work and travel shirts and pants, my cone-shaped skirt and dressy shirt, and the black handbag containing the tear gas. These items have rested comfortably in my room at Misgav Am so long that I've practically forgotten about them —forgotten that for a year and a half straight, I wore this uniform almost every day. As I lift them out of my duffel bag, I press them to my face and breathe in the smell. As I do memories come rushing in: of Eshbal, Shitim, Base Camp 80, and the Brigade.

"C'mon, Dorit," Svetlana says, "let's get a move on. Stop getting so sentimental."

"I can see you're starting to tear up, too, Svetlana," I say, wiping my eyes. "Don't start!"

"Well, it's bittersweet. But hey, we're out. That's it. We're finished. We're finally done!"

As part of the checkout protocol, the soldier in charge runs through a list and checks off the items I've just placed on the counter. When all is clear, he takes my boots and dumps them in a large box with all the other boots that have just been returned. *What are they going to do with all those boots?* I wonder. *Recycle them?*

I'm allowed to keep my dogtag and the sewing kit, but that's it. At the end of this formality, I'm given my *hoger*—identity card—with my release date stamped on it: January 4, 1993. There's no need for female reservists in the Nahal unit and I don't have a highly specialized job, so my time with the IDF officially stops here. I'm free. But to do what?

∽

SINCE ARRIVING AT SUFA ON NOVEMBER 1990, I'VE PUT in a little over two years and two months of service in the IDF. Two years and two months. It's hard to believe.

Eina goes back to Sufa to stay with Carlos, and eventually they get married. Dalia goes home to Denmark to visit her family, but she plans to come back to live in Israel permanently. Svetlana returns to Ashqelon to live with her family.

Many of the guys we've served with are released a few months later. Almost all of the guys in our garin stay in Israel.

Following my release, I decide to stay at Misgav Am for a few more months, where I continue working at the children's house. I'm intimidated by the idea of going back to the States. I'm aware of how much I've changed in the last two and a half years, and I know this might feel like a threat to Mom—which, in turn, feels like a threat to me, because I have so much on the line. I don't want to go back to the way things were. I need to protect my newfound independence.

After talking to a family friend who is an English teacher, I decide to apply to Oranim College of Education here in Israel, where I will study to become a certified English teacher. Classes will start in six months—October 1993, which will mark more than three years since I arrived in Israel. All my courses will be in English, but I'll be here, exploring what's next for me in Israel. There is a great need for English teachers. I'll be employable, and the Ministry of Absorption will pay for my education. It feels like the best of both worlds.

I go for an interview at the college, and a few weeks later I get an acceptance letter. I take the letter to the Ministry of Absorption, where they stamp my immigrant card. My rights are now ticking away: I'll be soon studying for my first degree on their tab. A lot of paperwork is involved, but the process goes smoothly.

To celebrate my release from the service and my college acceptance, I take a two-and-a-half-month trip back to the States.

∞

AS I TURN THE LOCK, I HEAR MOM RUSHING DOWN THE STAIRS.

"Who is it?" she asks anxiously.

"I'm home, Ma!" I shout, slamming the door behind me. We hug each other tightly, even though I'm not quite sure what might follow next. There's something forgiving about this moment, as if we were never really at odds at all.

I look around at the pastel wallpapered closets, Mom's 1932 Steinway grand, and the sheet music strewn all over the room's chairs and desks. I'm still hopeful that something has changed between us, but I won't fight the way she is now. I've thought about this homecoming time and again, and in some ways, I realize, I've outgrown my mom. I thought I wanted to see her so badly, but the truth is, I just wanted the reassurance that things haven't changed in my absence—that this familiar apartment is still here, just the way I left it.

I'm only twenty-two years old, but I'm already starting to see how time is elastic—how familiar everything feels, even after such a long time away. In some ways, it's as if I'd never left. But I'm different now, I know that. I have found my own voice and power. Being here confirms for me that I did the right thing by choosing to stay in Israel. If Mom starts exhibiting her usual worry signs, this time I'll know how to handle it.

∾

IT'S ODD TO BE BACK IN WESTBETH WITH MOM. ONE night during my stay I'm back in my old room watching the wavy images on the ceiling I used to get lost in as a child, and Mom walks in and says, "Dorit, you're a pretty solid kid."

I'm surprised to hear these words from her. I am amazed that she's recognizing me in a positive way. I'm stunned that she's able to voice this compliment, too. Could it be she's capable of change after all?

She doesn't ask me questions about what I experienced as a soldier, but she seems to be grateful and happy that I'm home.

Later that day, she walks up the tiny staircase to my room and brings me some unopened letters and mail she's been saving for me for the past few years. It's now September 1993, and my studies don't begin until October, right after Succott, the Jewish holiday for the festival of the Harvest.

"I'm so glad you're continuing your studies," she chirps. "You're a somebody with a college degree."

"I told you I would pursue my education." I sit up and look at her. "You know that. You get yourself all worried about these things. I'm not stupid. It just doesn't always happen at the pace you want it to happen."

Silence.

I reassure her. "You have nothing to worry about, Mom. I'm going to be all right."

"I know it," she says. "You're a good cookie. I have all the faith you're going to do good things."

Even though I know she'll never understand me, or try to comprehend what I've lived through in Israel, I'm grateful for this moment and that for once we're not arguing or fighting.

A few weeks later, when it's time for me to fly back to Israel, Mom lets me take the A train to JFK airport by myself and doesn't try to force a sweater on me. She just lets me go. We've come a long way since those earlier days.

In my travel bag, I carry two bottles of Estée Lauder perfume she has gifted me. After getting through security, I breathe them both in. They remind me of my girlhood.

Look how far you've come already, Dorit.

I may be my mother's daughter, but now I know I won't ever turn into her. I've developed into my own person, free to make my own decisions—free to live my life.

A few hours after we say our goodbyes, I'm buckling my seatbelt next to some Russian businessman and listening to the security announcements, first in Hebrew and then in English. Although I feel a bit guilty leaving Mom, I hold her words and voice in my heart—the same words she said three days ago: *"It's gonna be alright. You're gonna be alright."*

And I will.

EPILOGUE

IT'S OCTOBER 12, 1993, AND ALTHOUGH I WAS RELEASED from the army over nine months ago and I'm fresh from my trip to the US, it surprises me yet again that I'm on my own. There's no Eina or Svetlana speaking in Russian and snickering to one another—in fact, there aren't any Russian students enrolled in our core group of students here at the Oranim College of Education.

It's the first day of my BA studies, and it seems I've been given a fresh start. For as long as I can remember, I've listened as Mom has admonished me to "become a somebody" by getting a college education—and now I'm studying to become a teacher. But it's because it's what I want to do, not because she's pushed me into it.

Before my trip back to the States, I decided that when I came back to Israel, I would stay for an extended period of time. I can get a free college education here, and I can study in both English and Hebrew. Oranim College School of Education fits the bill perfectly for me: it's the only place in the north of Israel that offers a liberal arts education alongside a rigorous teacher education program, and which also has a large, diverse student body. My previous college experience was with kids who were mostly from Long Island and with whom I didn't connect culturally. But I hadn't ever pushed beyond my comfort zone back then. I hadn't learned the power of taking risks, stretching my faith, and listening to my heart.

I've risked so much to be here. Making a conscious effort to not be like my mom—to be my own person instead of adhering to her patterns—hasn't been easy. Now, unlike at SUNY, I want to be here at school for all the right reasons; I'm craving a different kind of academic experience. After my IDF service, I believe I'm more focused, and I feel ready to propel my life forward. I've finally broken away from the pressures I felt, back home in New York City, to conform to the status quo.

∞

From the first day, I can tell already how different this place is from SUNY at Albany. First, it's much smaller than any of my classes were there. I'll be with this same core group of students for the next four years, so already it's expected we'll be a nucleus, soon to be like family. My experience with serving in a garin will help me to succeed here as I learn British and American literature, pedagogy, writing and education alongside this small group of students for the next four years. I feel lucky to have gone through the IDF before this; otherwise, I might find myself rebelling against this close-knit mentality. While the garin experience was tough, being forced to develop close-knit relationships while in the military will serve me now.

I now understand that living in Israel requires a group mentality. Israelis thrive in groups in a way that Americans do not. Where Americans take pride in their individuality, Israelis don't strive to be singled out—they prefer the cohesion of the whole, whether in military, religious, or secular life. They've earned their reputation for traveling in "wolf packs" because they tend to hang out in largish groups. And this carries over into my academic life.

On my first day of class, I take in the first few early moments before my first teacher walks in to observe how two native English speakers and kibbutz members chat with each other in English. One's from England and the other's American. A male Druze student behind me speaks in Arabic with several other Arab Christians and Muslims, while native-born Israelis chat in Hebrew. We are twenty-four female students and just one male student: the Druze.

No one here knows I'm American with an Israeli name yet, or that I left New York City to volunteer in the Israel Defense Forces, but I don't plan on staying quiet for long. I now have an insider mentality, and I feel prepared to navigate this cross-cultural landscape, both linguistically and emotionally. Serving in the military has given me a social and cultural foundation. For the last year, I have felt more connected to Israel as my second home. I was special in the military because I was a lone American soldier for some time and now that special feeling continues. I have the best of both worlds: I can stay in this country I now call home and still study almost exclusively in English.

In a matter of hours, I find my multicultural tribe. I code-switch between English and Hebrew with some of the native Israelis, or speak Hebrew exclusively. When I'm feeling a bit nostalgic for home, I hang out with the two English-speaking mothers from a nearby kibbutz. After two and a half years of living hell trying to get along with the members of my military garin, I finally have found what I'm looking for: a cohesive, more accepting "academic garin." We have regular group assessments, and when I share ideas with my group, I am taken seriously. I can be silly and have intense academic conversations at the same time.

It feels strange to speak English here in Israel after mostly speaking in Hebrew while serving in the military. I tried during that time to acclimate quickly to the *sabra* mentality, but at Oranim, I enjoy the fact that I can just be me. I can chat in either English or Hebrew. I'm American, but I'm also Israeli—not just by virtue of knowing the language or having lived here for a few years, but also because I feel at home.

∞

In less than four years, I will complete my BA with a decent GPA and take up a full-time teaching post teaching elementary school children at Beit Shean, a development town in the Jordan Valley that consists of many low-income families. Later I will be told that this is one of the most difficult places for someone like me—someone who wasn't born in Israel—to teach, because the population is largely homogenous and culturally removed from my world. I will struggle with classroom management and discipline, which the *chutzpah* and rowdiness of the children—many of whom have never heard English—make quite difficult. I will be committed to making this teaching assignment work, but no one will know how professionally isolated and overwhelmed I feel.

I will be brought to tears when a teaching colleague (the only other English teacher at the school) refuses to collaborate with me even though we teach the same grades. At twenty-six years old, I will be surrounded by veteran Israeli teachers who chirp about culturally removed subjects in the teacher's room and wait anxiously for retirement. I will be given a taste of the real world, beyond the protective "ivory towers" of Oranim, and each night I will hug my tear-stained pillow knowing that tomorrow I will have yet another "cultural test" to go through. I will try to convince myself that it will get easier over time. I will often wonder how my life would have been if I had pursued my academic studies in the US and if this extra toil is worth it.

Over the years, despite my misgivings, I will "stick with it," and I will eventually move up from teaching middle school to high school in various town and city schools, before pursuing an MA in English literature. In 2000, I will land a high school teaching position at a dreamy kibbutz situated alongside the Jordan River, smack in the middle of the Hula Valley in the Upper Galilee—an area I had only observed from a distance before now—and one year later, I will meet my husband, a member at another nearby kibbutz. He'll propose to me under the rose bush garden on the east end of the river, and six months later we'll get married alongside the Jordan River—one of the first picturesque places I fell in love with when first coming to live in this area.

Our son, Ivry, will be born in the mystical city of Tzefat in 2004; our daughter, Ayala, will be born in 2013 in Pittsburgh, seven years after we leave Israel for good and just four months after Mom has died after a sixteen-year battle with Alzheimer's disease.

Even though Mom won't recognize me in the end, I will know that if she could, she would commend me for the "somebody" I've become.

I will have made it.

And every single milestone will have been hard-earned.

ACKNOWLEDGMENTS

Tough love. That's what I learned from my editor, coach, and publisher extraordinaire, Brooke Warner of She Writes Press, each time my manuscript came back with more questions and comments. Translating the experience of serving in a foreign country into story material was often frustrating. A voice inside said not to give up. Another voice told me to believe in my story. Brooke, thank you for encouraging me to "stick with it" so I could tell the best possible story. Special thanks to Caitlyn Levin who guided me every step of the way to make this memoir the best it could be.

My deepest gratitude and respect to my husband, Haim Sasson, also a former IDF soldier, who intuited my driving force to give voice to this story. Dearest friend, I salute you for loving and supporting me in my writing life and beyond.

A special, heartfelt shout-out of thanks goes to Krissa Lagos, my amazing copyeditor, who trimmed all the "fat" of my manuscript so my story of courage and transformation could shine. I'm indebted to you a thousand times over.

Thank you to the team over at She Writes press for your advice, counsel, and support. I'm extremely grateful to be part of an amazing community of female writers.

A zillion thank-yous go to my pool of dedicated beta readers: Kathy Pooler, Victoria Marie Lees, Clarike Bowman-Jahn, Christine Rosas, and Judi Resick Csokai. Thank you all for being stellar readers and providing heartfelt yet constructive feedback during the later stages of the manuscript.

I'm indebted to the many supporters who supported *Accidental Soldier* when it launched as a crowdfunding campaign. I'm especially grateful to Nicole Vandestienne—thank you for stepping up to the plate and sharing the news of my crowdfunding campaign with your network. Jennifer Vandestienne Gillow and Kathy Pooler, thank you so much for supporting my campaign and believing in me and my book's vision from the very beginning. Aaron and Donielle Morgenstern, Marcie Mitre and Ken Levin, I'm indebted to you for your amazing generosity and support toward my Pubslush crowdfunding campaign.

I'm deeply grateful to the friends who have supported and nurtured me. I'm very fortunate to know you, including those who schlepped and took care of my kids while I worked against the clock to write. You know who you are. In particular, I'd like to thank those who helped me in numerous ways while I wrote this book: Frank Thomas, Judy Siegal Henn, and Elan Elvaiah for keeping me grounded. And again, Kathy Pooler of *A Memoir's Journey*—you are a gem. Thank you for believing in my book and validating my heroine's journey.

A major hug to my children, Ivry and Ayala, who took my absence in good strides when I took off to write. They always helped me remember how much I loved them.

A heartfelt thank-you to my dad and Lynn for encouraging me to take the path least traveled and to leave my comfort zone for the sake of immigrating to Israel and serving in the Israel Defense Forces. Had I stayed in New York City, I wouldn't have been able to put my courage into action, and this book never would have been written.

Lastly, I would like to remember my garin friend Svetlana Baskin, whom I wrote about in this book. She turned out to be a good friend toward the end of our service in the Israel Defense Forces, but unfortunately I lost contact with her over the years. I hope that one day we'll get to see each other again.

ABOUT THE AUTHOR

Dorit Sasson was born in New York City and immigrated to Israel at age nineteen. She holds an MA in English Literature from Haifa University and teaches memoir writing workshops at the Pittsburgh Center for the Arts. She writes for a wide range of print and online publications, including *The Huffington Post*, and *The Writer*, and speaks at conferences, libraries, and community centers. She is the author of a featured chapter in *Pebbles in the Pond: Transforming the World One Person at a Time* and the host of the podcast, Giving Voice to Your Courage. She lives in Pittsburgh, PA, with her husband and two children. Visit her at:

www.GivingaVoicetotheVoicelessBook.com
www.DoritSasson.com

BOOK DISCUSSION QUESTIONS

1. When Dorit decides to volunteer on a kibbutz in Israel, she says that she has "finally managed to tap into that 'higher-up'" that she today calls her "Jedi" voice and has conquered her fears about Israel. Later, she struggles with the decision of whether to stay at college. What do you think her reasons are for immigrating to Israel to serve in the Israel Defense Forces?

2. At the beginning of the book, Dorit struggles to "live with the questions." How does she mature during the course of the book?

3. The term "sabra" is a symbol for cultural and linguistic transition. Dorit feels uprooted after leaving her New York City home. What helps her transition better to this "prickly pear" culture? Are there things she does or says along the way that help her cope more effectively?

4. The apple orchard at Kibbutz Malkiyyah is a symbol of freedom for Dorit. How does working at the orchard change her and the way she sees her relationship with her mother?

5. Of Shawna, Dorit writes, "[Shawna] triggers fears I've inherited from my mother—mainly her fears of authority and the unknown." She is speaking about her fear about Israel. To defeat that fear, she tries to build "feel-good connections" by reassuring herself through inner dialogue, thoughts, and actions that Israel is a safe country and that she's doing the right thing by serving in the IDF. What do you think about this "feel-good approach?" What are some of her other ways of overcoming fear?

6. At one point, Dorit tells herself, "trust that everything will work out." It's a darker moment of uncertainty and doubt, and yet she tries to believe in herself. How do the things Dorit believes about herself, including during the most challenging of moments, support or damage her while she's serving in the Israel Defense Forces?

7. During her first few weeks serving in the Israel Defense Forces, Dorit writes, "Somehow, this pressed travel uniform I'm wearing indicates to me that there will be serious lessons that will test the limits of my courage, faith, and endurance beyond random kibbutz work." Throughout the book she talks about getting along with other soldiers and garin members, taking commands, learning to shoot a gun, and getting punished—all in a new language and culture. How does this new military life help her cope with the emotional hurdles she faces?

8. At the beginning of her service, Dorit writes, "I feel as if I've lost my voice; I wait for someone else to speak up." Later, in the desert, she uses her musical ability to sing. The concept of "voice" is a perfect literary metaphor: Dorit can either be silent or be heard in this new foreign and militaristic country. Are there other ways she "gives voice" to other experiences that help her connect more deeply to Israel as a new immigrant?

9. All throughout her service, Dorit struggles with the label she has been given as the "goofy American." What does she mean by this, and how does her relationship with the garin in the Israel Defense Forces intensify these feelings?

10. Think about the things Dorit associates with being a sabra —Israeli born. What are they? How do they impact the change in her identity?

11. Dorit writes that her mother's approach to dealing with Israel has always been to respond in fear and panic. How does Dorit change this trajectory of living in fear of Israel while serving in the IDF?

12. What does starting on Kibbutz Sufa mean for Dorit? What does the new garin represent to her?

13. Why does Dorit identify herself as "an outsider" in Darren's presence? Are there other situations where she identifies herself as an outsider? How does she cope with these feelings, if at all?

14. Why is it so crucial that, even after finally feeling free in the desert, Dorit continues to refer it as a "lonely crater"?

15. Leaving her mom plays a tremendous role in how Dorit copes in the IDF, and yet her mom doesn't show much emotional support. In what ways does this absence of a maternal figure help Dorit finish her IDF service?

16. In which moments do you feel that Dorit accepts the fact that her mother will never become the "mother she always wanted?" At what point does she fully transform?

17. *Accidental Soldier* is a story of transformation. The person Dorit starts off as is not the same person she ends up as. What kind of meaning has she come to by the last lines of the book, "Even though Mom won't recognize me in the end, I will know that if she could, she would commend me for the 'somebody' I've become"?

SELECTED TITLES FROM SHE WRITES PRESS

She Writes Press is an independent publishing company founded to serve women writers everywhere.
Visit us at www.shewritespress.com.

Fourteen: A Daughter's Memoir of Adventure, Sailing, and Survival by Leslie Johansen Nack. $16.95, 978-1-63152-941-2. A coming-of-age adventure story about a young girl who comes into her own power, fights back against abuse, becomes an accomplished sailor, and falls in love with the ocean and the natural world.

All the Ghosts Dance Free: A Memoir by Terry Cameron Baldwin. $16.95, 978-1-63152-822-4. A poetic memoir that explores the legacy of alcoholism and teen suicide in one woman's life—and her efforts to create an authentic existence in the face of that legacy.

Learning to Eat Along the Way by Margaret Bendet. $16.95, 978-1-63152-997-9. After interviewing an Indian holy man, newspaper reporter Margaret Bendet follows him in pursuit of enlightenment and ends up facing demons that were inside her all along.

Postcards from the Sky: Adventures of an Aviatrix by Erin Seidemann. $16.95, 978-1-63152-826-2. Erin Seidemann's tales of her her struggles, adventures, and relationships as a woman making her way in a world very much dominated by men: aviation.

Gap Year Girl by Marianne Bohr. $16.95, 978-1-63152-820-0. Thirty-plus years after first backpacking through Europe, Marianne Bohr and her husband leave their lives behind and take off on a yearlong quest for adventure.

This Is Mexico: Tales of Culture and Other Complications by Carol M. Merchasin. $16.95, 978-1-63152-962-7. Merchasin chronicles her attempts to understand Mexico, her adopted country, through improbable situations and small moments that keep the reader moving between laughter and tears.